DOSTOEVSKIJ AND THE
BELINSKIJ SCHOOL OF LITERARY CRITICISM

SLAVISTIC PRINTINGS AND REPRINTINGS

edited by

C. H. VAN SCHOONEVELD

Indiana University

64

1969

MOUTON

THE HAGUE · PARIS

DOSTOEVSKIJ AND THE BELINSKIJ SCHOOL OF LITERARY CRITICISM

by

THELWALL PROCTOR

Humboldt State College

1969

MOUTON

THE HAGUE · PARIS

LIBRARY OF CONGRESS CATALOG CARD NUMBER: 68-57402

Printed in The Netherlands by Mouton & Co., Printers, The Hague.

for my aunt
Jennelle Porter Proctor

ACKNOWLEDGEMENTS

The author embraces this opportunity to express his appreciation to those members of the Department of Slavic Languages and Literatures at the University of California whose counsel and support abetted his work in its early stages: the late Professor Wacław Lednicki, Professor Francis J. Whitfield, and, most especially, Professor Emeritus Gleb Struve, under whose direction the original version of this work was completed.

The author's thanks for courteous and helpful assistance are also due to the staffs of the Library of the University of California, of the Reading Room of the British Museum, of the Bayerische Staatsbibliothek, of the Slavic collections of the New York Public Library and of the Library of Congress, where the bulk of the research for this work was accomplished.

To the publishers Harper and Row I am indebted for gracious permission to use the quotation from Aldous Huxley's *The Genius and the Goddess*.

FOREWORD

This work is an attempt to study the literary criticism of a relatively limited group of eminent critics, Belinskij, Černyševskij, Dobroljubov, Pisarev, and Mixajlovskij, representative of that current of socio-literary criticism which was such a prominent feature of the history of Russian nineteenth century literature and which, in a somewhat different form, continues to be predominant in Soviet criticism, with particular attention to the theoretical and practical problems involved in the mutual relationships of writer, critic, and reader, illustrated by the treatment accorded by these critics to the work of Fedor Mixajlovič Dostoevskij.

Dostoevskij's work was chosen to illustrate the practice of these critics for two reasons. First, with the exception of Černyševskij, all of them wrote influential articles on Dostoevskij; it is thus possible to compare and contrast their treatment of him. Second, the equivocal character of Dostoevskij's work lends itself to a variety of interpretations. The German novelist, Hermann Hesse, speaking of *The Brothers Karamazov*, remarks, "Jedes Symbol hat hundert Deutungen, deren jede richtig sein kann. Auch die Karamasoffs haben hundert Deutungen, meine ist nur eine davon, eine von hundert." [1] Aldous Huxley doubtless had something similar in mind when he began a recent novel in the following fashion:

"The trouble with fiction", said John Rivers, "is that it makes too much sense. Reality never makes sense."

"Never?" I questioned.

"Maybe from God's view", he conceded. "Never from ours. Fiction has unity, fiction has style. Facts possess neither. In the raw, existence is always one damned thing after another, and each of the damned things is simultaneously Thurber and Michelangelo, simultaneously

---

[1] Hesse, *Blick ins Chaos*, p. 12.

Mickey Spillane and Thomas à Kempis. The criterion of reality is its intrinsic irrelevance." And when I asked, "To what?" he waved a square brown hand in the direction of the bookshelves, "To the Best that has been Thought and Said", he declaimed with mock portentousness. And then, "Oddly enough, the closest to reality are always the fictions that are supposed to be the least true." He leaned over and touched the back of a battered copy of *The Brothers Karamazov*. "It makes so little sense that it's almost real." [2]

This essential ambiguity of Dostoevskij's work had also been remarked by Russians. For example, in the eighties of the last century, Arsenij Vvedenskij wrote, "Not only at the beginning of Dostoevskij's career, but even at its very end, literary criticism, influenced by the intellectual currents and enthusiasms of the time, did not find it easy to appraise its real significance." [3]

If the significance of Dostoevskij's work was obscure, the Russian critics felt it imperative to remedy this defect, and since Dostoevskij's work is open to varying and contradictory interpretations, it has, accordingly, received them. Indeed, from one point of view, the reactions of many critics to Dostoevskij's work are not dissimilar to those of persons exposed to Rorschach ink-blots. Their reactions often reveal more about themselves than about Dostoevskij's work.

Since these varying interpretations are not so much the result of individual whims of critical taste and vagaries of discernment as of shifting intellectual currents in Russian life, is has seemed necessary to situate the critics studied against the background of the development of intellectual life in Russia during the course of the period involved, to indicate their relationship to it, and to sketch their general ideological position, so as to set each critic's appraisal of Dostoevskij's work in the context of that critic's general orientation.

---

[2] Huxley, *The Genius and the Goddess*, pp. 9-10. Cf. Ortega y Gasset: "Dostoevski is a 'realist' not because he uses the material of life but because he uses the form of life", *The Dehumanization of Art*, p. 72.
[3] Vvedenskij, *Literaturnye xarakteristiki*, p. 90.

TABLE OF CONTENTS

I

INTRODUCTION

As an incidental result of extended isolation from Western Europe, Russia was relatively late in developing those literary genres common to Western European culture. Especially was this true of literary criticism, which requires a corpus of native literature upon which to exercise and develop its powers. A contributing factor was the slow development of the Russian periodical press; not until early in the nineteenth century did it begin to function on a scale approximating that achieved in Western Europe almost a hundred years earlier.

As a genre, literary criticism was not without roots in early Russian tradition. A recent Soviet historian detects the expression of an impulse toward literary criticism in such varied sources as Russian folklore, the literature of the Kievan period, and the works of Nil Sorskij, Iosif Volockij, Maksim Grek, Andrej Kurbskij, Ivan Timofeev, Simeon Polockij, and Avvakum. In the eighteenth century, late Renaissance literary theory is reflected in the work of Feofan Prokopovič; and Prince Kantemir, whose satires touch upon literary subjects, was familiar with the theories of Boileau.[1]

It has, however, been traditional to begin the history of Russian literary criticism a little later, with Lomonosov as the key figure, preceded by Tredjakovskij and succeeded by Sumarokov, at a time when the most pressing tasks confronting Russian literature were two: the assimilation of neo-classicism, borrowed from France, and such progress as could then be made in the creation of a vernacular literary language. To the accomplishment of both of these tasks, Lomonosov, and Tredjakovskij and Sumarokov as well, made significant contributions. Until a viable literary language was created and coherent canons of composition were established, other literary questions were of necessity of secondary importance.

[1] Akademija nauk SSSR, *Istorija russkoj kritiki*, I, pp. 25-45, 50. Cf. Gorodeckij, "O sozdanii istorii russkoj literaturnoj kritiki", p. 316.

On the threshold of the nineteenth century, Karamzin (in the realm of prose) and Žukovskij (in the realm of verse) succeeded between them in creating modern literary Russian. Together with changes in the literary language came changes in literary style. The dominance of neo-classicism was broken by the advent, first of sentimentalism and then of romanticism. As Vetrinskij remarks, these changes in literary style were accompanied by new standards in literary criticism, introduced first by Merzljakov and Venevitinov and later developed by Polevoj and Nadeždin, the immediate predecessors of Belinskij. Merzljakov campaigned for a more organic theory of art, though in the main within the general framework of neo-classicism; Venevitinov advanced the claims of a philosophico-aesthetic approach to literature and asked for national coloration and originality. Polevoj, a theoretician of romanticism *à la* Victor Hugo, raised the problem of the socio-ethical and historical significance of literature, and Nadeždin voiced a demand for realism. Vetrinskij points out that the limitations of these critics were due to the fact that their taste had been formed before an independent Russian literature, as shaped by such masters as Puškin and Gogol', had taken definitive form. Thus, in the criticism of even the two later critics, there were many echoes of an earlier era, and neither Nadeždin's wide and deep erudition nor Polevoj's love of literature, his brilliance, and his special gifts as a journalist prevented them from expressing critical judgments which now seem wide of the mark.[2]

Also active among Belinskij's temporal predecessors, though without a decisive influence on succeeding developments in Russian literary criticism, was Prince P. A. Vjazemskij, to whom seems to belong the honor of being the first Russian critic to defend romanticism (according to Puškin), as well as that of having first used (in 1819) the Russian term *narodnost'*, defined as that which is both *populaire et nationale*.[3] The recent Soviet history of Russian literary criticism, which devotes a whole chapter to him, while emphasizing the fact that Vjazemskij was no revolutionary, nevertheless considers that his criticism has been underrated and calls him the most important critic active during Puškin's lifetime.[4] To approximately the same period belongs also the criticism of I. V. Kireevskij, an early ideological leader of the slavo-

---

[2] Vetrinskij, *V sorokovyx godax*, pp. 44-45.
[3] Puškin, *Polnoe sobranie sočinenij*, X, 55; Akademija nauk SSSR, *Literaturnoe nasledstvo*, XLIII-XLIV, p. 261, note 14.
[4] Akademija nauk SSSR, *Istorija russkoj kritiki*, I, p. 238. Cf. Mordovčenko, *Russkaja kritika pervoj četverti xix veka*, pp. 280-313.

philes, whose work, though interesting in itself, shared the fate of
Vjazemskij's in that it was without decisive later influence.[5]

Russian literary criticism was in considerable confusion when
Belinskij entered the literary scene. Družinin, with some obvious exaggeration, described the situation as follows: "In textbooks and dic-
tionaries of poetry the views of Batteux and La Harpe were put quite
clearly; however, their obsoleteness was visible to the naked eye. Along
with the romanticism of Žukovskij, there had come to us the weak
efforts of the critics of the German romantic period, the most fruitless
of all periods. In the *Biblioteka dlja čtenija* (*Library for Reading*), as
we said, it was possible to find traces of British views on art, but views
significantly altered and even falsified by the incomprehensible caprice
of reviewers and translators. Add to this the last voices of the defenders
of French medieval romanticism, the rhapsodies of devotees of the
purity of Russian style, the chatter of the elders about the traditions
of Karamzin's sentimentalism – and before you appears a strange
picture of ideas and conceptions which had not grown to their full
development, perishing from age but not having passed off the scene
as yet." [6]

While, on the one hand, partisans of an older order had not yet been
reduced to silence, on the other, no new synthesis of critical ideas
persuasive enough to command wide acceptance had as yet emerged.
This lack Belinskij was to supply, and the critical tradition which he
established, as adapted by his successors, remained dominant throughout the greater part of the nineteenth century in Russia. Toward the
end of the nineteenth and at the beginning of the twentieth century,
this tradition was challenged, but under the Soviet regime, one of its
collateral descendents gained official support; thus the school of literary
criticism dominant today in the Soviet Union, when displaying its
family tree, counts Belinskij as its progenitor.

In the history of Russian literature and Russian literary criticism,
Belinskij holds a unique position. He is regarded as the founder of a
specifically Russian school of literary criticism and as the fountainhead
of a stream of ideas about and attitudes toward literature still abundantly flowing in the Soviet Union. Isaiah Berlin goes so far as to say:
"As anyone knows who has read at all widely in his works, he is the

---

[5] Lebedev-Poljanskij mentions Kireevskij's interest in the social implications of
literature and his demand for "reality", *V. G. Belinskij*, p. 26.
[6] Družinin, *Sobranie sočinenij*, VII, p. 211.

father of the social criticism of literature, not only in Russia but perhaps even in Europe." [7]

Did Belinskij, in fact, create this tradition, this stream of ideas, or was he but the instrument through which it expressed itself? For example, Černyševskij, Belinskij's successor, wrote: "If Belinskij was the spokesman of criticism at this time, that was only because his personality was precisely that which historical necessity demanded." [8] Isaiah Berlin, on the other hand, takes the opposite point of view: "Whether for good or ill [Belinskij's influence] transformed Russian writing – in particular criticism – radically, and, it would seem, forever." [9] The question is complicated by the existence of what may be called the Belinskij Cult. Belinskij's name came to be associated with a cultural myth potent in Russia in the nineteenth century and beyond. Although, to the supporters of autocracy, orthodoxy, official nationalism, and "pure" literature, his very name was anathema, both radical and liberal Russian writers proudly claimed descent from him and invoked his authority to lend support to their own ideas. Belinskij's status as a myth, a symbol, raises trying problems. For example, it is necessary to disentangle his actual position from what it is alleged to have been. This problem is further complicated by the rapid and complex evolution of his ideas; his early death, before his ideology had acquired stability and coherence; and by the conditions under which he worked: on the one hand, journalistic pressure, which encouraged the expression in print of ideas only partly worked out, and, on the other, a censorship which to some extent inhibited full and explicit exposition.

Abundant evidence of his influence upon his contemporaries has survived.[10] After his death, for some years censorship forbade even the mention of his name in print. His reputation was revived and the foundation of the Belinskij Cult was laid later, at the end of the fifties and the beginning of the sixties, by Černyševskij and his disciple, Dobroljubov. Lavrov and Mixajlovskij, Plexanov and Lenin, all of the Russian radicals in succession (not to mention the liberals), made their pious contribution to his reputation. In the Soviet Union, Belinskij's position is secure. Edmund Wilson goes so far as to refer to Belinskij as "The patron saint of the dogmatic Soviet criticism which made every work of literature a move in the game of propaganda and tried

[7]   Berlin, "A Marvellous Decade", December, 1955, p. 24.
[8]   Černyševskij, *Očerki gogolevskogo perioda*, p. 227.
[9]   Berlin, *op. cit.*, November, 1955, p. 29.
[10]   For a marshalling of such testimony, see Poljakov, *Vissarion Belinskij*, pp. 436-438.

to rule on the attitude of the author as 'correct' or 'incorrect'." [11]

The tradition linked with Belinskij's name differentiates Russian literary criticism from that of Western Europe. Acting upon and acted upon by Russian literature as it developed, this tradition was one of the factors which helped to give Russian literature its characteristic coloration and its peculiar place in Russian culture. The Russian attitude toward and expectations of literature came to be rather different from those of Western Europe, and peculiar demands were laid upon literature, upon the writer, and upon the critic.

What are the characteristics of this specifically Russian attitude toward literature which has been attributed to Belinskij's influence? Most conspicuous, perhaps, is the close linkage of literature and society. As Pypin puts it: "From [Belinskij's] time on, the relationship of literature to society substantially altered; literature ceased to be a sort of accidental appurtenance, an external decoration of social life. – On the contrary, it was closely linked with it; different schools, disagreeing in their most fundamental opinions, do not quarrel over the fact that reality, life, society should be the sole content of literature and the elucidation of them its essential task." [12] This close linkage of literature and society has meant that in Russia social and literary criticism have become inextricably mixed. At least in part, this development was due to the specific conditions obtaining in Russia early in the nineteenth century. Writing of this period, Mixajlovskij observes: "L'impression des livres rencontrait des difficultés insurmontables. Les journaux quotidiens n'existaient presque point. Il n'y avait qu'un genre de littérature qui se frayait chez nous le chemin et qui s'incarnait dans les revues mensuelles. C'est là que se groupaient les écrivains et les poètes, enfin tous ceux qui sentaient la necessité de parler au peuple russe et de faire valoir leurs idées. On y trouvait des poésies et des romans et surtout la critique littéraire, qui a fini par gagner une importance politique." And he goes on to comment: "Cet état de choses subsista même bien longtemps après l'émancipation des paysans." [13]

Limited to the monthly magazines as an avenue, the expression of ideas was further encumbered by the existence of a press censorship which sought to limit the dissemination of ideas, particularly those of a political and social character. Inhibiting as the Russian censorship could be, on occasion, it was more consistently nearsighted, frequently

[11] Wilson, "Comrade Prince", p. 15.
[12] Pypin, *Istoričeskie očerki*, p. 426.
[13] Mixajlovskij, "Le mouvement littéraire", p. 92.

either sluggishly inefficient or calculatedly lenient, with the result that social and political ideas found no insuperable difficulty in making their way into print under the light disguise of literary criticism. The role of the official Russian censorship in forging close links between literature and social and political thought has traditionally been emphasized by Russian literary historians, yet still another influence needs to be taken into consideration.

Both Isaiah Berlin and Herbert E. Bowman call attention also to the influence of the romantic movement as it found expression in Germany. The German romantic concept of organicism tended to blur or to obliterate the boundaries traditionally separating various aspects of national life – social, political, and artistic – and to include them all in a single inseparable whole. This point of view was enthusiastically adopted in Russia, with the result that it became the function of the Russian intelligentsia to maintain watch over and to pass critical judgment upon Russian national life as a whole, rather than upon its specific segments. As time went on, the Russian intelligentsia became more and more conscious that the key problem in Russia was social. The sense that the national life was organic and, consequently, needed to be viewed as a whole, plus the sense that the central problem for Russia was social, in combination with a situation which impeded the expression and dissemination of social ideas except in the guise of literary criticism led to a combination in Russia of the roles of social and literary critic.[14]

A close linkage of literature and society is justified, according to the theories of romantic nationalism, by the contention that literature is the more or less unconscious expression of the institutions peculiar to a particular national society. From this point of view, literature is expected to express and to assist in the definition of the nation as an organic social whole. This is, perhaps, a satisfactory position so long as the nation remains ambiguous and as yet not fully defined and, in addition, a generally accepted aesthetic canon is in existence. Under these conditions, aesthetic quality in a work of art may well seem the best available guarantee that the work does, indeed, express and define the nation. Aesthetic quality is the index of the degree to which a given work of art expresses the national spirit.

But this was not the situation in Russia toward the end of Belinskij's life. The schism of the intelligentsia into Westernizers and Slavophiles

[14] Berlin, *op. cit.*, November, 1955, p. 28; Bowman, *Vissarion Belinskij*, pp. 6-11.

was the result of competing definitions of the character of the national spirit and destiny. Under these conditions, given the high prestige of the artist as a leader, it was natural that both parties should turn to literature to find support for their opinions. Unfortunately, the appeal to literature took place at a time when aesthetic ideas were in flux and when aesthetic evaluations differed as sharply as opinions about the nation. But if the proposition that the aesthetically best art most correctly expresses the life of the nation is accepted, this formula can be reversed, and then correct definition of the national life becomes the index of aesthetic quality. Aesthetics becomes a function of ideology. In this situation, a denial of aesthetic quality becomes an attack upon ideology and *vice versa*. Quarrels over aesthetics, under conditions which, as in Russia, forbade open discussion of social and political problems, became quarrels over social ideology fought on the grounds of aesthetics largely because no other terrain was so readily accessible. Once the aesthetic quality of a work of art is conceived as a function of ideology and an ideology has been arrived at, literature as an unconscious expression of national life seems inadequate and there appears a demand for a more consciously oriented literature.

But in romantic aesthetics, the function of art is not alone to express and define the nation; art also has a function as an instrument of progress, the means by which the artist, in his function as prophet and seer, exercises his powers as a national leader. The two functions overlap significantly: if the national life is conceived organically and dynamically (that is, in terms of progress), then what the nation is furnishes indications of what the nation will be. Quarrels over interpretations and analyses of contemporary life are also, by implication, quarrels over what the nation will be, over the national destiny.

If literature is viewed as an instrument of progress, it is expected that it influence, act upon the national life. Once this proposition is accepted, art becomes committed to the realization of a program. In other words, the most effective propaganda is the best art. Another extra-aesthetic criterion has appeared, by means of which art is judged. Contributing to the importance of literature as propaganda, as a motivating power of social and political change, were the social and political conditions in Russia which made literature the only available propaganda instrument by means of which such changes might be effected.

Thus in Russia art was originally conceived of as the leader of the general cultural rather than the specifically social and political life of the nation. But given an organic conception of the national life and an increasing sense that the social problem was the determinant factor in that national life, cultural progress seemed impossible without social change. The emphasis began to shift from art as a leader of the national cultural life to art as a leader of the national social and political life, since the two were bound up one with the other and since art seemed the only available lever for setting in motion the necessary social and political changes.

The artist, especially the writer, had a unique role in German romantic aesthetic theory. According to the tenets of this system of ideas, it was every man's duty to dedicate himself to a cause. This obligation was particularly binding upon the artist. Of him was expected utter dedication, because of his exalted and responsible function as leader of the national life. This special dedication of the artist did not absolve him, as it has served to do at other times and places, from normal social obligations. Rather, it served to intensify them. In part, this was a result of the application of the romantic idea of organicism. From this point of view, man is one. His various roles as private individual, artist, public citizen, cultural, social, and political leader become fused. None of his activities can be considered in isolation from the others, and the touchstone by which all his activities can be judged is his personal integrity, the purity and disinterestedness of his motives. Commenting on this peculiarly Russian emphasis upon and interest in the personal integrity of the artist, John Middleton Murry writes: "The Russian mind does not live naturally under the reign of law. The act has not for it, as it has for us, a fixed and final importance in itself. The act is only a manifestation of a thought or a belief or a desire; and often conversely, what a man thinks or believes, that he must act. Just as the spiritual and the temporal were inextricably knit in the Russian empire under a Caesar who was himself the embodiment of State and Church together, so in the individual Russian, act and belief were one: there is no separation between the practical and spiritual man." [15]

Thus there was, in Russia, no separation of the writer's roles. What he was as a man, as an artist, as a citizen, as a national leader were inextricably bound up with one another. That a writer might be a bad man, an inadequate citizen and national leader, and at the same time a great artist was an unthinkable proposition from the Russian point of view. The result of this fusion of roles was to place the artist in a

[15]   Murry, *Discoveries*, p. 54.

peculiarly vulnerable position. His authority was dependent upon his integrity, and this was vulnerable to attack on the basis of his conduct as a man, as a citizen, as a national cultural and socio-political leader, and as an artist. The artist was thus exposed to a particularly merciless and searching scrutiny.

The close linkage of literature and society gave a specific coloration to Russian literary criticism; as it is traditionally put, literary criticism came to be not so much criticism of literature as criticism of life, not so much criticism of artists as criticism of men. This accounts for the tone peculiar to much of Russian literary criticism. When a work of art is praised, what is praised is not so much the work itself as what it stands for, the attitude toward life which it reflects, the man whom it expresses. When a work is condemned, at one and the same time the attack is directed against the work as a work of art, against the attitude toward life which it represents, and against its author as a responsible member of society.

Criticism of literature as criticism of life is an attitude which has both advantages and curious dangers and pitfalls, as illustrated by the way in which this idea worked itself out in Russia. On the one hand, this approach to literary criticism has the attractive advantage of insisting upon the importance of literature. The Russian critics with whom we will be concerned were consistently hostile to the idea of art as an end in itself as a doctrine which tended to vitiate the importance of art. On the other hand, this point of view toward literature has the difficulty that the importance of literature, great though it is, is defined in terms of something else, its relationship to society. Thus there is a tendency for the center of interest, the focus of attention, to shift from literature to society.

The concept of the artist as a socio-political as well as a cultural leader also leads to difficulties of a peculiar kind. So long as the meaning and direction of society, the nation, are undefined and still to seek, the artist is unchallenged as seer and prophet, leader of his people. The artist, the critic, and the people are united in a common search in which the artist leads the way because of his unique endowments. The critic gratefully accepts the intuitive insights of the artist, explores, clarifies, and expounds them to the people. At the base of this situation are the assumptions that there is but one true path of progress, that the artist is uniquely endowed to find it, and that his importance and significance lie in this service to his society, his nation. Goriély remarks: "En Russie, la fonction publique d'écrire fut toujours un

apostolat et la littérature, une arme de combat. Aussi l'écrivain tient-il
à la fois du grandprêtre et du preux." [16] So long as the artist is regarded
in this way by the critic, so long as the critic seeks enlightenment of the
artist as to the meaning and direction of society, literature remains the
unique source of enlightenment to which critic and public alike turn.
A sort of partnership exists between the critic and the artist, but the
authority and prestige of the artist remain unquestioned by the critic
and the public alike.

But when, as happened in Russia, the critics arrive at convictions
which do not coincide with those of the artists, the situation alters
drastically. No longer does the critic turn to the artist for illumination,
for illumination has been found, and it has been found not among the
artists but among the critics. The authority of the artist, at least for
the critic, is destroyed. Zajcev put the situation succinctly in an article
published in *Russkoe Slovo* (*The Russian Word*) in 1864: "Criticism
is related to literature exactly as literature is related to society. Literature depicts society, judges its condition, expresses its desires, tendencies, and needs. Exactly in the same way, the critics judge the condition of literature, describe its position, and evaluate all the individual
phenomena constituting it. But criticism, of course, must also study the
position of society, know it, understand its needs and tendencies. Without this knowledge, it cannot judge truly about literature." [17] A subtle
struggle for authority develops between the critic and the artist. The
original partnership is broken. The critic, instead of accepting the
leadership of the artist, attempts, on the one hand, to guide and influence the artist, and, on the other, to usurp the artist's role of seer,
prophet, leader of the people. As Borozdin observes, "The critic changes
from a simple commentator into a leader of society." [18]

This new situation creates complications for the critic. The critic
may take the position that the artist is a false prophet; then, by definition, he cannot be a good artist, a good citizen, or a good man. The
critic's attack may thus take several lines, alternatively or simultaneously. A direct challenge of the artist's authority, however, has several
disadvantages. On the one hand, it tends to alienate the artist, to make
him suspicious of the critic, to increase the critic's difficulties in influencing him. On the other hand, so far as the public is concerned,
a direct attack upon the prestige of the artist involves denial of the

[16]   Goriély, *Science des lettres soviétiques*, pp. 54-55.
[17]   Zajcev, *Izbrannye*, I, p. 166.
[18]   Borozdin, *Literaturnye xarakteristiki*, II, Part I, pp. 5-6.

basic proposition that the artist is the cultural and socio-political leader of the nation, a prejudice presumably ingrained, and the assertion of the critic's right to that role, an issue which the critics, on the whole, preferred to fight out obliquely rather than directly.

Rather than to attack the prestige of the artist directly, the critic chose often, rather, to maintain the prestige of the artist with the public. This tactical line had the advantages of preserving communication between critic and artist and not disturbing the public's prejudices. But instead of devoting himself to the exposition of the artist's ideas, the critic sought to interpose himself between the artist's work and the public and to impose upon the public not the artist's work but the critic's vision of it. The critic himself becomes a creative artist of a sort, using materials furnished by the artist as his raw material. As an example of this procedure, one thinks of the fate of Bazarov in Turgenev's *Fathers and Sons*. Is the Bazarov who exists in the minds of the Russian reading public Turgenev's or Pisarev's; Tatjana, Puškin's or Belinskij's; the Kingdom of Darkness, Ostrovskij's or Dobroljubov's? The answer to this question is clearly put by the Soviet critic Dmitrieva: "It is possible to assert, for example, that the significance of Dobroljubov's essay, 'Kogda-že pridet nastojaščij den?' ('When Will Real Day Dawn?') was almost greater than the significance of Turgenev's novel *Nakanune* (*On the Eve*), an analysis of which was included in this essay. Not because Dobroljubov added something of his own to what Turgenev showed. No, Dobroljubov took the very same phenomena of life which Turgenev depicted, accepted the same imaginative conception, in the same artistic aspect as Turgenev, but drew from them extreme revolutionary conclusions such as the author himself did not wish to draw and, indeed, could not, since he did not stand at the height of Dobroljubov's *Weltanschauung*." [19]

In this struggle for influence over the reading public, the critic needs the artist as an indispensable tool. When the artist voices the critic's ideas, the critic exalts the artist and supports his prestige in order to use it in the interest of ideas advanced not as his own but as the artist's. The prestige and authority of art are pressed into the service of the critic's ideology. The critic shelters cozily behind the authority of the artist. When the artist does not voice the critic's ideas, the critic may attack the artist, but, as has been pointed out, tactical complications make him reluctant to do this except in cases of absolute necessity.

[19] Akademija xudožestv SSSR, *Voprosy teorii sovetskogo izobraziteľnogo iskusstva*, p. 238.

Rather, the critic is apt to take the oblique method of demonstrating that the artist does not understand his own creation. Because of his unconscious powers of intuition, the artist has been able to grasp and to express reality, life, but he misinterprets the sense of what he himself has done, a misinterpretation which the critic undertakes to correct. The artist is simultaneously praised as a sort of unconscious medium and condemned as a conscious ideologue. His prestige is exalted, but the significance of his work is re-interpreted. The role of cultural and socio-political leadership thus comes to be divided: the artist remains a prophet, but an unconscious one. The conscious ideological leader has come to be the critic.

The results of this situation are curious. The artist remains on his pedestal; his prestige is maintained. But at the same time, his direct contact with the reading public is broken. He is now not so much a prophet as an oracle whose pronouncements are venerated but danger-ous until interpreted by the critic. But if the artist has been isolated from the public and his direct contact with it broken, at the same time the critic remains dependent upon the artist, either to give powerful expression to the critic's ideas or to furnish raw material for the critic's creative re-interpretation. Both critics and artists found this situation unsatisfactory. On the one hand, the critics were tempted to try their hands as artists. One thinks of Černyševskij's novel, *Čto delat'? (What is to be Done?)*, Gercen's *Kto vinovat? (Who is to Blame?)* – though Gercen was a social rather than a literary critic – and Mixajlovskij's abortive attempt at a novel. On the other hand, the artists attempted to invade the critic's domain with such works as Dostoevskij's *Dnevnik pisatelja (The Diary of a Writer)*, or, like Lev Tolstoj, calculatedly abandoned the role of artist for that of national ideological leader, pure and simple.

The final product of this stubborn struggle between artist and critic is the situation existent today in the Soviet Union, where the artist has been brought firmly to heel and the authority of the critic as ideological leader is flatly assumed. This is quite clear, for example, from the remarks of Bursov in a recent book on Černyševskij: "A critical essay is addressed to two individuals: the reader and the writer. Consequently, the goal of criticism is double: to influence both the reading public and literature. The goal of criticism in relationship to the reader is either to strengthen, or to weaken, or, perhaps, altogether to neutralize the influence upon him of one or another literary work. ... The goal of criticism in relationship to the writer must be viewed, obviously, as a

desire to help him either to confirm himself in the way he has taken
or to leave it and change over to another." [20]

The Belinskij tradition experienced considerable growth and development in the course of its career. What, specifically, did Belinskij lay
down as a foundation? In the first and most important place, Belinskij's
critical activity shifted the center of gravity of Russian literary activity
from aesthetic toward social concerns. This truism in the history of
Russian literary criticism is, perhaps, most clearly and convincingly
put by K. D. Kavelin, who considered himself Belinskij's devoted
disciple: "Belinskij symbolizes the change from a purely aesthetic
orientation of our literature and criticism to one which is social and
political, so far as the latter is possible. ... Each of us knows and
remembers how, in Belinskij's views, at first purely and strictly literary
and aesthetic, there gradually began to predominate a social, publicistic
element which little by little forced the aesthetic point of view into the
background." [21] Though a shift in the center of interest in Belinskij's
work is clear, even those critics in general unsympathetic to his school
emphasize that it was not complete. Volynskij, for example, remarks:
"Belinskij erred, fell into multifarious contradictions, but never ceased
to be a critic of literature." [22]

Belinskij's attitude toward society was composed of several elements.
On the one hand, there was an awareness of society as a developing
organism and the sense of man as a part of and something determined
by society, at least partially. On the other hand, there was an idealistic
sense of man as intrinsically good but warped by the society of which
he was inescapably a part. Thus there was a conflict between man and
society, or rather, between what man intrinsically was, ought to be,
and would be under more favorable social conditions and what society
encouraged or forced him to be. Belinskij came to the conclusion that
the resolution of the conflict depended upon the alteration of society
so as to enable man better to realize himself.

In order to encourage man to alter society, it was necessary to convince him of two main propositions: that man was the product of
society and that society, as then organized, did not satisfy his needs,
that is, did not permit man to be what, intrinsically, he was, what he
both ought to be and would be under more favorable conditions. Once
convinced of these propositions, man would rouse himself and alter

---

[20] Bursov, *Masterstvo Černyševskogo-kritika*, pp. 7-8.
[21] Kavelin, *Sobranie sočinenij*, III, p. 1100.
[22] Volynskij, *Russkie kritiki*, p. 155.

the organization of society to a more propitious pattern. Literature had an important role to play in helping to convince the public of the validity of these propositions.

The theme of sociological determinism, the contention that man as he is is the product of the society in which he lives, caused Belinskij to encourage writers to devote their attention to contemporary society, to sociological analysis. But sociological analysis was only the first step. It was necessary to show not only what society was but that what society was determined what the individuals who comprized it were, a demand which was to be satisfied, in part, by the work of such Russian novelists as Turgenev and Gončarov.

The application of this procedure was calculated to produce the following effect: if the individual is a product of society and if that individual is morally reprehensible, then moral indignation is directed not so much at the individual as at the society of which he is the inevitable product. Thus Belinskij arrived at a concept of literature as social protest, a literature which tended to show man in an unfavorable light, the so-called "negative" aspect of Russian literature, but in which moral indignation is directed, implicitly or explicitly, not at man himself but at the social conditions which have produced him. For whatever was bad in man, society was indicted, not man.

Together with sociological determinism, another theme was developed, that of humanitarianism. Now the reader's attention is directed to the intrinsic dignity of man, to the awakening and extension of moral sympathy, to the broad proposition that all men are brethren, that no social group enjoys a monopoly of moral virtue, and that all men are potentially (and some, actually, even under unfavorable conditions) possessed of morally admirable qualities. The effect is intended to be as follows: if the individual, despite inimicable social conditions, is yet morally admirable, is not this the strongest possible testimony to man's innate moral goodness?

Unfortunately, this line of reasoning tends to cancel out, or at least to call in question, the idea of sociological determinism. If, under admittedly intolerable social conditions, man is yet good (at least, on occasion), this fact may be interpreted as evidence of man's fundamental virtue, but what, then, becomes of the doctrine of sociological determinism? Humanitarianism, however, is related not to sociological determinism but to the idea of social justice, to the idea that society ought somehow to reward (or, at least, not to persecute) moral virtue. Again society is condemned, not because it produces bad men, for humanitarianism tends to emphasize the fact that men may be good, whatever society does to them, but because it is unworthy of man.[23]

It is important to note that the motivation of Belinskij's rejection of society, whether based on sociological determinism or on the idea of social justice, is a high ideal of man, an ideal the realization of which is frustrated or inhibited by the current organization of society. Belinskij's writing is permeated with a note of moral and ethical fervor, a note which was to leave a strong mark on Russian literary criticism. Combined with this ethical intensity was a certain lack of caution and restraint. These personal qualities of Belinskij's were at least as influential as his ideology.

At the base of the Belinskij tradition, then, we find a close linkage of literature and society, a precarious balance of literary and social interests already beginning to tip toward the predominance of the latter. Belinskij put a high value on literature, but he based this value on the service of literature to the common good of mankind and of the nation, conceived in broad terms. As a result, Belinskij opposed the theory of "art for art's sake", an attitude which marked the whole tradition descended from his work. At the same time there is, in Belinskij's work, scarcely a hint of that distrust of and hostility toward art which later found full expression, for example, in the work of Pisarev. Edel'son, writing of Belinskij's quarrels with the supporters of "pure" aesthetics, observes: "He carried on the struggle without questioning the very basis of poetry, without casting any suspicion either upon the independence of artistic creation or upon its deep significance in human life. He simply pointed out the high importance of poetry, realized in the best works of human creativity, demanded of it not simply amusement but serious content. Poetry itself and art he valued highly; their activity he placed on the same level as thought." [24]

Passionate and intemperate as Belinskij was, he was yet a rationalist in the sense that he believed, ultimately, in the capacity of reason to solve human problems, a faith which links the Russian adherents of his school to the French encyclopedists of the eighteenth century. His rationalism sets him off, in many ways, from the typical romantics. Because of his rationalism and his devotion to the idea of sociological determinism, he rejected the conventional romantic interest in the

---

[23] Plexanov stresses this ideological inconsistency in Belinskij's thinking. *N. G. Černyševskij*, p. 232.

[24] Denisjuk, *Kritičeskaja literatura o proizvedenijax N. G. Černyševskogo*, I, p. 120.

atypical, the fantastic, the inexplicable. On the same rationalistic grounds, he rejected metaphysics and theology, and he sought a rational organization of society, which he thought he had found in Socialism. The rationalism of Belinskij and his followers tended to turn them into doctrinaires who attempted to cram the world into the straightjacket of theory and to rebuild the world so as to conform to that theory.

Like the more typical romantics, Belinskij was a nationalist, but his nationalism was not mystical in its basis nor did it tend to exalt national particularity as an end in itself. Rather it tended to emphasize a rationalistic approach to the problem of the nation and to demand of the artist intellectual stature. In this same rationalistic spirit, as a critic, Belinskij devoted his attention to the anomalies of Russian culture as constituted in his day.

That Belinskij established a critical tradition and a school, there is substantial agreement. As to just which critics are members of his school, there is less agreement, understandably, since Belinskij's ideas were so varied and complex that, as has been pointed out, almost anyone in any degree opposed to the Russian *status quo* could claim Belinskij as an ancestor. Any selection of names is thus somewhat arbitrary, but for the purposes of this study, the Belinskij School will be considered as comprising Belinskij, Černyševskij, Dobroljubov, Pisarev, and Mixajlovskij. Marxist and Soviet critics are indubitably related to it, but they represent a synthesis of ideas which it is difficult to believe that Belinskij could have accepted or approved.

The epithets applied to the school of critics descended from Belinskij reflect various facets of the school as it developed. All of these facets are implicit in Belinskij's work, but they became more explicit as Belinskij's heritage was exploited by his successors. Their work is most frequently referred to as *publicističeskaja kritika* ("publicistic" criticism) or as *kritika po povodu* (criticism *à propos*), sometimes as *utilitarnaja kritika* ("utilitarian" criticism) (by Dostoevskij, for example) or as *tendencioznaja kritika* (*tendencioznj* or "tendentious" criticism.)

It is impossible to determine precisely what any of these terms means, since they are rarely defined. Further, rather than being employed simply as descriptive epithets, they tend to assume a pejorative function.[25] Such definitions of the terms as can be gleaned from Russian

---

[25] This pejorative function is clearly the issue when Lebedev-Poljanskij writes: "All those who write of his criticism as criticism *à propos* keep company with his enemies, who had a class interest in depreciating his literary authority and social

critical writing are not conspicuously helpful. Kavelin, for example, simply uses *publicističeskij* as a synonym for *obščestvennyj* (social).[26] Kirpotin defines a *publicističeskij kritik* ("publicistic" critic) as one who "discusses the phenomena of literary life from the point of view of their social significance."[27] Protopopov defines *publicističeskaja ili utilitarnaja kritika* as "that criticism which is guided not by aesthetic or metaphysical criteria but by the idea of rational sociality, the demands and needs of real life."[28] Evlaxov writes of "So-called 'publicistic criticism', i.e., criticism not based on the data of aesthetics, *unscientific* criticism, i.e., *non*-criticism."[29] Družinin in 1860 defined a *kritik-publicist* (critic-publicist) as one who, "*à propos* aesthetic works (sometimes important, sometimes unimportant) finds it possible to touch upon the most important questions of contemporary society, not developing them, due to not having the requisite space, but sustaining thought of these questions in the mass of thinking people and a salutary attitude toward them."[30] D'jačenko lists as *publicističeskie motivy* ("publicistic" motifs) a close link between literature and society, support for high moral ideals and education, and the use of literature as a lever for social progress.[31]

Steklov traces the term *kritika po povodu* back to Černyševskij and quotes his remark, "For a true critic, the work scrutinized is often only *a pretext for the development of his own view of the subject,* which is treated only superficially or one-sidedly."[32] The term *utilitarnaja kritika* is apparently derived from "utilitarian" philosophy and thus connected with Černyševskij, who was well known as a propounder of its tenets, though Dobroljubov is usually credited with having introduced "utilitarian" criteria into aesthetics. Sometimes the term is hyphenated: *uzko-utilitarnyj* (narrowly-utilitarian).[33] Lebedev-Poljanskij defines a *tendencioznyj kritik* as one "who seeks in the analysis of a literary work first of all proof of his own ideas".[34] Often the term is used where

influence." Lunačarskij and Lebedev-Poljanskij, *Očerki po istorii russkoj kritiki,* I, p. 174.

[26] Kavelin, *op. cit.,* p. 1100.
[27] Kirpotin, *Radikaľnyj raznočinec D. I. Pisarev,* p. 190.
[28] Protopopov, "Iz istorii našej literaturnoj kritiki", p. 139.
[29] Evlaxov, "Principy èstetiki Belinskogo", p. 1.
[30] Družinin, *op. cit.,* p. 603.
[31] D'jačenko, "Èvoljucija literaturnyx i obščestvennyx vzgljadov Belinskogo", p. 297.
[32] Steklov, *N. G. Černyševskij,* I, p. 338.
[33] Volynskij, *op. cit.,* p. 214.
[34] Lebedev-Poljanskij, *N. A. Dobroljubov,* p. 115.

we would use the term "propagandistic". A recent Soviet dictionary of terms used in aesthetics attempts to rehabilitate the adjective, at least partially. On the one hand, *tendencija* is distinguished from *tendencioznost'* as the difference between the actual and the intended effect of a work of art. On the other, *tendencioznost'* is defined as "The clearly expressed ideational orientation of a work of art, the obvious reflection in it of the class and ideational positions of the artist." *Tendencioznost'* may be either progressive or reactionary, and only reactionary, bourgeois *tendencioznost'* is condemned as conducive to distortion. "The works of art of socialist realism, permeated with the party spirit, are *tendencioznyj* in the better sense of the word." [35]

By whatever name it was called, this literary criticism was dominated by an interest in contemporary society based on the conviction that that society was in need of improvement. Sometimes this interest expressed itself in social analysis (usually designed to point out defects in the social structure), sometimes in the search for answers to pressing current social problems, sometimes in propaganda for socio-political panaceas. In any case, the critics sought to produce social effects, either through education, since education was regarded as a prerequisite for social improvement, or through propaganda for ideas which were expected to produce the same result. To this end the critics sought to enlist also the aid of creative writers.

Numerous objections against this variety of literary criticism have been raised, some dealing with the theory, some with its practice. If literature is used as a means for social analysis, then it is necessary to equate literature with life, art with reality, and the dangers of this procedural method have been pointed out.[36] It has been alleged that Russian literary criticism did succeed in eliciting from literature answers to current social problems. Mixajlovskij, for example, writes, "[La critique littéraire] . . . est arrivée, avec un rare talent, à tirer des créations artistiques des réponses pour les complications ambiantes." [37] But Nikolaj Solov'ev objects to the method on grounds of effectiveness and speaks of "the Danaidean labor of solving political problems by means of literary criticism and *belles lettres*".[38] The conventional answer to this objection, of course, is that those who used the method did not consider it ideal but rather the best *modus operandi* available. For ex-

[35]　Lebedeva, *Kratkij slovar' po èstetike*, pp. 369, 371-372.
[36]　Dobroljubov, *Polnoe sobranie sočinenij*, III, p. 19.
[37]　Mixajlovskij, *op. cit.*, p. 94.
[38]　N. I. Solov'ev, *Iskusstvo i žizn'*, I, p. x.

ample, writing ostensibly in reference to Polevoj, Nadeždin, and Belinskij, as well as to German literary critics of the late eighteenth and
early nineteenth centuries, but with obvious applicability to himself,
Černyševskij remarked, "They consecrated themselves to the service
of aesthetics willingly and calculatedly, not specifically because the
composition of reviews was for them a particularly attractive pursuit
but simply because it was the best of the means available to them for
acting on the life of society." [39] A preoccupation with social questions
tended to limit the critic's choice of works for discussion to those
which best served his ends, and the works chosen for discussion were
often distorted or simply ignored. In the latter case, Plexanov describes
the result as follows: "The critic busies himself not with what is said
in the work which he analyses but with what might have been said in
it if the author had shared the critic's social opinions." [40] When the
motif of using literary criticism as a means for public education comes
to the fore, literary criticism may be dominated by the need to dis-
seminate useful information. Certainly the temptation was great. The
critics whom we shall discuss were excited by new ideas and impatient
to share them with the reading public, which otherwise would have
remained uninformed of matters about which the critics felt that information must be broadcast without delay. Much of the influence of
the school of critics with which we are dealing resulted from this purely
publicistic aspect of their activity. Kotljarevskij notes, "Belinskij,
Černyševskij, Pisarev, Mixajlovskij were involuntary encyclopedists." [41]
Perhaps the commonest complaint against the school is its relative
neglect of aesthetic values. For example, Družinin, writing in 1856,
remarked: "No sooner had our criticism of the 40's become carried
away by the new didacticism than it deprived itself of the right to be
artistically fastidious. If a work analyzed by it contributed directly to
the education of the contemporary reader, developed an exciting idea,
and did not offend the rules of grammar, it was considered satisfactory
and remarkable." [42] A predominant interest in social values led inevitably to the displacement of aesthetic values as criteria.

Recently M. Kagan has objected to aspects of the Belinskij tradition
as inhibiting the proper development of general Soviet aesthetics: what

[39] Akademija nauk SSSR, *Literaturnoe nasledstvo*, XXV-XXVI, p. 141.
[40] Plexanov, *V. G. Belinskij* (1923), p. 196.
[41] Kotljarevskij, "Iz istorii obščestvennogo nastroenija šestidesjatyx godov:
Nikolaj Aleksandrovič Dobroljubov", p. 248.
[42] Družinin, *op. cit.*, p. 228.

might be termed literaturocentrism, a predominating interest in literature to the detriment of the other arts; lack of attention to the specific content of art which distinguishes it from science; and a consequent neglect of the whole problem of artistic value. Typically, he calls on the authority of Belinskij himself in support of his protest against the Belinskij tradition.[43]

---

[43] Kagan, "O putjax issledovanija specifiki iskusstva".

II

VISSARION GRIGOREVIČ BELINSKIJ (1811-1848)

1

Vissarion Grigorevič Belinskij was born on 30 May (11 June, new style), 1811 in Sveaborg, where he remained until 1816, when his family moved to Čembar. Here he finished his elementary schooling and then entered the gymnasium in Penza, where he did not complete his studies. In the fall of 1829 he entered the University of Moscow, where he was a student until 1832, when he was expelled, ostensibly on account of ill health and native unfitness for academic pursuits, but possibly, at least in part, as a result of his having written *Dmitrij Kalinin,* a play rejected by the censor. Belinskij had begun to publish in the Moscow press as early as 1831, and in 1833 he joined the staffs of *Teleskop* (*The Telescope*) and *Molva* (*Rumor*) as a protégé of N. I. Nadeždin. In 1834 (September-December) his first major piece of literary criticism, "Literaturnye mečtanija" ("Literary Reveries"), appeared in *Teleskop*. Unfortunately, in 1836 the publication of *Teleskop* was suspended as a result of the appearance in its pages of Čaadaev's "Filosofičeskoe pis'mo" ("Philosophical Letter"), and Belinskij was without regular literary employment until the spring of 1838, when he became the editor of *Moskovskij nabljadatel'* (*The Moscow Observer*). This journal survived only a year, but in 1839 the publisher Kraevskij invited Belinskij to Peterburg, where he took over the critical and bibliographical sections of *Otečestvennye zapiski* (*Fatherland Notes*). Belinskij retained this position until 1846, when he joined the staff of *Sovremennik* (*The Contemporary*), of which Panaev and Nekrasov had gained control, and his articles appeared there through 1847 and the first quarter of 1848. On 26 May (7 June, new style) 1848, having long endured increasingly poor health, Belinskij died.

The evolution of Belinskij's ideas was rapid, kaleidoscopic, and complex. Beginning by the assimilation of the philosophical ideas current among the intellectually enterprizing individuals of his day in Russia, he was influenced by a succession of German and French thinkers, and his philosophical and literary theories experienced continuous revision. In order to understand Belinskij's position at the time when he came in contact with Dostoevskij (in 1845, three years before Belinskij's death), it is necessary to sketch the genesis and evolution of his ideas, rather summarily so far as the earlier part of his career is concerned but in greater detail for the period when the two men were acquainted with each other.

In the course of sketching the evolution of Belinskij's ideas, it will be noted that these were consistently influenced by Western European sources. In this respect Belinskij was no exception among the Russians of his day. Indeed, Isaiah Berlin goes so far as to write: "Scarcely one single political and social idea to be found in Russia in the nineteenth century was born on native soil." [1] Pre-Soviet Russian literary critics and students of Russian intellectual history admitted this fact, but they emphasized the adaptations to which Western European ideas were subjected in Russia, and Belinskij's ideas were cited as an example of the process. In general, Soviet critics make a more chauvinistic plea for Belinskij's intellectual independence and originality, though they are often forced to admit that the ideas which he propagated were borrowed from Western Europe. At one time, Soviet criticism attempted to forge a link between Belinskij and Radiščev and the Decembrists, ignoring their intellectual indebtedness to the West and seeking to create an impression of a purely Russian ideological succession. Recently a more balanced viewpoint has been evidenced. [2]

At the time when Belinskij began his activity, German influence permeated the Russian intellectual atmosphere. The general effect of the German philosophers was to produce an exhilarating sense of intellectual liberation as a result of a shift from mechanistic categories of thought to a different intellectual mode. Instead of conceiving the universe as fundamentally static, a mechanism which, though in movement, was essentially unalterable, these thinkers conceived the universe as a living organism, activated by a vital impulse which eluded ration-

---

[1] Berlin, "A Marvellous Decade", June, 1955, p. 33. Cf. Wellek, *A History of Modern Criticism*, III, p. 244.
[2] Ščerbina discusses the zig-zags in the Soviet interpretation of Belinskij's ideological indebtedness to western sources in Akademija nauk SSSR, *Belinskij i sovremennost'*, pp. 6-8. Gul'jaev insists on Belinskij's debt but also upon his innovations. See *V. G. Belinskij*, pp. 2-4.

alistic analysis and comprehensible only in mystical and metaphysical terms, through intuition and spiritual insight rather than intellection.

The conception of organic growth as a cosmic principle entailed a new attitude toward history. Instead of the fundamentally irrelevant play of immutable principles in a closed system, change without progress, history was conceived as the successive unfolding of what was essentially new, an eternal progress. The peculiar calling of the philosopher was to discern the direction in which progress was moving, not through the observation of phenomena, not through logical deduction, but by intuitive contemplation. Once having perceivéd the direction, the relevance of history, the individual became one with it. The focus of the system, however, was not so much upon the individual as upon the social organism of which he is a part and by means of which he realizes his destiny. The individual and the social organism with which and within which he interacts are mutually dependent, and neither can realize itself, fulfill its mission, without proper definition of its historical role. Hence that obsession with the importance of getting in step with history which marks so much of Russian thought down to our own day. This point of view tended to stress the social role of the individual, both as a means by which the individual is able to realize his historical role and as a means by which society achieves its destiny, and it inspired that sense of active social idealism which marked Russian intellectual life in the 20's and 30's.

For the Germans the nation was that social organism of which the individual was a part, without which his existence was meaningless and through which, only, he could find self-realization. The Germans insisted that the human ideal was universal, rather than national, but that it was only through the national that the universal could be approached. This paradox provided a respectable basis on which any relatively homogeneous ethnic group could erect a nationalistic philosophy, an opportunity which the Russians were prompt to grasp.

This complex of ideas of German origin had unique impact in Russia, where the intellectual climate was quite different from that of Western Europe. Russian society, which had been isolated historically from the intellectual ferment of the Renaissance and Reformation, was unaccustomed to that competition of contending ideologies long prevalent in Western Europe. The situation was aggravated by a relative paucity of educational opportunity and by official hostility to new ideas. Coupled with a relative lack of intellectual sophistication, there existed in Russia at this time a passionate eagerness for new ideas, a sense of the unresolved problems of an enormous land, and a desire to play a significant role in the pageant of world history.

The results of this combination of circumstances were various. On the one hand, due to official suspicion, study of the new philosophical currents was driven underground, thereby acquiring all the seductive attractions of forbidden fruit, and, in addition, those interested in philosophy assumed an attitude of hostility toward existent Russian social and political institutions. On the other, lack of a tradition and the experience of the free competition between ideas contributed to extremism. Writing of this period, de Voguë remarks, "Les cheveux que les Allemands coupaient en quatre, on les recoupa en huit à Moscou." [3] This extremism did not confine itself within the limits of abstract thought but expressed itself in an enthusiastic desire to translate ideas into action as speedily as possible, without having first integrated the ideas into a logically consistent system. A further contributing factor to the Russian state of mind was a certain messianism derived partly from Herder and Schelling, an intoxicating sense of vocation, of an historical mission embracing both the individual and the nation.

Russian intellectuals enthusiastically accepted German leadership in two related fields of thought: the philosophy of nationhood and the philosophy of art. The two were intimately related. It was the artist, rather than the systematic philosopher, who, due to the superior sensitivity of unconscious artistic intuition, was able to discern and express national individuality. Hence the high position accorded the creative artist, both in Germany and in Russia.

But though the critics, the theoreticians of art, proclaimed the supremacy of the artist, at the same time they tended to usurp his function as seer and prophet under the guise of systematizing, making explicit and orderly, the traits of national character which the artist revealed. Speaking of the Germans, Isaiah Berlin writes: "The romantic critics in some cases supposed themselves not merely to be revealing the nature of types of knowledge or thought or feeling hitherto unrecognized or inadequately analysed, but to be building new cosmological systems, new faiths, new forms of life, and indeed to be direct instruments of the process of the spiritual redemption, or 'self-realization', of the universe." [4] This ambiguous but imposing function was inherited by the Russian literary critics; the role of literary critic be-

---

[3]   de Voguë, *Le roman russe*, p. 63.
[4]   Berlin, *op. cit.*, November, 1955, p. 23.

came confused with that of social prophet, a role which the Russian literary critics were only too willing to assume (and which Russian society seemed only too willing to grant them).

The German philosopher whose ideas were most influential at the beginning of the period under discussion was Schelling. His influence appears to have been predominant until approximately 1836. Schelling conceived of the universe as a unitary organism evolving through successive spiritual stages which found their most complete expression in man. Individuals were but single cells, infinitesimal living parts of an organic whole. As such, they were, in part, able to understand the whole, its growth and direction, not by rational processes but by the operation of sympathy, insight, intuition. Schelling's stress upon intuition rather than upon reason as a means of knowing caused him to place art more or less on a level with philosophy. Speaking of Schelling's ideas, Wellek writes: "Both the philosopher and the artist penetrate into the essence of the universe, the absolute. Art thus breaks down the barrier between the real and the ideal world. It is the representation of the infinite in the finite, a union of nature and freedom, for it is both a product of the conscious and the unconscious, of the imagination which unconsciously creates our real world and consciously creates the ideal world of art", though he goes on to say, "Schelling's views on the exact relationship between philosophy and art shift: at times philosophy and art and truth and beauty are completely identified; at other times they are conceived of as related like archetype and image." [5] To Schelling must be credited, in large part, the typically romantic idea that artists are more sensitive to the significance of their time than others who seek to interpret it by more purely rational means, for artists are peculiarly responsive to factors in the environment which escape ratiocination. Thus the artist is the guide, *par excellence*, to the significance of a given historical moment.

Belinskij became acquainted with Schelling's ideas when he associated himself with the Stankevič Circle in Moscow after his expulsion from the university in 1832. Since the study of philosophy was discouraged in Russian universities, intellectually enterprising individuals organized themselves into informal groups for the purpose of pursuing studies in which they could not engage formally. The most prominent and influential of these groups were those led by Gercen (Herzen) and Stankevič. The Gercen Circle devoted itself principally to politics, whereas philosophy was the center of gravity in the Stankevič Circle,

[5] Wellek, *A History of Modern Criticism*, II, p. 75.

though neither group was exclusively narrow in its interests and associations. The studies conducted were neither systematic nor scholarly. Some of the members were more or less familiar at first hand with German philosophy, while others (Belinskij, for example) contented themselves with illumination received at second hand. The dominant personality in the Stankevič Circle was that of its leader. Stankevič held that artists and scientists were both engaged in the same pursuit: a search for the eternal order concealed by the flux of events. Like Schelling, he gave a preeminent position to art because it alone embodied partial insights into the nature of eternal order, and he considered art and philosophy as but two aspects of a single truth.[6]

Because of the purely personal nature of the relationship between the two men and because all of the members of the group made contributions to its discussions, it is difficult to assess the extent of Stankevič's influence upon Belinskij, but it is perhaps significant that the room in which Belinskij worked was graced with a good portrait of Stankevič. The ideas prevalent in the Stankevič Circle were expressed in Belinskij's first influential critical article, "Literaturnye mečtanija", and left enduring traces in Belinskij's thought. The high position Belinskij assigned to the artist, whose powers of intuition, expressed through unconscious creativity, made him the surest guide to truth, clearly derives from Schelling's ideas, which reached Belinskij through the medium of the Stankevič Circle.[7]

Together with the ideas prevalent in the Stankevič Circle, the influence of Belinskij's predecessor, the literary critic Nadeždin, needs to be mentioned. In his *Očerki gogolevskogo perioda* (*Studies in the Age of Gogol'*), Černyševskij devotes more than a chapter to Nadeždin. To him is attributed the introduction into Russian literary criticism of the aesthetic principles of German philosophy. Černyševskij points out that Nadeždin and Belinskij shared this common point of departure, discerns traces of Nadeždin's influence in some of Belinskij's attitudes, especially his consistent opposition to French romanticism, and calls Nadeždin Belinskij's teacher (*obrazovatel'*). Trubačev points to the first thesis of Nadeždin's dissertation: "*Ubi vita, ibi poësis*" as the source of Belinskij's proposition: "*Gde žizn' – tam i poèzija*" ("Where there

---

[6]   For a discussion of the Stankevič Circle and the ideas prevalent there about 1835, see Kornilov, *Molodye gody Mixaila Bakunina*, pp. 118-128.
[7]   Poljakov, in two books on Belinskij published in 1960, strongly discounts the influence of Stankevič and his circle. See *Vissarion Grigor'evič Belinskij*, p. 78, and *Vissarion Belinskij*, pp. 110-119. For a recent and cogent study of the relationship between Stankevič and Belinskij, see Brown, *Stankevich*, pp. 83-114.

is life, there also is poetry") and to the third thesis: *"Formae poeseos, qua viget, aetatis ingenio determinantur"* as foreshadowing Belinskij's demand that art forms reflect contemporary life, but most writers make a moderate estimate of the extent of Nadeždin's influence upon Belinskij.[8] In any case, after the suppression of *Teleskop,* Nadeždin abandoned literary criticism (though he later wrote on other subjects for the periodical press), so that his active influence could only have affected the beginning of Belinskij's career. Nadeždin's ideas were sufficiently related to those of the Stankevič Circle so that the two influences reenforced each other and are extremely difficult to differentiate.

Thus, at the beginning of his career as a literary critic, Belinskij was not conspicious as an innovator; rather, he gave public expression to a group of related ideas derived ultimately from Schelling which, though new to the general public, had already gained acceptance in other quarters. Belinskij's almost immediately recognized preeminence as a critic resulted not from the freshness and originality of his ideas but from his ability to express effectively and attractively the intellectual currents of his day. In addition to giving vigorous expression and an individual turn to ideas which he had made his own, Belinskij waged unremitting warfare against those critics who continued to defend earlier points of view.

In 1836 the influence of Schelling upon Belinskij was succeeded by that of Fichte. As was the case with Schelling, Fichte was not swallowed whole in Russia, and the effect of Fichte's ideas was that of filling out and completing those of Schelling. Though the influence of Fichte upon Belinskij lasted only about a year, it was important in strengthening the ethical element in Belinskij's thinking and a symptom of increased interest in ethical problems on the part of the Russian intelligentsia.

The brief ascendancy of the influence of Fichte upon Belinskij was succeeded by the influence of Hegel in 1837 and coincided with the departure of Stankevič from Russia, leaving the leadership of his circle to Bakunin, who now served as the filter through which the ideas of the German philosophers reached Belinskij. Bakunin's interest in Hegel

[8]   Trubačev, "Predšestvennik i učitel' Belinskogo", p. 511; Filippov, "Sud'by russkoj filosofii, VI", September, 1894 (directed principally against Trubačev); Miljukov, *Iz istorii russkoj intelligencii,* p. 211; D'jačenko, "Èvoljucija literaturnyx i obščestvennyx vzgljadov Belinskogo", p. 297; I. N. Ždanov, *Sočinenija,* II, pp. 208-211; Mezencev, *Belinskij i russkaja literatura,* pp. 49-63. Polevoj is even less frequently seen as a forerunner of Belinskij, but see Gul'jaev, "Literaturno-èstetičeskie vzgljady N. A. Polevogo", p. 75.

had been aroused early in 1837, and his interest in this philosopher's ideas soon became serious. Unlike the shift in influence from Schelling to Fichte, which did not involve a change in basic philosophical position, the shift from Fichte to Hegel produced a considerable revolution in the ideas influencing the Russian intelligentsia and involved the abandonment of old positions and the acquisition of new ones.[9]

Perhaps the most influential of Hegel's ideas, so far as Russia was concerned, was his theory of history. Schelling had conceived of history as a more or less continuous progress. Hegel, on the contrary, saw history as progressing not continuously but by a "dialectical" process, a struggle between "thesis" and "anti-thesis" resulting in a "resolution" which became a new thesis, giving birth to a new anti-thesis, and so on, infinitely. Instead of relying principally upon intuition to understand the process of history, as Schelling had done, Hegel attempted to reduce the movement of history to a rational process, logically analyzable and predictable.

As Bakunin interpreted Hegel at this time, the *status quo* was logically inevitable. It was thus idle to complain or to rebel, since things as they were could not possibly be otherwise. It was in this sense that Belinskij understood Hegel, and, for a relatively brief period, he attempted to come to terms with things as they were. Hegel's idea was, of course, susceptible of a different interpretation, and, ironically, Belinskij perhaps came closer to it later on when he professed to be rejecting it. In any case, Belinskij seems to have acquired from Hegel's influence, as filtered through Bakunin's interpretation, a conviction that the march of history was discernible, not intuitively and imaginatively as Schelling had taught, but rationally and logically.

Hegel's ideas on aesthetics also influenced Belinskij, who was acquainted with them through a translation-adaptation made by Katkov. Belinskij's formula that art is "thinking in images" derived ultimately from Hegel.[10] For Belinskij, as for Hegel, the content of art was that of philosophy and religion. Perhaps more important was Hegel's idea of a work of art as an expression of a given historical moment, rather than as an expression of transcendent and timeless truth, and its

---

[9] For discussions of the impact of Hegel's ideas in Russia, see Filippov, *op. cit.*, November, 1894, pp. 41-56; Kovalevskij, "Šellingianstvo i gegel'janstvo v Rossii"; Čiževskij, *Gegel' v Rossii*; Koyré, *Études*, pp. 103-170. Poljakov denies the influence of Bakunin on Belinskij and argues that the significant influence was rather the reverse. See *Vissarion Grigor'evič Belinskij*, p. 108.

[10] Brown points out that this idea is to be found in Stankevič's letters. See *op. cit.*, p. 51.

function in the process of social change. For Hegel content was decisive in a work of art, but this implied no neglect of aesthetic form. However, there was in Hegel a certain anti-aesthetic element. Wellek writes: "As always, Hegel's attitude is ambivalent. From the point of view of his Hellenic ideal, modern art is inferior. But he sees its historical necessity, its implication in the social process moving toward middle-class society." [11]

From his exposure to Hegel's philosophy as expounded by Bakunin, Belinskij acquired certain ideas and attitudes to which he clung even after his general infatuation with Hegel was at an end. From this source Belinskij got the notion that the march of history could be perceived logically and not only intuitively, as Schelling had taught, and became even more strongly interested in the history of literature. So far as his aesthetics was concerned, to Schelling's idea of the work of art as a revelation of national character, Belinskij, influenced by Hegel, added the idea of the work of art as the expression of a given historical moment and an agent for social propulsion. Like Hegel, he continued to show keen appreciation of the formal aesthetic values of a work of art but began to feel that other values were, perhaps, more important.[12]

Belinskij did not long remain true to Hegel's general philosophy as he interpreted it. His philosophical position began to shift in 1841, though this change in viewpoint was expressed in letters rather than in his published articles, and by 1843 it was complete. The new intellectual influences which succeeded Belinskij's infatuation with Hegel were principally two: French Utopian Socialism (as expressed in the novels of George Sand and the works of such theorists as Pierre Leroux, Cabet, Saint-Simon, Proudhon, Louis Blanc, and Fourrier) and "left Hegelianism" (especially as expressed by Feuerbach). Almost everyone who has written about the evolution of Belinskij's ideas has commented upon his dramatic shift from a contemptuous attitude toward French thought to one of respectful adulation, and in this respect, as in so many others, Belinskij was typical and representative of the period. The influence of left Hegelianism upon Belinskij has been emphasized, quite understandably, by Marxist writers, but it has by no means been ignored by critics of other persuasions. The personal in-

---

[11]   Wellek, *op. cit.*, pp. 327-328. Plexanov points out that this was also Belinskij's attitude. See *V. G. Belinskij* (1923), pp. 183-184.
[12]   For Hegel's influence on Belinskij, see von Laziczius, "Fr. Hegels Einfluss auf V. Belinskij". Cf. Gul'jaev, *V. G. Belinskij*, pp. 58-74.

fluence of Gercen should also be mentioned. In Belinskij's overt rejection of Hegel, there is, as Boborykin points out, a paradoxical element: "If Belinskij himself, in his last articles, speaking of the vital problems of literature, considered himself an anti-Hegelian, then he was plainly mistaken, through absent-mindedness or incomplete knowledge of the sense and of the relevant passages in Hegel's aesthetics." [13]

Since it was in this final period in the evolution of Belinskij's ideas that he wrote on Dostoevskij, it is important to fix his final position as firmly as possible. This is by no means easy to do, and different students of Belinskij's life and work have offered widely differing interpretations, whereas some have simply thrown up their hands in bewilderment. The explanation for these divergent, sometimes contradictory, sometimes defeated attempts to systematize Belinskij's thought seems to lie in the fact that Belinskij was never a narrow and doctrinaire thinker, that it was impossible for him to confine his ideas within any straight-jacket, whether of his own or of another's manufacture. His ideas were in constant turbulent evolution, and his point of view never remained constant long enough for him to overhaul his ideas systematically and reduce them to consistency. Thus, in Belinskij's criticism, one is apt to find, at one and the same time, traces of abandoned philosophical positions and hints of developments to come as well as the expression of a currently favorite position.

This lack of system in Belinskij's ideas has been explained in various ways. Some writers, for example, attribute it to the unfavorable journalistic conditions under which Belinskij was forced to work, whereas others explain it as the result of Belinskij's inability to reconcile the antipodal attractions of German philosophical and French social thought or the opposed influences of aesthetic sensibility and social conscience. Baltalon emphasizes the conflicting influences of German theoretical aesthetics and the actual achievements of Russian literature as it developed before Belinskij's eyes. [14] The existence of official censorship also doubtless played some part by inhibiting the open and complete expression of Belinskij's ideas. His letters contain frequent complaints of the censor, and Soviet critics, particularly, insist upon the deleterious effects of censorship on Belinskij's work. However, taking the official censorship into consideration, it is often puzzling to account

---

[13] Boborykin, "Krasota, žizn', i tvorčestvo", pp. 105-106.
[14] Examples of these various views may be found in Vetrinskij, *V sorokovyx godax*, p. 43; Baltalon, *Èstetika*, p. viii; *Principy*, pp. 8-9, 13-14; Lavreckij, *Èstetika Belinskogo*, p. 11.

for much that did find its way safely into print. Dostoevskij, writing of the censorship of the period, remarked, " 'Dreadful things' used to slip through (for example, all Belinskij slipped through)." [15]

In any case, Belinskij has often been acknowledged as the central figure of his time. (His chief competitor in this respect is Gercen.) The reason for this lies rather in the representativeness than in the consistency of his ideas. This centrality of position accounts, at least in part, for Belinskij's influence during his lifetime, and it has a bearing upon the lack of a comprehensive system in his thinking. Apollon Grigor'ev wrote: "Belinskij would not have been Belinskij, would not have been a critic of genius, had he not responded to everything which moved the generation whose mighty voice he was." [16] In his work, all the ideas of his period, all those opinions which were to result later in wide divergences of position, found expression.

If the centrality of Belinskij's ideological position helps to explain his influence upon his contemporaries, it also helps to explain Belinskij's prestige with posterity. Precisely because of the diversity of the ideas which he expressed at one time or another, succeeding generations of writers of a wide spectrum of convictions have been able to appeal to him as an authority. Both the Slavophiles and the Westerners treated Belinskij's memory with respect, and as new parties formed, Belinskij's prestige remained substantially intact. All parties appealed to him as an authority, though each was eager to deny that its opponents had any right to share that prestige and insisted that it, alone, was the true heir to his mantle. [17] Much as the parties squabbled as to which of them was rightful heir to the inheritance, they united in a desire to preserve that inheritance, the possession and significance of which they contested. A situation of this sort is hardly likely to produce a dispassionate evaluation of Belinskij's work, a situation about which Družinin complained as early as 1856, at a time when Černyševskij began a campaign to popularize Belinskij's views. [18] The Belinskij "myth" persisted through the turn of the century when Belinskij's authority was challenged by critics who wished to substitute or to

[15]   Dostoevskij, *The Diary of a Writer*, I, p. 344.
[16]   Grigor'ev, *Sočinenija*, I, p. 232.
[17]   An exclusively possessive attitude toward Belinskij's legacy is clear from such a passage as the following: "Like Dobroljubov and Černyševskij, Belinskij was, of course, a predecessor of Marxist thought and in no way of *narodnik* thought." Lunačarskij and Lebedev-Poljanskij, *Očerki po istorii russkoj kritiki*, I. p. 214.
[18]   Družinin, *Sobranie sočinenij*, VII, pp. 189-242.

create a new critical inheritance,[19] and it has been stubbornly buttressed by Soviet literary policy.

At the base of Belinskij's critical position in the final period of his career lies a fundamental ambiguity: as Bowman puts it, in reference to Belinskij's conception of the writer's role, "He is ... teacher and poet at the same time", and goes on to comment, "This compound definition of the literary artist and his function led Belinskij to make statements on this subject throughout the forties which often seem to contradict each other." [20] This ambiguity in Belinskij's literary criticism is the result of the interplay of two forces, often pulling in opposite directions: on the one hand, an extraordinarily sharp and penetrating aesthetic flair; on the other, a need to integrate art into a comprehensive philosophical pattern. That Belinskij's aesthetic sense was acute and perceptive there can be no doubt. Unerringly he detected major literary talents as they appeared. (His immediate support of Dostoevskij is a case in point.) At the same time he campaigned against literary mediocrities. The grounds upon which he justified (or rationalized) his views have been questioned, but the fact that he was able to single out the significant figures of Russian literature as they appeared has not.

2

What were the general philosophical ideas which conditioned Belinskij's theories about literature? The central philosophical problem which dominated Belinskij's activity was an attempt to find some satisfactory relationship between the ideal (the good, the true, the beautiful) and that reality which Belinskij saw all about him and which he found to be bad, false, and ugly. He came to believe that "The only rational reality is the universal progress of humanity which evolves behind the appearance of the visible world." [21] This reality was not only rational, but moral. P. Kogan writes: "To the end of his literary activity the idea of moral justice as lying at the basis of developing life never left him. To the end he kept the idealistic point of view and applied his

[19] See Sakulin, "Psixologija Belinskogo", and Lebedev-Poljanskij, *V. G. Belinskij*, pp. 353-354, for discussions of Volynskij and Ajxenval'd, especially, as opponents of the Belinskij legend.
[20] Bowman, *Vissarion Belinski*, p. 150. Bowman rejects Plexanov's attempt to synthesize Belinskij's aesthetic pronouncements into a system. See p. 46.
[21] *Ibid.*, p. 203.

own moral, subjective standards to the phenomena of reality." [22] In reference to Belinskij, Dostoevskij wrote, "He knew that moral principles are the basis of all things." [23]

This philosophical position clearly derives elements from the German romantic idealist philosophers. It involves a dualistic attitude toward the world. On the one hand, there is the world of visible appearances, but, on the other, an ideal world (both rational and moral) only imperfectly realized in the visible world. Of the two, it is the ideal world, the world of things as they *ought to be* and only imperfectly *are*, that is the more significant, the more *real*. The ideal world is conceived of as in the process of being realized in the world of visible appearances; what *ought to be* not only *ought to be* but *will be*.

So far as the present is concerned, what *is* is only in part what *ought to be*. Only what both *is* and *ought to be* is *real*. What *is* and *ought not to be* will either pass away or be transformed into what *ought to be*. The future is, from this point of view, more *real* than the present. In consequence, it is easy to understand the strong orientation of Belinskij's thought toward the future. At the same time, discontent with the present is justified on philosophical grounds. This position satisfied two of Belinskij's strong needs: faith in the future and dissatisfaction with the present.

The idea of progress involves change moving toward a goal. Though the future may be hidden, the past is, at least in theory, more accessible, and study of it may reveal clues as to the direction in which progress lies. If history is, in any sense, an orderly march, then by determining the past route, the future route may be extrapolated. Thus, much as Belinskij's thought was oriented to the future, it was also obsessed with the appeal to history, to the past as the gauge of the future. Belinskij's emphasis on the historical development of Russian literature has often been listed as one of his most important contributions to the tradition of Russian literary criticism.

Together with faith in the future and rejection of the present, yet another motif makes itself felt in Belinskij's thought. This is the impulse to act upon, to change what *is*, to accelerate the arrival of what *ought to be*, to speed up the march of history. Belinskij and, especially, his successors were unable to resist this temptation.

On the one hand, they saw the problem as one of education, of enlightenment, an attitude which links them with the French *philosophes*

---

[22]   Kogan, *Očerki po istorii novejšej russkoj literatury*, I, p. 152.
[23]   Dostoevskij, *op. cit.*, I, p. 6.

of the eighteenth century. Like them, Belinskij and his followers had enormous faith in reason. If only man could perceive what was both rational and moral, he could not but abide by the dictates of reason and morality. Evil becomes equated with ignorance. On the other hand, the influence of the French Utopian socialists stimulated Belinskij's interest in social justice and the problems involved in the organization of human society. Belinskij and his followers were willing to admit that, strong as the imperative of reason and morality was, man was not always able to abide by it. In addition to ignorance, they saw an unjust social organization as an obstacle to the realization of what was moral and rational. Here, too, the notion of progress played its role. The current state of Russian social organization was not what it *ought to be* or what it would be in the future; thus the contemporary Russian social organization was condemned in the name of the future, of what was *real*, of what both *ought to be* and *would be*.

In any case, Belinskij and his followers clung to the conception of man popularized by Rousseau. Man was *really* good, what he *ought to be*. If, in actuality, he was not what he *ought to be*, then ignorance, or the social organization, or both together were responsible, not man himself. It is difficult not to reach the conclusion that the theories of Belinskij and of the men who shared his point of view were the result less of a desire for logical consistency than of need to justify their basic conviction that men were good and that society, as organized, was bad.

Belinskij's general philosophical position clearly influenced and helps to explain his theories about literature. From the German romantic idealist philosophers Belinskij derived a high regard for the role of the artist, particularly the literary artist, whose work is an expression of universal culture in concrete terms of national particularity.

In order to be equipped to express the national life in this fashion, Belinskij demanded that the artist be well educated so as to be able to take a broad and comprehensive view of the national life. Not only must the artist give expression to what *is* (Černyševskij was to express this idea by writing that it is the function of art to "reproduce" life); he must place what *is* in the perspective of the truth which lies behind it and beyond it, of what *ought to be* (Černyševskij was to express this idea by writing that it is the function of art to "explain" life). In this perspective, what *is* and *ought not to be* is condemned in the name of what *ought to be* (Černyševskij's pronouncement that art "judges").

These explanatory and judgmental functions have a theurgic aspect. If ignorance is regarded as an impediment to progress, then the reduction of ignorance acts to hasten progress. If what *ought not to be* in national life is condemned, then dissatisfaction with actuality is aroused. For Belinskij, if what *is* is demonstrably what it *ought not to be*, then it is incumbent upon the individual to do whatever lies within his power to transform what *is* into what *ought to be*. To expedite progress thus becomes part of the artist's function, either by reducing ignorance or by arousing dissatisfaction with the current social order. In either case, the artist's function is not only to express, explain, or judge the national life but also to change it by such means as are at his disposal. When the theurgic motif, the desire to act upon the national life becomes paramount, art becomes *tendencioznyj* ("biased", "tendentious").

If the national life is in need of transformation and progress toward that end is to be expedited, then new difficulties appear: toward which of possible ideal goals should society move? (This problem split the Russian intelligentsia into rival camps, Westernizers and Slavophiles, during Belinskij's lifetime.) And even if a general goal is agreed upon, what are the most efficacious means of moving toward that goal? (This problem split the Westernizers into rival camps, liberals and radicals, during the careers of Belinskij's successors, Černyševskij and Dobroljubov.)

The difficulty of such a complex attitude toward art as Belinskij's lies in reconciling these assorted functions: expressive, educative, judgmental, and theurgic. Belinskij's interest in the expressive function of art led him to champion realism; his interest in the educative and judgmental functions led him in the direction of publicistic art; his interest in its theurgic function nudged him in the direction of *tendencioznyj* literature. The difficulty of reconciling these functions is already implicit in Belinskij's criticism; it was to become more explicit in the work of his successors.

The multiplicity of functions which Belinskij assigned to the artist accounts for the contradictions apparent in Belinskij's aesthetic theory. It proved impossible to juggle these functions in such a way that balance between them was maintained. Perhaps the fundamental problem was that of the autonomy of art. Is art an end or a means? Is the artist an independent, objective observer, or is he an advocate and propagandist? Is his concern simply with what *is,* or is he an active agent of change?

Belinskij was unable to resolve this problem satisfactorily. As Bowman remarks, "All the ambiguities in Belinskij's final critical doctrine have their origin in his conception of literature as playing a part in the general progress of humanity, in his conception of the artist as a warrior against whatever impedes the historical march of Reason. As Belinski himself was well aware, such a doctrine requires a precarious balance to be maintained between the urgent protest which he was concerned with making and the human truth in whose name the protest was to be made. The artist could be the spokesman of humanity only by being a faithful witness to human truth. Such an ideological requirement could never be met unless the integrity of the artist was maintained; yet at the same time it imposed upon the artist a militant conception of himself." [24]

From its inception the Belinskij school was, in a certain sense, anti-aesthetic. Belinskij energetically opposed "pure" art, art divorced from any except aesthetic considerations. Theoretically, Belinskij took the position that such art had never existed and could not exist. The attempt to limit art to purely aesthetic expression meant to clip its wings, to impose upon it humiliating and artificial limitations which merely crippled it. As we shall see, this basic position was adopted by Černyševskij. Belinskij followed Hegel in considering Greek art as closest to the ideal of "pure" art but felt that the development of art was gradually moving further and further away from this ideal. Belinskij's aesthetic sense, however, did not permit him to regard asthetic considerations as irrelevant, though they ceased to be paramount. Theoretically, according to Belinskij, a work of art could satisfy both aesthetic demands and social needs. The balance of aesthetic and social interests proved unstable, even for Belinskij. Though Belinskij frequently protested against didactic art, toward the end of his life, as we shall see, he was willing to admit privately that if a choice had to be made between aesthetic quality and social relevance, then he was willing to sacrifice aesthetic quality.

Belinskij's literary theories tended to encourage realism. Writers were urged to devote their attention to life as it was lived around them, to focus their interest on contemporary Russian life and its problems, to forge a close link between literature and life. Through such social analysis, literature fulfilled its function of assisting in the definition of the national life. But, much as Belinskij was interested in encouraging writers to describe and analyze contemporary life, he was not interested solely in objective description, in recording, classifying, defining. It was characteristic that Belinskij welcomed writers who described Russian life in such a way as to arouse dissatisfaction with it. Thus the

[24]   Bowman, *op. cit.*, p. 151.

writers of whom Belinskij approved and those who were influenced by his attitudes tended to be, implicitly or explicitly, highly critical of the Russian life to which they gave expression, and a "condemnatory" tone colored a good deal of Russian writing from Belinskij's day on. It is not surprising that Belinskij encouraged such works, for his own conviction was that the conditions of Russian life were intolerably unsatisfactory, and his theory of art emphasized the role of the artist as the implacable critic of what *is* and *ought not to be*.

Related to the condemnatory aspect of literature was Belinskij's cultivation of humanitarianism, his sympathy for human suffering, his interest in enlarging and extending the bounds of human sympathy, his emphasis on man's inhumanity to man, his demand for social justice.[25] As humanitarian sympathy broadened, additional areas of Russian life came to be treated in literature. One aspect of Belinskij's humanitarianism was his insistence that Russian literature, which had devoted its principal attention to the upper social classes, give more attention to the lower layers of the social hierarchy. This demand, in addition to expressing Belinskij's humanitarianism, also tended in the direction of realism, as this term is usually understood.

Both Belinskij's attitude toward Russian life and his demands on Russian literature implied, it is true, a criticism of Russian life, but this criticism was not purely negative and destructive, as some of his opponents contended. If Belinskij himself criticized, protested against, condemned the actualities of Russian life, this was only a denial of what *is* in the interests of what *ought to be*. Ironically enough, as Kogan remarks of the "realist" Belinskij, "Up to the end he spoke more of what ought to be than of what is".[26]

At the time when Belinskij was writing, the question as to whose was the greater authority, the critic's or the writer's, had not yet become pressing. Belinskij's position was that both critic and artist serve the nation. Final authority thus resides in the nation, and neither critic nor

[25] The same motif appeared slightly later in English literature. Both Mario Praz and Basil Willey point to G. H. Lewes's article in the *Westminster Review* (July, 1852) which Willey summarizes as follows: "Fiction ... should enable readers to share a profounder realization of the feelings and plight of common humanity." Willey, *Nineteenth Century Studies*, p. 246. Cf. Praz, *The Hero in Eclipse*, p. 323. This idea is reflected in George Eliot's letter to Charles Bray (1 July, 1859): "The only effect I ardently long to produce in my writings is, that those who read them should be better able to *imagine* and to *feel* the pains and joys of those who differ from them in everything but the broad fact of being struggling, erring, human creatures." Cross, *Life of George Eliot*, pp. 306-307.
[26] Kogan, *op. cit.*, I, p. 154.

artist is exclusively invested with oracular preeminence as the voice of the nation. The critic and the artist are envisaged as proceeding, hand in hand, toward the same goal, though either may be momentarily in the lead. In general, in consonance with romantic canons, the artist leads the way. Though Belinskij held that the critic could help the artist by pointing out his defects, he believed that criticism was based upon art, rather than *vice versa*. He argues that the most significant criticism is that which attempts to arrive at new theory based on the artist's practice. Though he later shifted his position, he at one time argued that the critic should not approach a work of art with preconceived standards but should be particularly sensitive to what is new. On occasion he maintained that the artist should ignore the critic, though Lebedev-Poljanskij points out that in this case Belinskij's remarks were directed against the critic Ševyrev.[27]

In Belinskij's view, the principal duty of the critic lay in acting as the artist's interpeter (a position which subordinates the critic to the artist). He referred to the critic as the *guverner* (mentor) of society, and in this role, the critic's function is to exert influence upon the public, not upon the artist. In this role, it is the critic's business to discern the basic idea of a work and then to show how that basic idea animates the whole. Still, one can discern the seeds of a different position in Belinskij's contention that the task of art is to represent what exists – that of the critic, to determine whether or not he has done so. So long as the critic and the artist substantially agree, as has been pointed out, no difficulty arises, but in case of serious disagreement, the critic has declared his right not to accept the artist's version of reality.

Belinskij's attitude toward literature is thus a peculiar and unstable mixture of elements. If publicistic literary criticism is defined as the attempt to analyze, define, and understand the national life with the assistance of literature, then the fact that Belinskij's own *Weltanschauung* was in many respects fluid, that he was constantly testing new theories and relating them, on the one hand, to Russian literature as it developed and, on the other, to the life around him helps to explain the publicistic element present in much of Belinskij's discussion of literature. On the other hand, insofar as Belinskij's *Weltanschauung* was fixed, so far as his attitude toward life was already defined and he turned to literature simply to seek illustration for and demonstration of his own ideas or to use literature as a lever of social progress in

---

[27]   Lebedev-Poljanskij, *op. cit.*, pp. 139-140.

order to move society in a pre-determined direction, it was *tendencioz

nyj*. Thus Belinskij's work served as a point of departure for both
publicistic and *tendencioznyj* literary criticism, though the latter note is
to be heard only tentatively and toward the very end of Belinskij's
career.

In both cases, Belinskij's literary criticism was polemical. As a publicist, in order to be able to search for new ideas, it was necessary to
convince oneself and others that old theories were inadequate. In this
case, the polemics are purely destructive, a matter of clearing the
ground and creating space in which new theories can grow. When new
ideas are advanced, they must be tested against, opposed to old ideas
in order to see which group seems more satisfactory. And as soon as a
conviction is reached that the new ideas are more satisfactory than the
old ones, then the old ones must be attacked, no longer simply to clear
ground but to make way for new ideas; the motive is not simply destructive but also constructive, the attempt to replace one idea with
another. From the beginning to the end of Belinskij's career, his articles
had a marked polemical tone, either simply destructive of old ideas as
outworn or combatting them in the interest of new ideas, more or less
specific. The polemical tone was one of Belinskij's lasting legacies to
Russian literary criticism.

The heritage which Belinskij left to Russian literary criticism was
thus rich, complex, and composed of unstable, contradictory elements.
To it must be attributed a shift from a predominantly literary point of
view toward one oriented to a concern with society. However, in spite
of his hostility to the idea of "pure" art, aesthetic considerations were
of sufficient importance to Belinskij so that they have been considered
as basic in his attitude toward art by more than one student of his work.[28]

That the literary criticism of the sixties is closely related to that of
Belinskij, there can be no doubt, but the extent and character of the
relationship has been variously interpreted. Plexanov goes so far as to
declare that "Belinskij, in the final period of his life, regarded art exactly as Černyševskij, Dobroljubov, and other progressive people of the
sixties later regarded it",[29] but many students of Russian literary criticism have regarded Belinskij's successors as, one way or another, onesided and partial (if more consistent) exponents of Belinskij's ideas.

---

[28] Baltalon and Plexanov agree that formal aesthetic considerations were fundamental in Belinskij's attitude toward art. See Baltalon, *Principy*, p. 28, and
Plexanov, *op. cit.*, p. 181.
[29] Plexanov, *V. G. Belinskij* (Geneva), p. 5.

The shift of interest in literary criticism from purely literary to socio-literary concerns was characterized by certain themes and attitudes which were to be echoed through the criticism of Belinskij's successors: his faith in inherent human goodness and in progress, his interest in a a juster and more humane organization of society, the orientation of his thought toward the future as well as an interest in history as in-dicating the path of progress, his condemnation of the present, his sense of the importance of art and the social function of the artist, his hostility to "pure" art.

Belinskij's legacy to Russian literary criticism was not only ideologi-cal. To it he contributed also certain of his personal characteristics and qualities: a receptivity to new intellectual currents as they made them-selves felt in Western European thought, ethical fervor and an urgent sense of dedication, extremism, an appetite for polemics, and a personal style.

Relatively little serious attention has been devoted to Belinskij as a stylist. Jurij Mann has called attention to what may now be considered its formal defects; the fact that his articles were seldom carefully planned and coherently worked out; that the sequence of his ideas was not always strictly logical; that the line between broad critical articles and simple reviews was often not observed; that Belinskij's language was frequently careless and flat; that the titles of his articles were unimagi-native and unrevealing; that he was given to extended quotation.[30] Yet in spite of its formal defects and logical inconsistencies, Belinskij's criticism has an effect of coherence for which it is not easy to account. Bowman finds this unifying element in Belinskij himself, in his per-sonality. As he puts it, "The fact that the principle of change resided more in the critic's private and emotional life than in any purely intel-lectual or aesthetic doctrine determines the outer disorder of his critical activity and at the same time its semblance of inner coherence".[31]

3

The sequence of events which led to Dostoevskij's spectacular debut in Russian literature is known from his own account, which appeared in *Dnevnik pisatelja* (*The Diary of a Writer*) for January, 1877, an ac-

[30]   Mann, "Poèzija kritičeskoj mysli", pp. 231-232.
[31]   Bowman, *op. cit.*, p. 46. Cf. Akademija nauk SSSR, *Literaturnoe nasledstvo*, LV, pp. 21-22; Merežkovskij, *Zavet Belinskogo*, pp. 25-26.

count substantially corroborated by other memoirs.[32] In the winter of
1844-1845, Dostoevskij wrote his first novel, *Bednye ljudi (Poor Folk)*.
In May, 1845, he showed the manuscript to D. V. Grigorovič, his only
friend with literary connections. Grigorovič advised him to submit the
novel to Nekrasov, who was planning publication of a miscellany. When
Grigorovič took the manuscript to Nekrasov, it so engaged the latter's
interest that he and Grigorovič sat up most of the night reading it and
were enthusiastic enough about what they had read to visit Dostoevskij
in the early hours of the morning in order to congratulate him. Nekrasov then took the manuscript to Belinskij, whose initial skepticism
speedily gave way to enthusiasm, and in June, Dostoevskij was introduced to Belinskij, who excitedly hailed the literary novice as an
authentic artist and a potentially great writer.

Belinskij's formal critical opinions of Dostoevskij's work are recorded
in three articles. The first of these is a review of Nekrasov's *Peterburgskij sbornik (Peterburg Miscellany)*, in which *Bednye ljudi* appeared on
15 January 1846. In addition to *Bednye ljudi*, Belinskij discusses in
this article "Dvojnik" ("The Double"), which appeared in the February
number of the *Otečestvennye zapiski*. The second of these articles,
"Vzgljad na russkuju literaturu 1846 goda" ("A Review of Russian
Literature for the Year 1846"), published in the *Sovremennik*, again
mentions *Bednye ljudi* but devotes more space to a defense of Belinskij's previously expressed opinion of "Dvojnik" and, in addition, discusses "Gospodin Proxarčin" ("Mr. Proxarčin"). Dostoevskij's story
"Xozjajka" ("The Landlady") is mentioned in the third article, "Vzgljad
na russkuju literaturu 1847 goda" ("A Review of Russian Literature
for the Year 1847").

These essays reveal a rapid and dramatic evolution in Belinskij's attitude toward Dostoevskij's work. In the first of them, Belinskij expressed unqualified admiration; in the second, published less than a
year later, he qualified his admiration with reservations; in the third,
published a year after the second, he condemned Dostoevskij's work
out of hand. Thus, in the space of approximately two years, Belinskij's
opinion of Dostoevskij's talent ran the gamut from fervid approbation
to perfervid reprobation. So drastic a revision of Belinskij's critical
opinions was not an altogether isolated phenomenon. There is the

---

[32] Dostoevskij, *op. cit.*, II, pp. 584-588. Cf. Annenkov, *Literaturnye vospominanija*, pp. 447-450; Grigorovič, *Literaturnye vospominanije*, pp. 139-147; Panaev,
Literaturnye vospominanija, pp. 404-405; Turgenev, *Literary Reminiscences*, p.
130.

even more dramatic case of Gogol', whose stalwart champion Belinskij long had been but whom Belinskij did not hesitate to castigate in his famous "Pis'mo k Gogolju" ("Letter to Gogol' "). Belinskij was acquainted only with Dostoevskij's early work; he died shortly after Dostoevskij's literary career began. Conceivably, had he survived to read the novels of Dostoevskij's later years, Belinskij's opinion might again have changed. Personal relations between the two men ran through a parallel evolution. Accepted enthusiastically, at first, as a member of the literary circle which centered on Belinskij, Dostoevskij's personal relations with the members of the group soon cooled.[33]

Dostoevskij's story, "Dvojnik", which seems to be the origin of Belinskij's disillusionment as to Dostoevskij's talent, though begun in the latter half of 1845, was finished only on 28 January, 1846. According to Dostoevskij, in December, 1845, he read part of the story at a soirée at Belinskij's. By the first of April, 1846, Dostoevskij was aware of Belinskij's dissatisfaction with the story.[34] Despite Belinskij's unfavorable reaction to "Dvojnik", personal relations between the two men seem to have remained cordial. Fom April to October of 1846, Belinskij was travelling in southern Russia and out of touch with Peterburg literary circles. His wife was in Reval, and some of his letters to her were addressed in care of Dostoevskij, who was visiting his brother Mixail there.[35] By the time Belinskij returned to Peterburg, Dostoevskij was on bad terms with *Sovremennik* (a magazine of which Nekrasov had gained control and with which Belinskij was closely associated), and in November he quarreled with Nekrasov, though not, as yet, with Belinskij. In December of 1846 and January of 1847, Dostoevskij was still visiting the Belinskijs, but the cooling of relations between the two men is evident in Dostoevskij's confession, in a letter to his brother, that, though he knew that a child had been born to the Belinskijs, he had not dared to enquire whether the infant was a boy or a girl. At the same time, Dostoevskij complained of bad reviews, perhaps a reference to Belinskij's second article mentioning Dostoevskij.[36] From May to

---

[33] For a discussion of Dostoevskij's uncomfortable position in the Belinskij group, see Čukovskij, "Dostoevskij i plejada Belinskogo".

[34] See Dostoevskij's letters to his brother Mixail dated 1 February and 1 April, 1846 (Dostoevskij, *Pis'ma*, I, pp. 86-90), and *op. cit.*, II, p. 883. Cf. Annenkov, *op. cit.*, pp. 448-449.

[35] Belinskij, letter to M. V. Belinskaja, 4 September, 1846. *Polnoe sobranie sočinenij* (1953-1959), XII, p. 316.

[36] See Dostoevskij's letters to Mixail, end of October, 26 November, 17 December, 1846 and January-February, 1847 (Dostoevskij, *Pis'ma*, I, pp. 99-108).

September of 1847, Belinskij was abroad, and references in his letters to Dostoevskij's work are uniformly hostile. The definitive break between the two men apparently occurred after Belinskij's second article and before his departure abroad.

Why did Belinskij greet *Bednye ljudi* with such overwhelming enthusiasm? The answer to this question is to be found in Belinskij's theories about literature at the time when he became acquainted with the manuscript. We are fortunate in having his "Mysli i zametki o russkoj literature" ("Ideas and Notes on Russian Literature"), published in the *Peterburgskij sbornik* at the same time as Dostoevskij's *Bednye ljudi*. It is thus possible to form a clear idea of Belinskij's attitude toward literature at the period when he first read Dostoevskij's novel.

Belinskij's preoccupation with the social role of literature is clear from this essay. In Belinskij's opinion, Russian society, originally a social organization split into sharply defined social classes, showed evidences of an evolution toward a more organic structure welded together by common moral concerns, similarity of ideas, and an equal level of education, all of which enabled its members to transcend class interests. As evidence of such a trend, Belinskij pointed to the emergence of the intelligentsia as a social grouping (a grouping of which Belinskij was himself a typical representative) composed of members originating in various social classes but united, as Belinskij thought, by a common understanding of intrinsic human dignity, an attitude which Belinskij designated by an adjective usually translated as "humanitarian" (though "humane" would be more accurate). Dobroljubov later used the word "humanitarian" to designate the same quality. In the awakening of this attitude and the consequent creation of the intelligentsia as a social group, Russian literature had, in Belinskij's opinion, played a decisive role and would long continue to do so.

As Dostoevskij remembered it, on his first meeting with Belinskij, the humanitarian aspect of *Bednye ljudi* had kindled Belinskij's enthusiasm. Belinskij's idea of the social role of literature and the social significance which he attributed to the sense of human dignity help to explain what Belinskij meant when he exclaimed to Annenkov, referring to *Bednye ljudi*, "This is our first attempt at the social novel".[37] The "little man" as a literary theme was by no means a new one, having been used by Puškin in "Stancionnyj smotritel'" ("The Station Master")

37 Annenkov, *op. cit.*, p. 447.

and "Grobovščik" ("The Undertaker") as well as by Gogol' in "Zapiskı sumašedšego" ("Notes of a Madman") and "Šinel'" ("The Overcoat"), not to mention such writers as Pogodin, Polevoj, and Pavlov, and it became particularly popular just at this time.

Another of Belinskij's ideas about literature is reflected in his initial reaction to Dostoevskij's novel: his idea that art was the product of unconscious creativity. As Dostoevskij remembered his first meeting with Belinskij, the latter's almost first words were: "But do you, yourself, understand . . . what you have written. . . . You may have written, guided by immediate instinct, as an artist, but did you yourself rationalize all this dreadful truth which you have pointed out to us? It is impossible that at your age of twenty you could have understood it." [38]

Belinskij's idea that artists think in images (while philosophers think in words) was also expressed: "We, publicists and critics, we merely deliberate; we try to explain this with words, but you, an artist, with one trait, with one stroke, in an image, you set forth the very gist, so that one can feel it with one's own hand, so as to enable the least reasoning reader to grasp everything at once. This is the mystery of art!" And as the quotation of Belinskij continues, another of his ideas about literature comes into play: his conception of the relationship between truth and art and the role of the artist as prophet and seer. "This is the truth of art! This is the artist's service to truth! To you, as an artist, truth is revealed and declared; it came to you as a gift. Treasure, then, your gift, be faithful to it, and you will become a great writer!" [39]

Belinskij's initial reaction to Dostoevskij's work is perhaps reflected in an article which he wrote at approximately the time when he first met Dostoevskij and which was published in the July issue of *Otečestvennye zapiski*, a review of the maiden work of a young and aspiring poet, "Stixotvorenija Petra Štavera" ("The Poetry of Petr Štaver"). Belinskij wastes relatively little space on the work in question but, rather, devotes most of his article to avuncular advice. The humanitarian theme appears here clearly in connection with Belinskij's views on human nature and society. "In general, people are by nature more good than bad, and not nature but rearing, need, a false social life make them bad. Almost every one of them, even the worst, has his beautiful, human side, only it is difficult to espy and to discover it. The latter constitutes the noblest mission of the poet; to him belongs by right the

---

[38]   Dostoevskij, *The Diary of a Writer*, II, p. 587.
[39]   *Ibid.*

justification of noble human nature, as to him belongs by right the persecution of false and foolish bases of society, which distort man, making him sometimes a beast and most often a feelingless and feeble animal. People are brothers one to another, although the falseness of their relationship makes them enemies. Noble, great, and sacred is the calling of the poet who wants to be the herald of the brotherhood of men!" [40] Belinskij's distaste for the extravagant (an attitude which determined his later aversion to Dostoevskij's "Dvojnik") is also expressed: "Dear poet, learn not to get carried away only by what is enormous – it is often only monstrous and not great; learn not to get carried away only by what is astounding, effective, dazzling, brilliant. Everything true and great is simple and modest." [41]

Shortly before the appearance of *Bednye ljudi*, Belinskij again obliquely referred to Dostoevskij in the number of *Octečestvennye zapiski* for January, 1846, in the course of a review of a translation of George Sand's *Le meunier d'Angibault*. Here Belinskij hints at the imminent advent of an important new literary figure, a "teaser" generally understood as a reference to Dostoevskij. When Belinskij wrote his review of *Peterburgskij sbornik*, in his discussion of *Bednye ljudi*, the humanitarian theme is dominant: "Honor and fame to the young poet whose muse loves people in garrets and cellars and says of them to the inhabitants of gilded palaces: 'Truly, these too are people, your brothers!'" [42] Humanitarianism, exalted almost into a religion, was a common denominator in the systems of Utopian socialism, and this fact helps to explain the appeal of this theme to Belinskij and his contemporaries; that it acted powerfully upon the members of the Belinskij circle, there can be little doubt. Grigorovič, describing his initial reading of the manuscript of *Bednye ljudi* to Nekrasov, relates: "On the final page, when old Devuškin takes his leave of Varen'ka, I could no longer control myself and began to sob; I stole a glance at Nekrasov: tears were also streaming down his face." [43]

Allied to the humanitarian theme is another, characteristic of Belinskij. This is his concept of the "natural school", a literary tendency of which Gogol' was, in Belinskij's opinion, the founder and a school which he discussed at some length in an article which appeared shortly before his "Vzgljad na Russkuju literaturu 1847 goda". This article is

[40] Belinskij, *op. cit.*, IX, p. 175.
[41] *Ibid.*, p. 177.
[42] *Ibid.*, p. 554.
[43] Grigorovič, *op. cit.*, p. 141.

Belinskij's "Otvet 'Moskvitjaninu'" ("Answer to 'The Muscovite'"), and it is a good source for Belinskij's ideas about the natural school.

In Belinskij's view, the natural school was an inevitable and natural outgrowth of previous Russian literary development and a response to contemporary social needs. As a reaction against romantic idealism, it was characterized by an anti-idealistic attitude toward the depiction of life, an attitude which Belinskij understood as realistic, and its principal social value was the awakening of that humanitarian point of view which Belinskij discerned in *Bednye ljudi*. Since Russian society was, as a whole, deficient in the exercise of this point of view, the natural school was negative in its attitude toward Russian reality.

Belinskij accepted Dostoevskij as a member of Gogol's school. Not only did *Bedny ljudi* share its humanitarian point of view, but the novel was characterized by the stylistic qualities of realism, as Belinskij understood the term. Even the mixture of humor and tragedy which Belinskij notes in *Bednye ljudi* is a characteristic which Dostoevskij shares with Gogol'. Belinskij goes so far as to discern the influence of Gogol' even on Dostoevskij's turns of phrase, but at the same time Belinskij is careful not to impugn Dostoevskij's proper originality in respect to his conception of the whole work and the characters depicted in it. Though Belinskij praises Dostoevskij's strength and clarity of characterization, he makes a minor exception in the case of the heroine. Belinskij attributes the fact that Dostoevskij shares Gogol''s literary characteristics not so much to Gogol''s literary influence as to the fact that the two writers share the same source of literary materials. Belinskij's view of Gogol''s relationship to the natural school is put perhaps even more succinctly in a letter to K. D. Kavelin dated 7 December 1847: "Between Gogol' and the natural school there is a whole abyss; but, all the same, it proceeds from him; he is its father; he not only gave it form but also indicated its content. The latter it has used no better than he ... but only more consciously." [44]

It was in his review of the *Peterburgskij sbornik* that Belinskij's much quoted prophecy about Dostoevskij appeared: "His talent belongs to the order of those which are not at once appreciated and acknowledged. During the course of his career many talents which will be set up against his will appear, but in the end they will be forgotten by the time he achieves the apogee of his fame." [45] This statement has frequently been cited as an example of Belinskij's prophetic perspicuity, and cer-

[44] Belinskij, *op. cit.*, XII, p. 461.
[45] *Ibid.*, IX, p. 566.

tainly few literary prophecies have been more meticulously fulfilled. However, it is ironic that Belinskij, as we shall see, later regretted this confident prognostication. Critics who emphasize Belinskij's critical clairvoyance neglect, however, to mention observations such as the following: "At first glance it is obvious . . . that the predominant characteristic of his talent is humor." [46] On the basis of that portion of Dostoevskij's work which Belinskij had seen at the time he wrote, this is a just observation, but scarcely an indication of total clairvoyance.

The source of Belinskij's disillusionment with Dostoevskij as a writer lies in the difference between *Bednye ljudi* and "Dvojnik", but apparently Belinskij was at first able to accept this story as a tentative, experimental flight on untried literary wings, and he even professed to find in its difference from *Bednye ljudi* a source of commendation. But even in this article, Belinskij's attitude toward "Dvojnik" is quite different from that displayed toward *Bednye ljudi*. Though Belinskij declared that there was more creative talent and depth of thought in "Dvojnik" than in *Bednye ljudi* and was able to praise the choice of subject as daring and original and its realization as masterful, points upon which he was later to alter his opinion in print, he detected in the story numerous technical defects for which he excuses Dostoevskij on the grounds of inexperience: long-windedness, lack of harmony and measure, monotonous similarity in the speech of the various characters. On this last point Belinskij's opinion had enduring echoes. As we shall see, it was repeated by Dobroljubov and long remained a critical cliché as applied to Dostoevskij's work, though this opinion is no longer tenable. At this point Belinskij seems still to have regarded Dostoevskij as a literary protégé whom he hoped, by a judicious mixture of gentle reproof and solid encouragement, to lead back into the proper path from which he had momentarily strayed. This, at least, was Annenkov's impression. [47]

But when "Dvojnik" was followed by "Gospodin Proxarčin" and "Xozjajka", when it became obvious that "Dvojnik" represented not merely a momentary aberration but was symptomatic of a consistent line of development, Belinskij's disenchantment with Dostoevskij's literary work was complete. What Belinskij now objected to was Dostoevskij's abandonment of realism, with its attendant humanitarianism,

---

[46]   *Ibid.*, pp. 550-551. Kulešov makes an interesting observation on this point: "Humor, as Belinskij understood it, is stern indignation against evil, burning sympathy for the down-trodden man." *Natural'naja škola*, p. 56. Cf. p. 75.
[47]   Annenkov, *op. cit.*, p. 449.

and his use of melodramatic elements, the absence of which he had praised so highly in *Bednye ljudi*. This is quite clear from remarks which Belinskij voiced both in private letters and in print.

Belinskij's review of the *Peterburgskij sbornik* had appeared in *Otečestvennye zapiski*. His "Vzgljad na russkuju literaturu 1846 goda" appeared in the *Sovremennik*, a periodical of which Nekrasov had gained control and whose staff Belinskij had joined in the course of 1846. Belinskij's place as principal critic on *Otečestvennye zapiski* had been taken by Valer'jan Majkov, whose point of view on social questions was rather different from that of Belinskij, and a polemical relationship between the two critics speedily developed. Majkov saw Dostoevskij as a writer whose significance was more psychological than social, and he approved of both *Bednye ljudi* and "Dvojnik". Too, in the autumn of 1846, Dostoevskij had become intimate with the Beketov group, in which Majkov was a central figure.[48] Belinskij's "Vzgljad na russkuju literaturu 1846 goda" was in part a response to Majkov's "Nečto o russkoj literature v 1846 godu" ("Something about Russian Literature in 1846") and Mordovčenko attributes to Majkov's criticism of Dostoevskij and to the general ideological situation at the end of 1846 the alteration of Belinskij's attitude toward Dostoevskij.[49] It has also been suggested that Dostoevskij's story, "G. Proxarčin", offended Belinskij because he detected in it echoes of Max Stirner's *Der Einzelne und sein Eigenthum*.[50] It seems clear that Belinskij was disillusioned when he read the completed version of "Dvojnik"; Majkov's article, Dostoevskij's personal friendship with Majkov, and the ideological situation at the moment may have facilitated the expression of Belinskij's altered opinion of Dostoevskij in print.

Belinskij's "Vzgljad na russkuju literaturu 1846 goda" shows an evident cooling of enthusiasm toward both *Bednye ljudi* and "Dvojnik". Portions of the original manuscript have been preserved, and a comparison of these with the essay as it appeared in print shows consistent and significant toning down of superlatives, due in part to Nekrasov's

[48] Komarovič, "Junost' Dostoevskogo", pp. 16-17.
[49] Akademija nauk SSSR, *Istorija russkoj literatury*, VII, pp. 120-122. Cf. Akademija nauk SSSR, *Literaturnoe nasledstvo*, LV, p. 229. For a recent discussion of Majkov as a critic, his criticism of Dostoevskij, and his polemic with Belinskij, see Akademija nauk SSSR, *Belinskij i sovremennost'*, pp. 175-195. For Majkov's influence on recent Soviet criticism of Dostoevskij, see Kulešov, *op cit.*, pp. 132-135.
[50] Gus, *Idei i obrazy F. M. Dostoevskogo*, p. 62.

editorial emendations.[51] Even *Bednye ljudi* (described in his first article
as "all, in entirety, first-rate")[52] falls heir to accusations on the score
of longwindedness levelled originally by Belinskij only at "Dvojnik".
So far as "Dvojnik" itself is concerned, the position taken in the earlier
article is, on the whole, reaffirmed, but the emphasis on Dostoevskij's
lack of artistic restraint is stronger. At the end of his discussion, Belinskij delivers himself in print of his real opinion of "Dvojnik": "But
in it there is yet one more real defect: this is its fantastic coloration. In
our time the fantastic has its place only in insane asylums and not in
literature and is to be found in the care of physicians and not of
poets." [53] The acerbity of this observation carries conviction.

In his "Vzgljad na russkuju literaturu 1847 goda" Belinskij mentions
"Xozjajka", though he comments that, "Had it been signed with some
unknown name, we would not have said a word about it." [54] After a
scornfully caustic analysis of the content of the story, Belinskij is unable
to find a single good word for it and ends his remarks with a blanket
condemnation: "In the whole story there is not one simple and living
word or expression: everything is far-fetched, stilted, artificial, and out
of tune." [55] In a letter to V. P. Botkin dated 4-5 November 1847, before he mentioned "Xozjajka" in print, Belinskij included the story in
a list of "*bad things*",[56] and about a month later, he wrote to K. D.
Kavelin, perhaps with Dostoevskij in mind, "We have all one common
fault – the ease with which we manufacture geniuses and talents. . . . It
would appear that it is time to give up this rather childish habit and
be less lavish with laudatory epithets." [57] And in a letter to Annenkov
(dated 15-27 February 1848) Belinskij wrote: "I don't know whether
or not I wrote you that Dostoevskij has written a story, "Xozjajka" –
frightful rubbish! In it he wanted to reconcile Marlinskij with Hoffmann, having mixed in a bit of Gogol'. He has written something or
other after that, but each of his new works is worse than the last. In
the provinces they can't abide him; in the capital they express hostility
even to *Bednye ljudi*. I tremble at the thought of rereading it – it is so
easy to read! We deceived ourselves, my friend, on the score of the

---

[51] Belinskij, *Sobranie sočinenij* (1948), III, p. 890, note 444. Cf. Kulešov, *op. cit.*, pp. 81-82.
[52] Belinskij, *Polnoe sobranie sočinenij*, IX (1953-1959), p. 563.
[53] *Ibid.*, X, p. 41.
[54] *Ibid.*, p. 350.
[55] *Ibid.*, p. 351.
[56] *Ibid.*, XII, p. 421.
[57] *Ibid.*, p. 454.

genius Dostoevskij! . . . In this case, I, the leading critic, played the role of a perfect ass . . . ." [58]

Though Belinskij denied that tendency was a proper basis on which to found literary judgments and proclaimed that writers should not be limited in any way in their choice of material [59] (positions which we shall find reproduced in Dostoevskij's literary criticism), Belinskij's denial of any merit whatsoever to a writer whose tendency he no longer approved is indicative, at the least, of a certain disingenuousness. Belinskij's position in this respect is frankly expressed in a letter to V. P. Botkin dated the beginning of December, 1847, in which he says: "As far as I am concerned, poesy and artistic quality are necessary only so far as that the story be true, i.e., that it not fall into allegory or smack of a dissertation . . . . The important thing is that it raise questions, produce a moral effect upon society. If it achieves this goal and is altogether without poesy or creativity – to me it is interesting, *nevertheless* . . . . Naturally, if the story raises questions and produces a moral effect upon society together with high artistic quality, so much the better, so far as I am concerned, but with me the important thing is nevertheless the subject matter and not the trimmings. However artistic a story is, if it is not serious, then I am perfectly indifferent to it." [60] In this statement, a shift of interest from literature, as such, to social concerns is perfectly patent. The reader's attitude toward literary works is determined by extra-literary criteria. There is thus an inconsistency between Belinskij's private opinions and those which he chose to express in print. The problem of reconciling aesthetic and extra-aesthetic criteria as applied to literature was to trouble Belinskij's successors.

The shifts in Belinskij's critical attitude toward Dostoevskij are instructive. When he originally hailed Dostoevskij as a literary genius, as a seer and a prophet, ostensibly Belinskij was paying tribute to the artist's superior powers rooted in unconscious creativity. Actually, he was welcoming someone who, as he thought (and not without cause), shared his own point of view and expressed it forcefully and effectively. As it became obvious that Belinskij was mistaken as to the identity of his and Dostoevskij's *Weltanschauungen,* Belinskij first attempted to in-

---

[58]   *Ibid.,* p. 467. Mordovčenko notes that Apollon Grigor'ev had pointed out the influence of Hoffmann in his review of "Dvojnik". See Akademija nauk SSSR, *Literaturnoe nasledstvo,* LV, p. 220.
[59]   Ščerbina suggests that Belinskij's denunciation was directed against the patriotic tendency of such popular writers as Bulgarin and Kukol'nik. See "Problemy realizma v èstetike V. G. Belinskogo", p. 17.
[60]   Belinskij, *op. cit.,* p. 445.

fluence Dostoevskij, to encourage him to return to Belinskij's own viewpoint. When this goal appeared impossible of achievement, Belinskij simply condemned Dostoevskij out of hand.

Belinskij and Dostoevskij were on close personal terms over the span of approximately a year, succeeded by a year during which their relations cooled, and finally by a year during which they did not meet. Relatively short in duration as it was, Belinskij's impact upon Dostoevskij, nevertheless, left enduring traces. Dostoevskij himself, when he reminisced about Belinskij in his *Dnevnik pisatelja,* confessed the attraction which Belinskij exercised upon him and the influence of Belinskij's ideology at the beginning of his career, but echoes of Belinskij's influence are to be detected throughout Dostoevskij's life and work. The news of Belinskij's death seems to have provoked one of Dostoevskij's early epileptic attacks.[61] One of the incriminating charges brought against Dostoevskij in the Petraševskij Affair was his having read in public Belinskij's "Pis'mo k Gogolju". In Dostoevskij's deposition, written in prison, his attitude toward Belinskij is ambivalent, as it is in the articles devoted to Belinskij in *Dnevnik pisatelja.* Earlier, in 1867, when Dostoevskij was first abroad with his second wife, he unsuccessfully attempted to clarify his attitude toward Belinskij, but since the essay was never published and the manuscript appears to have been lost, the content of this essay remains unknown. Almost at the end of his life, in a letter written to an unidentified correspondent, dated 24 December 1880, recommending a list of books suitable for an adolescent reader, it is interesting to note that the only literary critic mentioned is Belinskij.[62] In an attempt to explain Dostoevskij's ambivalent overt references to Belinskij, Georgij Čulkov writes, "He judged Belinskij on various levels – now as a private citizen, now as a character, now as a 'phenomenon of Russian life', now as a religious type. . . . This is why in Dostoevskij one can find every shade of sympathy and hatred for this man." [63]

Echoes of Belinskij's theories on art are to be detected in Dostoevskij's own literary criticism, as we shall see, and his influence is reflected more significantly in Dostoevskij's work as a novelist. The influence of Belinskij's ideas has been laboriously traced throughout Dostoevskij's work by V. Kirpotin, who writes, "Dostoevskij treated

---

[61]   Yarmolinsky, *Dostoevsky,* p. 59.
[62]   Dostoevskij, *Pis'ma,* IV, p. 222.
[63]   Gosudarstvennaja akademija xudožestvennyx nauk, *Trudy, Literaturnaja seksija, vyp. III, Dostoevskij,* p. 63.

Belinskij not as a pupil treats a teacher. He did not repeat his lessons in formal logical completeness; he constantly thought them over, assimilated them, dissolved them in his consciousness, inspired himself with them, found in them points of departure for his own artistic creation." [64] The recent publication of Dostoevskij's preliminary drafts for *Podrostok* (*A Raw Youth*) makes clear how much Belinskij was on Dostoevskij's mind as he worked on this novel.[65] And when Dostoevskij discussed resuming publication of *Dnevnik pisatelja* in 1880, he remarked, "It will probably begin with Belinskij." [66] Belinskij's influence is perhaps most conspicuous in the novels *Besy* (*The Devils* or *The Possessed*) and *Brat'ja Karamazovy* (*The Brothers Karamazov*). Dostoevskij never succeeded in laying Belinskij's ghost.

[64]   Kirpotin, *Dostoevskij i Belinskij*, p. 17. See also Rammelmeyer, "Dostoevskijs Begegnung mit Belinskij".
[65]   Akademija nauk SSSR, *Literaturnoe nasledstvo*, LXXVII. Cf. Dolinin, *Poslednie romany Dostoevskogo*, p. 54.
[66]   Solov'ev, Vsevolod, "Vospominanija o Dostoevskom", p. 843.

III

NIKOLAJ GAVRILOVIČ ČERNYŠEVSKIJ (1828-1889)

Belinskij died on 7 June (new style) 1848, on the eve of a period of political reaction in Russian history induced by the European social and political events of that year. Indeed, just before Belinskij's death, his activities had attracted official attention, and while he was lying on his death bed, he was summoned to appear before the chief of the secret police in Peterburg, a pressing invitation to which his illness prevented and excused him from responding. Belinskij's funeral seems to have been observed by police agents, and, after the Petraševskij affair, L. B. Dubel't of the secret police is said to have expressed violent regret that Belinskij was dead, adding, "We would have rotted him in prison." [1]

In April of the next year Dostoevskij's literary activity was interrupted first by arrest, then by imprisonment, trial, and deportation to Siberia. It was not until August, 1857, that "Malen'kij geroj" ("A Little Hero"), a story which Dostoevskij had written in prison in 1849, finally appeared in print. Dostoevskij himself returned to Peterburg only at the end of 1859, after an interim of ten years. The period of Dostoevskij's enforced absence from the literary scene thus coincided with a period of political reaction, and when he returned to the capital and to literary activity, a new wave of liberalism had gained strength.

The period of political reaction in Russia extended from 1848 until 1855. The defeat of Russia in the Crimean War had exposed the inadequacies of the regime as then constituted, and Russian society began to look forward hopefully toward a series of political, social, and economic reforms. The spokesmen of these new hopes were Nikolaj Gavrilovič Černyševskij and Nikolaj Alexandrovič Dobroljubov, two names very closely linked in Russian intellectual history.

Černyševskij was the first of the two men to become active. His

---

[1] Kavelin, *Sobranie sočinenij*, III, p. 1094.

dissertation, *Èstetičeskie otnošenija iskusstva k dejstvitel'nosti* (*The Aesthetic Relations of Art to Reality*), was written 1853-55 and published in 1855. Before it appeared, he had already published in the *Otečestvennye zapiski* (No. 9, 1854) a review of the first Russian translation of the *Poetics* of Aristotle ("O poèzii") in which he enunciated ideas further developed in his dissertation. Two months after the appearance of his dissertation, he published, under a pseudonym, in the *Sovremennik* (No. 6, 1855) a review of his own book which reiterated and amplified the ideas expressed in it. Some thirty years later, apparently in 1887-88, when a third edition of the work was under consideration, he wrote a preface which was not published until 1906. Two other articles, "Kritičeskij vzgljad na sovremennye èstetičeskie ponjatija" ("A Critical View of Contemporary Aesthetic Ideas") and "Vozvyšennoe i komičeskoe" ("The Sublime and the Comic"), the latter unfinished, were written in 1854, at the time when Černyševskij was working on his dissertation, but these were published only in the twentieth century (the first in *Zvezda*, No. 5, 1924, and the second in *Pod znamenem marksizma*, No. 11, 1928). In 1856-57 Černyševskij published in the *Sovremennik* a series of articles on Lessing ("Lessing, ego vremja, ego žizn' i dejatel'nost' ") which have some bearing on aesthetic problems.

In the field of literary history, Černyševskij's most influential work, *Očerki gogolevskogo perioda russkoj literatury* (*Studies in the Age of Gogol'*) appeared first in the *Sovremennik* in 1855-1856. This had been preceded by a series of articles on Puškin which had appeared in 1855, and it was succeeded by one on Gogol' 's letters published in 1857. In addition, Černyševskij published reviews of various writers (Avdeev, Tur, Ostrovskij, Tolstoj, Ogarev, Grigorovič, Saltykov-Ščedrin, Ščerbina, Pisemskij, and Turgenev) between 1854-1858. In 1861 he published an article on Nikolaj Uspenskij.

From the above it can be seen that Černyševskij was active as a literary critic principally between 1854-1858. After this his attention was devoted mainly to questions of history and economics. His aesthetic theorizing and literary criticism occupy a position decidedly of secondary importance in the conspectus of his work. However, it is necessary to devote attention to his views on aesthetics since they served as the foundation of Dobroljubov's position as a critic and exercised, both independently and through their development by his successors, an enormous and continuing influence. Even more conspicuously than in the case of Belinskij, the critical ideas of the revolutionary democratic stream of thought find expression in Černyševskij's work. Many of the ideas of Belinskij's final period were revived by Černyševskij, and an attempt was made to bring them into some coherent relationship, an attempt, however, so unstable in its results that later critics, taking one or another aspect of Černyševskij's ideas, attempted to work them out more fully and satisfactorily. A study of Černyševskij's dissertation is thus necessary in order to understand the aesthetic ideas of the whole movement. Consequently, Černyševskij's aesthetic theories will be treated at greater length than the extent of his criticism of Dostoevskij would otherwise warrant.

Particularly in his *Očerki gogolevskogo perioda*, Černyševskij revived Belinskij's literary reputation and laid the foundation of that Belinskij Cult which, as has already been pointed out, marks Russian literary criticism to this day. This aspect of Černyševskij's activity was important, for during the period extending from 1849 into 1856, Belinskij's name had not appeared in print. (In the early installments of Černyševskij's study, Belinskij is referred to as "the critic of the Gogol' period" or by other circumlocutions.) Furthermore, Černyševskij established himself as the heir both to Belinskij's theories and to his influence, adapting Belinskij's ideas to his own ends before passing on the succession to Dobroljubov.

Černyševskij's dissertation, *Èstetičeskie otnošenija iskusstva k dejstvitel'nosti*, has two aspects: an attack upon Hegelian aesthetics and an attempt to establish aesthetics upon a new basis. Černyševskij's attack was launched from the materialist position of Feuerbach. A direct attack upon Hegel was tactically impracticable since the very mention of his name in print was at that time forbidden in Russia, so Černyševskij's fire was directed at Hegel's disciple, F. T. Vischer.[2]

Černyševskij's ideas on aesthetics were more systematically developed than Belinskij's, yet, as we shall see, Černyševskij's ideas on art, like Belinskij's, were by no means worked out into a coherent system. Of this Černyševskij himself seems to have been aware, for in his autocritique, he writes, "Mr. Černyševskij wrote his study when the process of the development of the ideas advanced by him was still taking place, when they had not as yet achieved full, well-rounded, definitive systematicity."[3]

---

[2] Hegel's ideas on art are, however, clearly reflected in Černyševskij's. See Astaxov, *G. V. Plexanov i N. G. Černyševskij*, pp. 134-149. Cf. Ljackij, "N. G. Černyševskij i učitelja ego mysli", October, 1910, pp. 149-156.

[3] Černyševskij, *Polnoe sobranie sočinenij*, X, Part II, p. 188.

In Černyševskij's opinion, Hegelian aesthetics as interpreted by Vischer was rooted in philosophical idealism. Beauty was conceived as an absolute, existing only in the world of ideals. Art was an attempt to realize this ideal by creating in works of art that perfection which cannot exist in the real world and an expression of man's thirst for perfection. Against this position Černyševskij made a series of objections. In the first place, Černyševskij argued that the real world was superior to the world of ideals. This was the attitude of Feuerbach's materialism as Černyševskij interpreted it. In the second place, the real world affords examples of beauty more satisfying than any work of art and is, in respect to satisfying man's desire for beauty, superior to art. In the third place, rather than having a thirst for perfection, man is satisfied simply with the good, of which a healthy man can find enough in the real world, without having recourse to ideals.

In place of the aesthetics which he criticized and rejected, Černyševskij proposed his own. Instead of defining beauty as an absolute value, Černyševskij approached his definition of beauty in terms of the effect which it produces. "The feeling produced in man by the beautiful is a bright joy like that which fills us in the presence of a creature dear to us." From the effect, Černyševskij proceeds to the cause: "What is common to that which is dear to man and the dearest thing in the world to him is life." Thus Černyševskij arrives at his famous definition: "Beauty is life." This definition is, however, too general to be very useful, so Černyševskij expands it as follows: "The definition of beauty, 'beauty is life', 'beautiful is that being in which we see life as it should be, according to our understanding, beautiful is that object which manifests in itself life or reminds us of life' – it would seem that this definition satisfactorily explains all of the occasions arousing in us the sense of the beautiful." [4]

As a result of Černyševskij's definition of beauty as life as it should be according to our understanding, one expects him to define the content of art as the depiction of life as it should be. For idealistic aestheticians, beauty had been an end in itself. Černyševskij, however, criticizes this attitude as unnecessarily and artificially limiting the content of art and specifically denies the beautiful as the sole object of art. (We shall see, later, why Černyševskij was forced to discard the beautiful as the content of art.) Instead, he proposes a different definition of the content of art: "All that variety of objects, events, questions,

---

[4]   Černyševskij, *Èstetičeskie otnošeni*ja, pp. 9-10.

aspects of life which interests man forms the content of art." [5] This point of view derives from Belinskij's late work and Černyševskij maintained it in his *Očerki gogolevskogo perioda*.[6]

If reality is superior to art, as Černyševskij maintained, why should art exist at all? Černyševskij answers this question by asserting that reality is superior to art but that reality is not always readily accessible, whereas art may be. Thus art is superior to reality in that it is more accessible. Another problem is the difficulty of simultaneously experiencing and reflecting upon life. Reality presented by means of art affords opportunity for reflection. Further, art serves to call attention to beauties in reality which would otherwise be missed. Thus Černyševskij tends to regard art as a convenient substitute for life: "Let art be ... in the absence of reality, a kind of equivalent for it." [7] This idea Dobroljubov was to develop further.

Černyševskij attempted to differentiate between the "reproduction" of life and the "imitation" of life, dear to the neo-classicists. As Černyševskij interpreted the doctrine, "Neo-classical theory really understood art as the imitation of reality to the end of deceiving the senses." In contradistinction, "Reproduction has as its goal to aid the imagination and not to deceive the senses, as imitation wants to do." [8] Lavreckij points out that Černyševskij was not always able to keep this distinction clear.[9]

In addition to "reproducing" reality so that art can serve as a convenient substitute for experience, art may have a second function, to explain experience. "Science and art (poetry) are a *Handbuch* for those beginning to study life; their significance is to prepare one for the study of sources and then, from time to time, to serve as a reference." [10]

Further, in addition to "reproducing" and "explaining" life, art must also "judge" it. "A poet or artist cannot, even if he wanted to, refuse to pronounce his judgment on the phenomena depicted, and this judgment is expressed in his work. This is another significance of art by which art becomes one of the moral activities of man." [11]

---

[5] *Ibid.*, p. 116.
[6] Černyševskij, *Očerki gogolevskogo perioda*, pp. 296-297.
[7] Černyševskij, *Èstetičeskie otnošenija*, pp. 128-129. Rjurikov attributes this statement to the exaggeration likely to occur in polemics. See *N. G. Černyševskij*, p. 103.
[8] Černyševskij, *Èstetičeskie otnošenija*, pp. 114, 154.
[9] Lavreckij, "N. G. Černyševskij – teoretik", p. 217.
[10] Černyševskij, *Èstetičeskie otnošenija*, p. 125.
[11] *Ibid.*, p. 123.

The ideas which have just been outlined were a consequence of Černyševskij's *Weltanschauung* and can best be appreciated in relation to it. Its main outlines are clear from what Černyševskij wrote in his dissertation, particularly as amplified by his auto-critique. Philosophically, the problem which lies at the heart of Černyševskij's thinking is the relationship of what *is* and what *ought to be*. Idealistic philosophy had taken the position that the real world was the world of ideas and ideals (what *ought to be*) and that the actual world in which we live (what *is*) could, at best, but approximate and never coincide with the ideal world. Černyševskij took the position that the world of ideas and ideals could (and, in fact, sometimes did) coincide with the actual world. The idealists had seen the world as both imperfect and imperfectible. For Černyševskij the world was composed of elements both perfect (what *is* and *ought to be*) and imperfect (what *is* and *ought not to be*), and was at least partially perfectible by the transformation of the imperfect into the perfect.

When Černyševskij argues the superiority of reality to art, that a living girl is more beautiful than any possible representation of her in art, he is, fundamentally, arguing that, in some cases, what *is* and what *ought to be* do, in fact, coincide. He does not argue that *every* living girl is superior to *every* representation of a girl in art. In other words, he does not argue that everything which *is, ought to be,* only that what *ought to be*, on occasion, *is*. It is true that when Černyševskij is arguing against the idealistic view of perfection as something that cannot exist in the actual world, in the attempt to persuade the reader that the perfect does exist in the actual world, he tends to exaggerate and to suggest that the actual world is perfect, that what *is, ought to be*. For example, he writes, "A man with uncorrupted aesthetic feeling delights in nature without reserve, finds no defects in its beauty." [12] It is important to note Černyševskij's limitation, "uncorrupted". We shall examine later what this term meant to him. It has been pointed out that in addition to tending to over-emphasize the perfection of what *is*, Černyševskij also, when he is arguing the superiority of life to art, tends to exaggerate the artificiality of art. [13]

For Černyševskij, reality was not only that which *is* and *ought to be*, but also that which *was, may be*, or *will be* and *ought to be*. "Reality includes not only dead nature but also human life, not only the present,

---

[12]   *Ibid.*, p. 85.
[13]   Lavreckij, *Belinskij, Černyševskij, Dobroljubov*, p. 216.

but also the past, insofar as it has expressed itself in action, and the future, insofar as it has being prepared by the present." Further, reality, for Černyševskij, includes not only what ought to exist, actually or potentially, in the objective world but also what exists subjectively, in man's subjective world of thought, insofar as it contributes to the transformation of the actual world into the "real" world. "Thought is not something in opposition to reality, because thought is born of reality and tends toward realization, and for that reason constitutes an indivisible part of reality." This position is repeated and emphasized in Černyševskij's auto-critique.[14]

Thus, to recapitulate, for Černyševskij, what was "real" was that which *ought to be*. What is real exists, in part, in the actual world, but more fully and completely in potentiality (in the actual world of the future, as transformed by man's activity), less fully and completely in the past (only insofar as the past has contributed to what is real in the present), also in whatever in the intellectual and moral life of man contributes to the transformation of what actually *is* and *ought not to be* into what *ought to be*.

Černyševskij's conception of the relationship of what *is* and what *ought to be* leads to apparently paradoxical results. Whereas, for the idealist, the opposition between what *is* and what *ought to be* had been absolute (what *is* could never be what *ought to be*), for Černyševskij, this opposition was relative, rather than absolute (what *is* may or may not be what *ought to be*), as Lavreckij emphasizes.[15] Černyševskij's "rehabilitation of reality" was effected simply by insisting that what *is,* on occasion and in part, coincides with what *ought to be*. But by no means all of what *is* is also what *ought to be*. That portion of what *is* which *ought not to be* is condemned in the name of what *ought to be*. Thus we arrive at the apparent paradox that a body of thought at once "rehabilitates reality" and "condemns and denies" reality. The reality which is "rehabilitated" is that which *is* and *ought to be* (what *is* and *ought to be* is declared superior to what *ought to be* but never *is*); the reality which is "condemned and denied" is what *is* and *ought not to be* (what *is* and *ought not to be* is condemned in the name of what *ought to be* and *will* or *may be*). In both cases, the standard is what *ought to be* (either actually or potentially). As Plexanov justly observes: "Concern with what *ought to be* predominates in Černyševskij's dissertation

---

[14] Černyševskij, *Èstetičeskie otnošenija*, p. 145. Cf. *Polnoe sobranie sočinenij*, X, Part II, p. 174.
[15] Lavreckij, *op. cit.*, p. 208. Cf. "N. G. Černyševskij – teoretik", p. 210.

over a theoretical interest in what *is*, at times, quite different." [16] To the extent that Černyševskij's thinking is concerned with what *ought to be* (rather than what *is*), he is, in a sense, an idealist. But Černyševskij locates the ideal not exclusively in a world discontinuous with the world around us, but in the world around us, so far as it both *is, was, will* or *may be* and *ought to be*.

Faith in progress, implicit in Černyševskij's thinking, when combined with his concept of the relationship of what *is* to what *ought to be,* also produces curious results. For Černyševskij, in the actual world only what *is* and *ought to be* is "real". Much of the actual world *is* and *ought not to be*. But what *is* and *ought not to be* is capable of being transformed by man's action into what *is* and *ought to be*. Černyševskij hoped for this transformation and his thought is oriented toward the future (what both *will be* and *ought to be*). Thus we arrive at another paradox: to the "realist" Černyševskij the actual world is less "real" than the future, which, in terms of the present, does not exist at all. The "realist" is concerned not so much with the actual world (except insofar as it coincides with what *ought to be*) as with what *ought to be* (insofar as it exists in the present or will exist in the future). But how can we be sure of what will exist in the future? Černyševskij solved this question by faith in progress. Later, the Marxists were to solve it with a "scientific" theory of history. Thus the Marxists were able to accept and to incorporate into their aesthetics much of Černyševskij's thinking.

Man and his needs are central to Černyševskij's *Weltanschauung,* and it was Černyševskij's view that it was not for man to adjust himself to the world as he finds it but rather to mold the world to his requirements. In his auto-critique, Černyševskij writes: "Nature does not always correspond to his needs; therefore man, for the peace and happiness of his life, must change reality objectively in many respects in order to adapt it to his practical needs." In order to change the world so as to make it correspond more closely to man's requirements it is necessary to determine what those requirements are, and for this purpose, it is necessary to select a criterion, a standard by means of which man's needs can be recognized. This criterion, for Černyševskij, was the ideal of man as he *ought to be* as a kind of absolute. Černyševskij's idea of the nature of man clearly derives from that point of view

---

[16] Plexanov, *N. G. Černyševskij*, p. 225. When Černyševskij is arguing against Hegelian aesthetics, he is apt to appeal to what *is*, but when he is attempting to erect his own system, he appeals, rather, to what *ought to be*.

popularized by Rousseau: that man is fundamentally good; if he is, in fact, bad, this condition is a result of his having been corrupted by circumstance. Černyševskij writes: "Intellectual and moral life (developing in a suitable way when the organism is healthy – that is, when the material side of man's life proceeds satisfactorily) – this is truly that life appropriate to man and most attractive to him." [17] Thus, for Černyševskij, given proper circumstances (a satisfactory material level of existence) man's life will be what it *ought to be* and at the same time what he both desires and needs.

This proposition seems reasonable enough, in the abstract, but in its historical context, the proposition raises difficulties. In Russia at that time the only social class whose life proceeded under relatively satisfactory material conditions was the aristocracy. Logically, the life of that class, according to Černyševskij's definition, should have represented the most immediate approximation of what *ought to be* and was most desirable and necessary. But the material welfare of that class depended upon the institution of serfdom, an institution which Černyševskij, together with numbers of other people, felt to be an abomination deserving only prompt liquidation. Therefore, the life of the aristocracy could not be accepted as the criterion of what *ought to be*.

How, then, ignoring the most obvious concrete example, are we to know what man *ought to be*? Černyševskij, in his dissertation, gives no very satisfactory answer to this question. Man as he *is* cannot serve as a criterion, for he is the product of a mixture of what *ought to be* and what *ought not to be* (serfdom, for example). Man's desires furnish no criterion. True, when man is what he *ought to be,* his needs and desires coincide, but since man is not what he *ought to be,* his present desires furnish no dependable indication as to his needs. Since neither man as he *is* nor his present desires can furnish an indication as to his needs, how are we to discover them? Černyševskij answers the question in these terms: "In part, instinct, yet more science (knowledge, thought, experience) give man the means of understanding what manifestations of reality are good and beneficial to him and consequently should be supported and encouraged by his action and which manifestations of reality, on the other hand, are injurious and damaging to him and consequently should be destroyed or, at least, weakened in the interests of human life." But this is scarcely science as we understand the term

---

[17] Černyševskij, *Polnoe sobranie sočinenij*, X, Part II, p. 188.

now, for Černyševskij goes on to say: "Science is not abstract and cold: it approves and disapproves, discourages and encourages – it approves noble people who concern themselves with the moral needs of man and who grieve, seeing them so often unsatisfied, as it approves also those who concern themselves with the material needs of their brethren." [18] Such a curious statement lends support to the conclusion of Charles Corbet: "Si Černyševskij soumet l'art à la science, il soumet la science à la politique. La science de Černyševskij n'est en réalitè qu'une science de seconde main, supposée *a priori* favorable aux desiderata politiques de l'écrivain." [19]

The orientation of Černyševskij's thought toward the future, combined with a faith in progress and "science", justified the urge to transform the world as it was into the world as it *ought to be* and *would be*, an impulse strong in the whole revolutionary democratic stream of thought. This impulse was bound to affect the aesthetics of the movement. As Plexanov remarks, "Our enlighteners did not in the least disdain poesy, but they preferred the *poesy of action* to every other." [20] As a result of this imperative urge to remake the world, the revolutionary democrats were tempted to consider art as a tool, a lever, an instrument, a means for effecting the hoped-for, necessary, and justified change. This tendency has been pointed out by numerous critics, and it was another element of revolutionary democratic thought which the Marxists were able to adopt.

What place does art have in such a *Weltanschauung*? Traditionally, aesthetics has been understood as the science of the beautiful and art as its embodiment. As we have seen, Černyševskij rejected beauty as the sole content of art and proposed rather the "interesting". What is Černyševskij's attitude toward beauty, if it is not to be considered as the principal content of art? As Ikov has forcefully pointed out, at times Černyševskij argues as if beauty were some sort of absolute value, at others as if it were simply a fundamentally irrelevant accident.[21]

For example, when Černyševskij is arguing the superiority of real life as opposed to art, he maintains that a living girl may be more beautiful than any possible artistic representation of her. If this is a valid reason for valuing a real girl above a representation of her, life above art, then beauty must be a kind of absolute value, a relevant

[18]   *Ibid.*
[19]   Corbet, "Černyševskij esthéticien et critique", p. 126.
[20]   Plexanov, *Literatura i èstetika*, I, p. 434.
[21]   Ikov, *Èstetika N. G. Černyševskogo*, p. 18.

standard by which one thing can be measured against another. Here, however, Černyševskij is attacking idealistic aesthetics in terms of its own system of values. Elsewhere Černyševskij argues the dependence of a sense of beauty upon other conditions. He points out that a peasant has a notion of beauty, and standards in this respect, quite different from that of an aristocrat. What the one finds beautiful, the other finds ugly, and vice versa.[22] Is beauty simply dependent upon a point of view? If so, how, then, can beauty be any kind of an absolute or standard? How is one to measure one thing against another in its terms, except to say that the one corresponds to the conception of beauty peculiar to one class and the other to that of another class? It would seem that we arrive at *de gustibus non est disputandum*, a position which, as we shall see, Pisarev was to adopt.

Černyševskij, however, was far from willing to leave the matter there. Though he is not explicit on this point, it is clear that for Černyševskij some sort of standard existed. He writes, "A passion for pale, sickly beauty is a sign of an artificial depravity of taste",[23] so his standard would seem to be what is not artificially depraved, spoiled, and unnatural. But by what standard is one to determine what is natural, unspoiled, healthy?

This is another point on which Černyševskij is resolutely unexplicit. The assumption would seem to be that a healthy, unspoiled taste is superior to an unhealthy or spoiled taste. Thus what is beautiful is that which appeals to such a taste. This introduces a further modification in Černyševskij's definition of the beautiful. Instead of "The beautiful is that being in which we see life as it should be according to our understanding", we get something on the order of "The beautiful is that being in which we see life as it should be according to our understanding, provided we see life from a healthy point of view." Such a formulation brings us to a situation of this sort: in life we are surrounded by things which may be either what they *ought to be* or what they *ought not to be*; a sense of beauty is no safe criterion by which to choose between them since we may have an unhealthy or spoiled taste; the relevant standard is a healthy or unspoiled taste (whether or not it corresponds with our own). Thus aesthetic questions tend to shift ground. The question which must be answered is not "Is this beautiful?" (Does this satisfy my understanding of life as it *ought to be?*)

---

[22] Čalyj traces this idea back to Majkov. See *Realizm russkoj literatury*, pp. 82-83.
[23] Černyševskij, *Èstetičeskie otnošenija*, p. 12.

but "Is this beautiful from a healthy point of view?" (Does this satisfy an understanding which is what it ought to be?)

The epithets, "unhealthy", "corrupt", etc., are usually applied by Černyševskij to the taste of the merchant class or the aristocracy. The implication is that the taste of the peasantry is healthy and unspoiled. But if this is so, then the life of the peasants must be what it *ought to be* since it has produced a taste which is what it *ought to be*. It is easy to see why Černyševskij does not develop this line of reasoning. His implied standard seems to be not so much the peasants as they *are* but as they *ought to be*.

Actually, the criterion seems to be reason. Černyševskij writes, "To gratify man's whims does not mean to satisfy man's needs. The greatest of these needs is truth." [24] Thus an aesthetics which started out as one based upon the reality of aesthetic emotion ("a feeling like that which fills us in the presence of a being dear to us") ends as a rationalist aesthetics based not upon what *is* but upon what *ought to be*, judged by rational criteria. It is difficult not to agree with Plexanov when he writes of Černyševskij's dissertation that "Its attention is concentrated not on what is and what was but on what ought to be and actually would be if people began to listen to the voice of 'reason'." [25] Another aspect of Černyševskij's attitude toward beauty will be discussed later.

According to Černyševskij's scheme, the function of art is to produce not the beautiful but rather the interesting. As Nikolaj Solov'ev tartly observes, "Instead of aesthetics, a science of the beautiful, something on the order of a science of the interesting makes its appearance." [26] And what is interesting? As we have already seen, Černyševskij was deliberately vague and ambiguous on this point.[27] In Russian, as in English: the adjective *interesting* suggests principally something attractive and engaging, in other words, something arousing our desires. But the noun *interest*, in Russian as in English, may mean profit, gain, advantage, in other words, something answering our needs. It is perhaps permissible to suggest that as Černyševskij used the adjective, both ideas are involved. To Černyševskij as a rational egoist what was interesting to man was what brought him advantage, gain, good. Need and desire coincide. But, as we have seen, desire is not a safe criterion

---

24   *Ibid.*, p. 104.
25   Ovsjaniko-Kulikovskij, *Istorija russkoj literatury*, III, p. 187.
26   N. I. Solov'ev, *Iskusstvo i žizn'*, I, p. 84.
27   Mirov particularly castigates this weakness in Černyševskij's system. See "Černyševskij i Plexanov", p. 23. Cf. Ikov, *op. cit.*, p. 58; Kagan, *Èstetičeskoe učenie Černyševskogo*, p. 96.

for determining man's needs, rather "science", a political ideology, reason, is the criterion.

Where the function of art is concerned, Černyševskij seems to be arguing from the point of view of things as they are, what *is*, rather than from the point of view of what *ought to be*. As we have seen, if man were what he *ought to be*, then his needs and desires would coincide, and art, which caters to man's desires, would serve also his needs. The beautiful and interesting coincide. But in the actual world, where man's desires are liable to corruption, his desires and needs may not coincide, and in this case the beautiful serves only man's desires to the possible detriment of his needs.

Černyševskij's distrust of man's desires is clear. In his dissertation we find, "Art strives to satisfy our inclinations, and reality cannot be subjected to our tendency to see everything in that light and in that order which pleases us or accords with our conceptions, often one-sided." On the other hand, Černyševskij does not maintain that aesthetic satisfaction necessarily runs counter to man's needs, for he writes, "Aesthetic satisfaction may be differentiated from material interest or a practical view of an object, but it is not opposed to it." [28]

What, then, is the situation at which we arrive, according to Černyševskij's theory? Art is life as it *ought to be,* according to man's understanding. If man's understanding were what it *ought to be,* man's needs and desires would coincide: but, due to the corrupting influence of a world which is only very partially what it *ought to be,* man is not what he *ought to be.* As a result, his understanding is not what it *ought to be,* and what he needs and what he desires may not necessarily coincide. Since this is the case, man's needs are to be served rather than his desires.

This situation puts the artist in an almost impossible position. The difficulty is that, in Černyševskij's system, the aesthetic effect of a work of art is dependent upon its serving man's desires. Man's desires, however, may be corrupt, and by serving them the artist may be sacrificing man's needs in order to achieve aesthetic effect, whereas man's needs should take precedence over his desires. If the artist serves man's needs rather than his desires, he runs the risk of failing to make the aesthetic effect at which he aims. Until man is what he *ought to be,* it seems impossible for art to be what it *ought to be.* This dilemma is never posed by Černyševskij, but it is implicit in his system.

[28] Černyševskij, *Èstetičeskie otnošenija,* pp. 103, 65.

One way out of this dilemma lies in improving man's understanding, for when man's understanding is what it *ought to be,* then man's needs and desires coincide. Thus it is in the interest of artists to help to transform man's understanding into what it *ought to be* by advancing the cause of "science". Through "science" man's understanding can be transformed into what it *ought to be,* and the problem of the artist is solved. (Not, it is true, in the present, where the artist's problem remains fundamentally insoluble, but in the future, which, since it is more fully what it *ought to be* than the present, is more real.)

Černyševskij wanted art to serve "science". He writes, for example, in his auto-critique, "Science is worthy of [filial love] because it serves man's good as art is worthy of it when it serves man's good. And art brings him very much good, because the work of an artist, particularly of a poet worthy of the name, is a 'textbook of life', . . . a text-book which everyone makes use of with pleasure, even those who know and love no other. Art should be proud of this lofty, beneficent significance." [29] It is perhaps worth pointing out that here Černyševskij justifies art not on the grounds of its serving the aesthetic impulse (as he himself defined it) but on the grounds of its deserving respect as serving the needs (though not necessarily the desires) of man. That Černyševskij wanted art to serve what he called science is perfectly clear. *How* it was to do so is perfectly obscure. If art depends for its effect upon catering to man's desires, then it is impossible to see how it can effectively serve man's needs, unless desires and needs coincide.

Černyševskij's emphasis upon art as a handmaiden to science was seized upon both by his opponents and by his successors. That art should subordinate itself to science was disputed by his opponents. One of his successors, Pisarev, not only supported Černyševskij's position but went on to ask a further question: what is the function of art once the public becomes educated? His answer was that art, having fulfilled its function, would simply disappear, a conclusion with which it is difficult to believe that Černyševskij could have agreed, since, as we have seen, when man is what he *ought to be,* his needs and desires coincide and what satisfies his interests is also beautiful.

Černyševskij's system poses other thorny problems to the artist in addition to those already mentioned. It will be remembered that Černyševskij gives three functions to art: to "represent" life, to "explain" life, and to "judge" life. These three functions are not altogether

---

[29]   Černyševskij, *Polnoe sobranie sočinenij,* X, Part II, p. 186.

compatible. In "representing" life, art presumably focuses its attention upon what *is*; in "explaining" and "judging" life, attention is focussed upon what *ought to be*. The problem posed for the artist is the difficult one of presenting life both as it *is* and as it *ought to be,* for life as it *ought to be* is only a part of life as it *is*. Art as an "explanation" of life also presents problems for the artist in a period of conflicting values. He can "explain" life only from one point of view. He must commit himself to the *Weltanschauung* of a party, and he thus becomes a committed partisan. He is in this position also when he "judges" life. Černyševskij, together with the other revolutionary democratic critics – not to mention the Marxists – emphasizes the bias of art.

Art, all art, comes to be regarded fundamentally as propaganda, more or less overt. In Russian critical literature, this quality of art, its propagandistic aspect, is often referred to as *tendencija*. A recent Soviet dictionary of literary terms defines *tendencija* as follows: "*Tendencija* in a work of art . . . is the idea, the conclusion toward which the author attempts to lead the reader by drawing pictures of life and characters in a work", and the writer goes on to comment: "In contrast to the sometimes hidden *tendencija* of bourgeois literature, attempting, by distorting the truth of life, to lead the reader to reconciliation with social injustice, to distract his thoughts from the necessity of struggle with capitalism, and to encourage in him a conviction in the hopelessness of that struggle, Soviet literature, correctly depicting life, not only does not hide its *tendencija,* its Communist direction, but attempts in every way that a work of art show an example of a real man, that it inspire the people to struggle for its happiness, that it help to build a Communist society." [30] For the revolutionary democrats, as for the Marxists, every work of art had a *tendencija,* a bias. The problem is not whether or not a work of art is propaganda; all art is propaganda; the problem is propaganda for what? Those who did not share this point of view tended to use the adjective *tendecioznyj* to describe, pejoratively, only that literature which adhered to the revolutionary democratic bias.

Aničkov points out that this emphasis on the propagandistic aspect of art (its *tendencija*) derives from the views of Young Germany and that its demand that art "judge" life runs counter to the demands of realism, if realism is understood as the depiction of what *is*.[31] Yet one

[30]   Timofeev and Vengrov, *Kratkij slovar'*, p. 130.
[31]   Aničkov, "Očerk razvitija èstetičeskix učenij", p. 185. Soviet literary critics profess to see no contradiction between *tendencija* and realism. For example,

aspect of *tendencija* does emphasize what *is*. The "condemnatory" aspect of Černyševskij's theory has already been mentioned. "Condemnatory" literature is the negative aspect of *tendencija*.

Let us see how "condemnatory" art fits into Černyševskij's system. If life as it *is* is composed both of elements which are what they *ought to be* and of others which are what they *ought not to be,* then when life is depicted as it *is,* some of it will be beautiful (since it corresponds to life as it should be according to our conceptions) and some of it will be ugly (since it does not so correspond). If art is concerned only with the beautiful, then it must ignore those elements of what *is* which are not what they *ought to be.* But these were precisely those elements in which Černyševskij was interested. Somehow he had to make room for the ugly as a suitable content for art. When he insists that the content of art should be the "interesting" rather than the "beautiful", he accomplishes this end. The depiction of the ugly is then justified, not because it brings aesthetic satisfaction, but because it does good by calling attention to what *ought not to be* (which must be ignored if the content of art is exclusively the beautiful), thus encouraging the person exposed to a work of art to attempt to eliminate or to transform the ugly (what *ought not to be*) into the beautiful (what *ought to be*). So long as the content of art remains exclusively the beautiful, art cannot be realistic (in the sense of depicting what *is,* insofar as it *ought not to be*). Černyševskij's theory encourages realism (the depiction of what *is*) in that he provides a justification for the inclusion in the content of art of what *is* and *ought not to be.* On the other hand, Černyševskij's idea that what *ought to be,* if only in potentiality, is "real", pulls in the opposite direction (toward the depiction of what *ought to be* but as yet *is not.*)

If all art is *tendencioznyj,* this fact, again, poses a difficult problem for the artist. It would seem that if the artist wished to serve man's needs surely, he must of necessity take care consciously to adopt the requisite *tendencija.* In his dissertation, Černyševskij specifically avoids committing himself on this issue. He writes: "Perhaps it is now more needful clearly to set forth the dependence of beauty on the conscious *tendencija* of the artist than to expatiate upon the fact that the works

---

Bursov writes, "Tendentious works, soaring above the facts of every-day life, do not cease to be realistic. Rather the contrary, their reality is heightened thereby." Černyševskij, *Èstetika i literaturnaja kritika,* p. vii. Cf. Lavreckij, *Èstetika Belinskogo,* p. 174. Clearly such critics share Černyševskij's conviction that only what *ought to be* is real.

of a truly creative talent always have a great deal that is unpremeditated, instinctive. Be that as it may, both points of view are familiar, and it is unnecessary to dwell upon them here." Although Černyševskij admits the efficacy of unconscious creativity, he also writes, "A poet worthy of the name usually wants to communicate to us in his work his ideas, his views, his feelings, and not exclusively only the beauty which he has created." He also betrays a certain distrust of the artistic instinct: "How often artists are mistaken in their understanding of beauty! How often even the artistic instinct deceives them!" [32]

Lunačarskij attributes Černyševskij's ambiguity on the issue of "unconscious creativity" versus *tendencioznost'* to Černyševskij's understanding of the difficulties involved. "If the artist does not feel himself to be free and instead of producing that which has ripened within him, that truth which he sees, he tries to stifle his truth – This is very bad for art. This is a delicate problem: here it is very easy to make a mistake and begin crassly to insist that the artist produce what we demand. Černyševskij admirably understood this truth." [33] Perhaps, but the understanding of the delicacy of this aspect of the problem may be more Lunačarskij's than Černyševskij's.

Protopopov explains Černyševskij's lack of dogmatism on this issue in a different, and possibly more convincing, way: he attributes it to Černyševskij's faith in man's goodness and quotes the passage: " . . . man, i.e., a creature by his nature inclined to honor and love truth and goodness and to abhor everything else, – a creature able to transgress the laws of goodness and truth only through ignorance, mistake, or the influence of conditions stronger than his character and reason, but never able, willingly and freely, to prefer evil to good." [34] Thus the artist, if left alone, will arrive, of himself, at the suitable *tendencija*. But, as Dostoevskij was to emphasize in *Zapiski iz podpol'ja* (*Memoirs from Underground*), man may be so constituted that he knows what is good and still desires what is evil.

If Černyševskij does not insist that the artist consciously adopt a *tendencija*, on the other hand, it is difficult to take very seriously those critics who maintain that Černyševskij stood unequivocally for artistic freedom. It has been pointed out that when Černyševskij voiced a demand for freedom of the artist, he was apt to have in mind the artist's freedom from the demands of idealistic criticism, as in the case

[32] Černyševskij, *Èstetičeskie otnošenija*, pp. 68-69.
[33] Lunačarskij, *Russkaja literatura*, p. 75.
[34] Protopopov, "Umnaja kniga", p. 106.

of his remarks about the poet Ščerbina.[35] That the problem of the freedom of the artist still troubles Soviet critical theory is evident. For example, Lavreckij writes of *tendencija:* "It cannot be imposed on an artist." But he goes on to say, "The artist creates freely, but his creation attains highest value only when it is permeated freely from within by the truest understanding of life." [36] If this is the case, then the canny artist, anxious to achieve work of the highest value, will take care to see that his work is suitably permeated. Even in this case, however, the artist's problems are not necessarily solved. A contemporary Soviet critic, Z. V. Smirnova, writes, "Immediate tasks in the development of Marxist aesthetics and Soviet art focus, in our opinion, on two main questions. One of them is the problem of the possibility of a lack of correspondence between the objective ideational content of a work of art and the subjective ideational intent of the writer. . . . So far as the second question is concerned, it may be formulated as the problem of the role of a progressive, scientific *Weltanschauung,* i.e., the Marxist-Leninist *Weltanschauung,* in the development of contemporary progressive art and especially of Soviet art." [37]

Neither in his dissertation nor in his auto-critique does Černyševskij say anything about the role and function of the critic. In a minor article, "Ob iskrennosti v kritike", ("On Sincerity in Criticism"), which answered objections raised by the *Otečestvennye zapiski,* Černyševskij protested against toothless criticism. He defines criticism rather conventionally: "Criticism is a judgement as to the merits and defects of any literary work." He then immediately goes on to say, "Its function is to serve as an expression of the opinion of the best section of the public and to cooperate in its further dissemination in the mass." Here we have a clear echo of Belinskij's concept of criticism as the mentor of society. Further, it seems clear that Černyševskij is trying to guide the writer in directions which he feels desirable: "But the defects from which Mr. Avdeev's talent suffers can vanish, if he seriously wants this, since they lie not in the genuineness of his talents but in the absence of those qualities necessary to the fruitful development of talent which are not given (like talent) by nature, which are acquired by some through the difficult experience of life, by others through science, by others through the society in which they live; to these conditions the *Sovremennik* tried to direct Mr. Avdeev through the whole

---

[35]   Akademija nauk SSSR, *Istorija russkoj kritiki,* II, p. 56.
[36]   Lavreckij, *Belinskij, Černyševskij, Dobroljubov,* pp. 214-215.
[37]   Smirnova, *Voprosy xudožestvennogo tvorčestva,* p. 153.

length of its review and expressed them as clearly as possible at the end." [38] Lavreckij calls attention to a letter in which Černyševskij confesses that he is trying to influence Tolstoj.[39] Thus the attempt, begun by Belinskij, to establish the critic as the mentor of the artist was continued by Černyševskij and, more particularly, by his successors.

As a practising critic, Černyševskij was bedevilled by the antithesis between what *is* and what *ought to be,* between the need to evaluate current literature and at the same time to legislate the literature of the future. As we shall see, *tendencija,* conscious or unconscious, was the decisive criterion in Černyševskij's evaluation of any work of art. Though he approved conscious *tendencija,* in his critical practice he more often attributed the effectiveness of literary works to the operation of "unconscious creativity", for example, in his discussion of Pisemskij's work as Lavreckij points out.[40] We shall find Dobroljubov and Pisarev (and Dostoevskij himself) behaving in an identical fashion, theoretically proclaiming the necessity of a proper conscious *tendencija* in a work of art but falling back on the theory of "unconscious creativity" in the discussion of specific works and writers. The practical and immediate critical problem for Černyševskij (as it had been for Belinskij and would be for Černyševskij's successors) was a dearth of works written with a *tendencija* of which he approved.

We have observed, in Belinskij's treatment of Dostoevskij's work, a disposition to treat beauty of form as a function of correct ideological content. It will be remembered that when Belinskij approved of the content of Dostoevskij's work, he also praised its form and that as he became disillusioned with its content, he became increasingly critical of its form. Černyševskij's attitude is similar. In his dissertation Černyševskij insists upon beauty of form, for he calls it "a necessary quality of every work of art".[41] Elsewhere than in his dissertation, Černyševskij writes: "In order to determine the artistic worth of a work, it is necessary to investigate, as strictly as possible, whether or not the idea serving as the base of the work is true or not. If the idea is false, there can be no question of artistic quality because the form also will be false and full of incongruities. Only works in which a true idea is incarnated are artistic, if the form perfectly fits the idea." [42]

---

[38] Černyševskij, *Polnoe sobranie sočinenij,* I, pp. 151, 156.
[39] Akademija nauk SSSR, *Istorija russkoj kritiki,* II, pp. 75; Lavreckij, *op. cit.,* p. 266.
[40] Akademija nauk SSSR, *Istorija russkoj kritiki,* II, p. 88.
[41] Černyševskij, *Èstetičeskie otnošenija,* p. 117.
[42] Černyševskij, *Polnoe sobranie sočinenij,* II, p. 459.

Obviously, for Černyševskij, more overtly than for Belinskij, form and content are not independent aspects of a work. Beauty of form is dependent upon correct ideological content and possible only when that content is acceptable. In determining artistic quality, content clearly takes precedence over form, and beauty is simply a function of content. This theoretical formulation Černyševskij applied in specific cases. Steklov calls attention to his treatment of the work of Ostrovskij. Černyševskij condemned Ostrovskij's play *Bednosť ne porok* (*Poverty is no Sin*) on both ideological and artistic grounds, but when a later play satisfied Černyševskij's ideological demands, he granted it both ideological and artistic merit.[43]

Černyševskij has been accused by both friends and foes of being the "destroyer of aesthetics". How far does he deserve this dubious distinction? Russian critics give conflicting answers to this question. The crux of the matter seems to be what is understood by the term "aesthetics". Aesthetics had been understood as the study of the beautiful and the importance of art was its exemplification of the beautiful. In place of this definition, Černyševskij sought to substitute the idea of aesthetics as the study of art, of which the beautiful was but one aspect and by no means the most important. If the term "aesthetics" means the idealistic aesthetic system, then Černyševskij, insofar as his theory was successful, is its destroyer. Though his attitude toward art (specifically literature) is fundamentally the same as Belinskij's at the end of his career, in Belinskij's work one seeks in vain for so thorough and reasoned a development of a theoretical position as inimicable to idealistic aesthetics as that to be found in Černyševskij. And if by "aesthetics" one has in mind the "art for art's sake" position, then, too, Černyševskij, like Belinskij before him, takes a position hostile to this point of view. In his *Očerki gogolevskogo perioda*, Černyševskij wrote: "History knows no works of art which were created exclusively by the idea of the beautiful; even if there are or were such works, then they attract no attention from contemporaries and are forgotten by history as too feeble, feeble even artistically.[44] For Černyševskij, as for Belinskij, the "art for art's sake" position was identified with an ideological position which they considered reactionary.

As has been pointed out in the discussion of Belinskij, the romantic idealists gave a leading cultural role to art (specifically literature). In Černyševskij's scheme of ideas, this function was transferred from art

---

[43]   Steklov, *N. G. Černyševskij*, I, p. 340.
[44]   Černyševskij, *Očerki gogolevskogo perioda*, p. 297.

to what he called science. With this transfer of primary importance, literature necessarily assumes a secondary, though by no means insignificant, role. The significance of art, while remaining great, consists of the services which it can render a greater interest: "science", or a political ideology.

Polemical considerations also complicate the question. When the successors of Černyševskij (Pisarev, in particular) were accused of being "destroyers of aesthetics", it was convenient for them to take refuge behind the authority of Černyševskij. Opponents who were unwary enough to take the bait faced the necessity of refuting Černyševskij before they could deal with their opponents, who had retired behind what might be called a defense in depth composed of red herrings. The result, as Aničkov remarks, was that "Both opponents and adherents look upon him as the destroyer of aesthetics and read into his book that aesthetics is utterly unnecessary, that neither true art nor a real understanding of it has anything to do with aesthetics." [45]

Like Belinskij, Černyševskij was by no means indifferent to aesthetic values. Rather than to deny the validity and importance of aesthetic values, he sought to establish them on what seemed to him a broader foundation. When this aspect of his views is not ignored, Černyševskij is seen to deserve the title "the destroyer of aesthetics" no more than Belinskij, and, in general, critics writing after the polemics of the sixties refuse him the right to it. Ivanov-Razumnik remarks: "It is necessary to give Černyševskij his due: in all this he showed a great deal of patience and the soundest relationship to the question of art in the whole period of the sixties." [46] Though Černyševskij seems not to deserve the title "the destroyer of aesthetics", at the same time, it cannot be denied that in Černyševskij's aesthetics the balance between ideological and aesthetic criteria shifts significantly, and with his successors, it shifted further. As Plexanov observes, "Critics who subscribed to Černyševskij's aesthetics were inclined to overlook the question of the aesthetic qualities of the works which they analyzed, focussing their principal attention on the ideas in these works." [47]

In Černyševskij's emphasis upon the importance of actual life, in his desire to act upon, to change the conditions of life as they then existed in Russia, and in his insistence that art lend its assistance and support

[45]   Aničkov, *op. cit.*, p. 184.
[46]   Ivanov-Razumnik, *Istorija russkoj obščestvennoj mysli*, II, p. 53.
[47]   Plexanov, *N. G. Černyševskij*, p. 216.

in this great task, one must, indubitably, take into consideration the historical situation at the period when Černyševskij devoted his attention to literature. Mixajlovskij, in an article published in France, summed up the historical situation as follows: "Nous avons eu chez nous, aux abords de l'année 1860, une idée grandiose, un problème immense qui mettait d'accord la volonté de tous et qui répondait en même temps à l'idéal et aux exigences pratiques de toute la nation russe. Cette grande idée, c'était l'émancipation de millions de serfs. ... À côté de la necésssité juridique de l'émancipation, il restait à résoudre le côté économique, la question agraire, si importante et si compliquée." [48] In a situation of this kind, it was not unnatural that matters of practical concern should come to the fore and tend to shoulder other considerations into the background. As Plexanov puts it: "For the progressives of the sixties, the question of art was first and foremost a moral question; they asked themselves: Have we the right to give ourselves up to the enjoyment of art at a time when the majority of our compatriots are deprived not only of this enjoyment but even of the possibility of satisfying the most elementary and at the same time the most fundamental, the most urgent needs?" [49]

Another factor, emphasized by some writers, is the emergence in Russian social life of a new class, the "raznočincy" (the déclassés), who had no place in the old social organization and were attempting to win for themselves a measure of recognition and influence. Belinskij has already been mentioned as an early example of this social group. Increasingly hostile to the "genteel" tradition in literary matters, this group rejected Russia's aristocratic cultural heritage, a rejection symbolized by the ideological tension which developed between Černyševskij and Gercen and eventually grew to the breaking point and by the withdrawal of a number of the older contributors from the *Sovremennik*.

It has been pointed out that Černyševskij considered himself (and has been considered by others) as the continuator and developer of the ideas of Belinskij's last period. In large measure this seems true. Černyševskij shared with Belinskij in his final period the influence of Feuerbach.[50] Černyševskij's definition of beauty, "The beautiful is life",

[48]   Mixajlovskij, "Le mouvement littéraire", p. 90.
[49]   Plexanov, *V. G. Belinskij* (Geneva, 1899), p. 4.
[50]   Some Russian critics, seeking to support the thesis of an independent Russian tradition, attempt to minimize the influence of Feuerbach upon Černyševskij and to stress rather that of Belinskij. For a recent Soviet discussion of this issue, see Astaxov, *op. cit.*, pp. 150-153; 166-175. Aničkov comments cogently on this problem. See *op. cit.*, pp. 183-184. Toward the end of his career, Belinskij was

seems to derive from Belinskij's "Wherever life is, there, too, is poesy". The three functions which Černyševskij gives to art: "reproduction", "explanation", and "judgment" of life are also foreshadowed in Belinskij. The orientation of art toward the future, the desire to use art as a lever to change the world ("the theurgic motif"), the conflict between aesthetic and ideological values and in artistic method between conscious *tendencija* and "unconscious creativity"; all of these are to be found in Belinskij. Contempt for "art for art's sake", and a preference for Gogol''s work (as he understood it) above Puškin's Černyševskij also shares with Belinskij. Together with sharing Belinskij's ideas, Černyševskij's writing is reminiscent of Belinskij's in its tone of indignant sincerity and its eager participation in polemics. We shall see later the treatment of this heritage by Dobroljubov, Pisarev, and Mixajlovskij.

During Černyševskij's lifetime, his published writing contained only one reference to Dostoevskij, a brief review of the first number of Dostoevskij's magazine *Vremja* (*Time*), published in the *Sovremennik* for January, 1861. Černyševskij credits the first installment of *Unižennye i oskorblennye* (*The Scorned and Insulted*), which first appeared in this issue of *Vremja*, with being the most important contribution to the literary contents of the magazine. (This is not necessarily high praise, for Černyševskij comments on the fact that the periodical does not have a stable of well-known contributors.) [51] Černyševskij remarks in the character of the heroine a streak of what we would probably now call masochism, a willingness to be humiliated by the man she loves in spite of her pride, an anticipation of a theme to be developed later by Mixajlovskij.[52] Over half of Černyševskij's review is devoted to an examination of what we would now probably call the program of the periodical as expressed in its contents, and Černyševskij recommends it to the attention of the reading public, remarking that "As far as we can judge by the first number, *Vremja* disagrees with the *Sovremennik* in its understanding of many of those questions about

influenced by Feuerbach, so it is not surprizing that Černyševskij's and Belinskij's views should be similar. See Ljackij, "N. G. Černyševskij i učitelja", pp. 160-163. Naumova stresses rather the differences between Feuerbach and Černyševskij and places Černyševskij and Dobroljubov, as philosophers, above Hegel and Feuerbach, but below Marx and Engels. See "Černyševskij i Fejerbax". Wellek sees Černyševskij (and Dobroljubov and Pisarev as well) as more influenced by Vogt, Moleschott, Büchner, and the English utilitarians than by Feuerbach. See Simmons, *Continuity and Change*, p. 388.

[51] Černyševskij, *Polnoe sobranie sočinenij*, VIII, p. 62.
[52] *Ibid.* Lavreckij cites this passage as an example of Černyševskij's critical

which there can be a difference of opinion in good society." [53] That Dostoevskij's magazine should have been greeted, though guardedly, by Černyševskij is not surprising. On his return from Siberia, Dostoevskij enjoyed the good will accorded by the radicals to one who had suffered for his political opinions, and the program, the *tendencija,* of his journal was not as yet well defined. That Černyševskij valued Dostoevskij's *Zapiski iz mertvogo doma* is evidenced by the fact that he entered into negotiations with Dostoevskij in the intention of publishing a cheap edition of extracts which he planned to select.[54]

That there should be only one reference to Dostoevskij's work published during Černyševskij's lifetime is not surprising, considering the fact that Černyševskij's most active period as a literary critic was over before Dostoevskij's return to Peterburg. In Černyševskij's posthumously published writing, however, there is a discussion of Dostoevskij's remarks on Nekrasov published in *Dnevnik pisatalja,* No. 12, 1877. These remarks of Černyševskij (first published in part in 1905 and in full in 1930 and again, slightly abridged, in 1951) [55] are concerned with defending Nekrasov's memory against what Černyševskij felt were unjustified insinuations. In 1886 Pypin requested Černyševskij to write his reminiscences of Dostoevskij, and in 1888 they were written. They were published only in 1930.[56]

Černyševskij and Dostoevskij met first in 1859 but seem never to have been more than casual acquaintances. As early as 1861 Dostoevskij had publicly expressed his opposition to Černyševskij and Dobroljubov in his essay, "G. -bov i vopros ob iskusstve" ("Mr. -bov and the Problem of Art"). Since Dobroljubov had, by that time, taken over, in the main, the responsibilities as literary critic of the *Sovremennik,* Dostoevskij's shafts were levelled ostensibly at Dobroljubov, though Dostoevskij was doutbtless aware of Černyševskij's position as leader of the movement. In May, 1862, Dostoevskij, alarmed by a revolutionary pamphlet found at his door and connecting it with a series of fires which were widely

---

acuity. See *Belinskij, Černyševskij, Dobroljubov,* p. 266, note 1. A reviewer in *Severnaja pčela* (No. 199, 1861) noted that the hero of the novel seemed to enjoy his sufferings. See Zamotin, *F. M. Dostoevskij,* I, p. 38.
[53] Černyševskij, *Polnoe sobranie sočinenij,* VIII, p. 66.
[54] Lejkina-Svirskaja, "N. G. Černyševskij".
[55] Pypin, *N. A. Nekrasov,* pp. 244-245; Černyševskij, *Literaturnoe nasledie,* III; *Èstetika i literaturnaja kritika,* pp. 507, 537-538.
[56] Černyševskij, *Literaturnoe nasledie,* III, p. 89.

believed to be of revolutionary origin, called on Černyševskij and asked him to use his influence in order to put a stop to these disturbances.[57] In June, however, two articles written for *Vremja* (either by Dostoevskij or his brother Mixail) were forbidden publication by the censor. In both of these articles it was argued that the fires had resulted from natural causes.[58] Dostoevskij's *Zapiski iz podpol'ja* (*Epoxa*, Jan., Feb., Apr., 1864) are clearly, at least in part, a reaction to Černyševskij's novel, *Čto delat'?* (*What is to be Done?*) In May, 1864, there appeared in *Epoxa* (The Epoch), Dostoevskij's "Ščedrodarov (otryvok iz romana)" ("Excerpts from the novel *Ščedrodarov*"). Though this parody was directed principally at Saltykov-Ščedrin, Černyševskij's aesthetic theories were a subsidiary target.[59] Dostoevskij's unfinished story, "Krokodil" ("The Crocodile"), (*Epoxa*, No. 2, 1865), was widely interpreted as an attack upon Černyševskij upon both ideological and personal grounds. Since at the time the story was published Černyševskij was in exile as a political prisoner and it was impossible even to mention his name in print, no rebuttal was possible. It was felt that the personal element in Dostoevskij's attack was particularly offensive, directed, as it was, against someone defenseless by someone who had himself been in the same position. In the issue of *Dnevnik pisatelja* in which Dostoevskij gave his version of his interview with Černyševskij mentioned above, he defended himself against this interpretation of his story, how convincingly is open to question.[60] Since "*Ščedrodarov*" and "Krokodil" were directed not only against Černyševskij but also against Dobroljubov and Pisarev as well, they will be discussed later in connection with Dostoevskij's essay "G. -bov i vopros ob iskusstve".

[57]   For Dostoevskij's version of this interview, see *Diary of a Writer*, I, pp. 23-25. Černyševskij's reminiscences of Dostoevskij's visit agree with an account recorded by one of Černyševskij's fellow exiles in 1882, before the reminiscences were written. See Oksman, *N. G. Černyševskij*, II, p. 121.

[58]   Lemke, *Političeskie processy*, pp. 624-630. Cf. Koz'min, "Brat'ja Dostoevskie". Grossman denies that either of the brothers was the author of these articles but admits that they must have known of them and may have instigated the writing of them. See *Dostoevskij*, p. 246.

[59]   For a discussion of this controversy and the principal relevant materials, see Matlaw (ed.), Dostoevskij, *Notes from Underground*.

[60]   Bel'čikov, "Černyševskij i Dostoevskij", pp. 43-51. Cf. Gosudarstvennaja akademija xudožestvennyx nauk, *Trudy, Literaturnaja seksija, vyp. III, Doestoevskij*, pp. 47-54.

IV

NIKOLAJ ALEKSANDROVIČ DOBROLJUBOV (1836-1861)

1

When the center of Černyševskij's activity shifted away from literature, his place as the principal literary critic of the *Sovremennik* was taken by his protégé, Nikolaj Aleksandrovič Dobroljubov. After having made his literary debut in July, 1856, in the *S.-Peterburgskie vedemosti* (*St. Peterburg News*) (under the *nom de plume* of Nikolaj Aleksandrovič), Dobroljubov, while still a student, had begun contributing to *Sovremennik* in the fall of 1856 (Aug.-Sept.) as well as to *Žurnal dlja vospitanija* (*The Journal of Education*). From 1857, when he began regular work on *Sovremennik,* until his premature death in 1861, he was the most prominent and influential literary critic writing for the periodical.

Those who have studied Černyševskij and Dobroljubov emphasize their close relationship. Even their early biographies are parallel in broad outline: both came from clerical families; both began their educations in seminaries and continued them in secular institutions; both had come under the influence of Feuerbach's philosophy. Dobroljubov was familiar with the work of such men as Rousseau, Prudhon, Bruno Bauer, Belinskij, and Gercen, and he had closely followed Černyševskij's early articles in the *Otečestvennye zapiski* and the *Sovremennik.* Thus, even before the two men met in the first half of 1856, biographical and ideological similarity provided a foundation for the close intellectual solidarity which rapidly developed between them. When Dobroljubov joined the full time staff of the *Sovremennik,* Černyševskij instructed his young protégé: "Write about whatever you like and as much as you like in the way you know how. There is no need to talk it over with you. I am satisfied that you understand things aright." [1]

[1] This much quoted remark comes from Černyševskij's autobiographical novel, *Prolog.* See *Polnoe sobranie sočinenij,* X, Part I, p. 210.

Like his mentor, Černyševskij, Dobroljubov thought of himself as a successor to Belinskij. So much is this true that recently an attempt has been made to establish as fact the assumption that a letter to N. I. Greč attacking the memory of Nikolaj I, echoing Belinskij's "Pismo k Gogolju", and signed Anastasij (i.e., Resurrected) Belinskij was written by Dobroljubov.[2] Though he contributed his share to the promulgation of the Belinskij cult originated by Černyševskij, opinions have differed as to how faithful to Belinskij's ideas Dobroljubov actually was. In an article published in 1878, Antonovič noted the attempt to dissociate the ideas of Belinskij from those of Dobroljubov and defended Dobroljubov as Belinskij's legitimate heir against Kavelin and Turgenev.[3] Lebedev-Poljanskij, for example, maintains that Dobroljubov simply went on from where Belinskij left off.[4] Skabičevskij, on the other hand, though he finds substantial agreement between Dobroljubov and Belinskij, granted such minor differences as resulted from the general ideological developments which had taken place during the interim dividing the activities of the two men, emphasizes the stronger publicistic flavor of Dobroljubov's criticism, as do Volynskij and Rozanov.[5] Bursov points out the influence of Belinskij on Dobroljubov's estimate of Puškin as well as on Dobroljubov's historico-literary conceptions. He notes that Dobroljubov devoted less attention than Belinskij to the problem of the creation of a national literature since, in the opinion of Černyševskij and Dobroljubov, that problem had already been solved.[6]

Dobroljubov considered himself a successor not only to Belinskij but also to Černyševskij. Like Černyševskij, Dobroljubov was influenced by Feuerbach, with whose work he had become acquainted while yet a student through Belinskij's "Vzgljad na russkuju literaturu 1847 goda" ("Survey of Russian Literature for 1847"), and in 1855, before he met Černyševskij, Dobroljubov began a translation of Feuerbach's

---

[2] See Akademija nauk SSSR, *Literaturnoe nasledstvo*, LVII, pp. 7-24. For a discussion of this article, see Efremenko, "Raskrytie avtorstva", pp. 70-79. Cf. Dobroljubov, *Sobranie sočinenij*, I, pp. xi-xii, where the assumption is not questioned and *Izbrannoe*, p. 7, where a more moderate view is taken.
[3] See Antonovič, *Izbrannye stat'i*, pp. 313-341; cf. pp. 298-312; Kavelin, *Sobranie sočinenij*, III, pp. 1099-1114; Turgenev, *Literary Reminiscences*, pp. 105-139.
[4] Lunačarskij and Lebedev-Poljanskij, *op. cit.*, II, pp. 171-172.
[5] Skabičevskij, *Sočinenija*, I, p. 550; Volynskij, *Russkie kritiki*, p. 15; Rozanov, *Literaturnye očerki*, pp. 173-174.
[6] Bursov, *Voprosy realizma*, pp. 304-305.

Todesgedanken.[7] Most of those who have studied the two men agree as to the dependence of Dobroljubov's aesthetic theories upon those elaborated by Černyševskij and emphasize their similarity in critical procedure, polemical style, and literary personality. Bursov points out even close textual similarities, and goes on to say, "At times it was as if one of them continued and developed ideas expressed earlier by the other."[8] If Dobroljubov's and Černyševskij's ideas were nearly identical in matters of aesthetics, they were equally close in socio-economic matters. On the staff of *Sovremennik*, the two men functioned as a united team, Černyševskij discussing socio-economic problems and Dobroljubov devoting himself to literature.

In full agreement with the ideas of Černyševskij as expressed in his dissertation, Dobroljubov placed life above art. Dobroljubov accepted Černyševskij's formula, "the beautiful is life", and the idea that "art reproduces whatever is interesting to man in life". Černyševskij had assigned three functions to art: to "reproduce" reality, to "explain" it, and to "judge" it. Of these three, Dobroljubov emphasized particularly the first. Dobroljubov's position, as interpreted by Pypin, was that "A genuine artist is truthful; his works reflect life truly and thus provide material for the study of life itself in its material and moral aspects."[9] For Černyševskij, one of the principal virtues of art was its accessibility. Dobroljubov tended simply to equate art with life, the difference being that art was life made more accessible through the intervention of the artist.

As to the question of artistic method, it will be remembered that Černyševskij refused to choose between conscious *tendencija* and "unconscious creativity". In his dissertation, he simply remarked the existence of the two theories. Nor did Dobroljubov pronounce unequivocally in favor of one theory or the other. For the most part, in his critical practice, Dobroljubov relied on the theory of "unconscious creativity". On the other hand, he demanded that the artist "keep abreast of life",

---

[7]   Rejser, *Letopis žizni i dejatel'nosti N. A. Dobroljubova*, p. 117. Aničkov points out that two early essays dating from 1855 show the influence of Feuerbach but also that of Černyševskij. See Dobroljubov, *Polnoe sobranie sočinenij*, III, pp. 14-15.

[8]   Bursov, *op. cit.*, p. 299. As Nikolaj Solov'ev points out, there was not originally agreement on this point. See *Iskusstvo i žizn'*, I, p. 98. For example, see Bibikov, *O literaturnoj dejatel'nosti N. A. Dobroljubova*, pp. 7-8. Putincev quotes an entry in Dobroljubov's diary dated 1857: "I like Černyševskij's dissertation very much, and it seems to be a very remarkable thing." Dobroljubov, *Izbrannoe*, p. 8.

[9]   Pypin, "Moi zametki", p. 28.

so that he be equipped to understand it aright, so that he not mis-interpret phenomena as he observes them, so that in taking an informa-tive "slice of life", he make the correct section.

The problem of artistic method involves the relationship of art to knowledge. Are art and science simply different and equally valid techniques for the apprehension of reality, or is one more valid than the other, and if so, which? In his attitude toward this problem, Dobroljubov harks back to Belinskij. The thinker (the scientist or philosopher) expresses his *Weltanschauung* in logical constructs; the artist (writer) expresses his in images. Both require an equally powerful intellect and creative ability. Their works are created in response to the environment surrounding them, but the artist, more liberally en-dowed with intuition, grasps significant facts before he comprehends them theoretically. According to this line of argument, employed earlier by both Belinskij and Černyševskij, it would appear that the artist has an advantage over the thinker, that he goes in advance as a road-breaker for the systematic thinker. This line of argument supports "unconscious creativity" as an artistic method.

On the other hand, when it is desired to support *tendencija,* quite a different line of argument comes into play. The demand is made that the writer keep abreast of contemporary thought (rather than in ad-vance of it) so that his work will correctly reflect the phenomena which strike his attention. As a consequence of this line of reasoning, knowl-edge ("science") is given the upper hand and becomes the standard guiding art. However, on occasion, Dobroljubov denied that he sup-ported *tendencija.* Charles Corbet, for one, points out the incompati-bility of these two lines of reasoning.[10]

In his critical practice, Dobroljubov was also inconsistent. As Aničkov points out, when dealing with the work of Marko-Vovčok (Mar'ja Aleksandrovna Markovič), for example, Dobroljubov seems to approve *tendencioznost',* but, on the other hand, in discussing Ostrovskij and Turgenev, he takes his more common stand on "un-conscious creativity".[11] Various attempts have been made to reconcile or explain this inconsistency. Lebedev-Poljanskij, for example, argues that, though Dobroljubov actually opposed *tendencija* in any narrow

[10] Corbet, "La critique de Dobroljubov", p. 51. G. Solov'ev defends Dobrolju-bov for not attempting to resolve this inconsistency. See *Èstetičeskie vzgljady N. A. Dobroljubova,* pp. 266-267.
[11] Aničkov, "Očerk razvitija èstetičeskix učenij", p. 185. Cf. Dobroljubov, *Pol-noe sobranie sočinenij,* V, pp. 13-14.

sense, at the same time, when he rejected *tendencija in toto,* he was carried away in the heat of argument with polemical opponents and misrepresented his real position.[12] Skabičevskij sees in this inconsistency a reflection of the ambiguity of Belinskij's position at the end of his career (an inconsistency shared by Černyševskij).[13] Aničkov detects an evolution of Dobroljubov's thought in the direction of *tendencija* (an evolution similar to that occurring in Belinskij and Černyševskij).[14] Perhaps we see here, rather, simply an alteration dependent upon the material discussed (a technique originated by Černyševskij and perfected by Pisarev). When material reflecting the requisite *tendencija* was available (in the case of Marko-Vovčok), it was invoked. When (as in the case of Ostrovskij) *tendencija* could not be invoked (a much more frequent situation), "unconscious creativity" was relied upon.

Černyševskij, in his dissertation, omitted discussion of the role of the critic. Dobroljubov was more explicit. Belinskij, at the end of his career, had seen the role of the critic as that of being not so much a critic of art as a critic of life. This position was adopted by Dobroljubov. As we have seen, he emphasized the idea that it was the function of art to reproduce life. The critic of art and the critic of life are one because art and life are one. Should it be necessary to make a choice between art and life, Dobroljubov left no doubt as to what his choice would be, for he wrote: "If one is to choose between art and reality, then let there be stories, not fulfilling the requirements of aesthetic theories but true to the meaning of reality rather than impeccable from the point of view of abstract art but distorting life and its true significance." [15] However, Dobroljubov did not feel that art and life were necessarily in antithesis. (Nor, it will be remembered, did Černyševskij.) In Dobroljubov's view, if a choice of the sort indicated had to be made, then the artist was at fault.[16] Dobroljubov, then, was interested first and foremost in life (that is to say, society), and he saw the function of literary criticism as being not to draw conclusions about works of art but to draw conclusions about society. In order to be able to do this, works which reproduced life were required.

It will be remembered that in Černyševskij's aesthetics, the second and third functions of art, in addition to "reproducing" life, were

12   Lunačarskij and Lebedev-Poljanskij, *op. cit.,* II, p. 184.
13   Skabičevskij, *N. A. Dobroljubov,* p. 83.
14   Dobroljubov, *Polnoe sobranie sočinenij,* V, p. 14.
15   Quoted in Lunačarskij and Lebedev-Poljanskij, *op. cit.,* II, p. 136.
16   *Ibid.,* p. 174.

"explaining" and "judging" it. These functions Dobroljubov transferred, in the main, from art to criticism. It was the function of the artist to assemble the necessary raw materials for arriving at an explanation and a judgment of life, but it was the critic who "explained" and "judged" life, not the artist. In this fashion, the critic arrived at a position of superiority to the artist.

Again we may have to do here with the practical problem of a critic obliged to exercise his skills upon work which does not embody his ideals but which he wishes to use for his own purposes. When, as in the case of the stories of Marko-Vovčok, Dobroljubov encountered work whose *tendencija* he approved, he was willing to surrender to the artist the right to "explain" and to "judge" life (since that "explanation" and that "judgment" coincided with his own).[17] When, on the other hand, he chose to discuss works whose *tendencija* was not his own, he reserved to himself the right of "explanation" and "judgment". In this case, Dobrojubov deliberately ignored the meaning which the author himself gave to his work, analyzed how far his "reproduction" of life corresponded to reality, and on the basis of this estimate, drew his own conclusions. In justification of this procedure, Dobroljubov writes, in his discussion of Ostrovskij, for example: "Sometimes the artist may even not understand the meaning of what he himself has depicted",[18] an opinion endorsed, significantly, by Gončarov, whose novel *Oblomov* had served as the pretext for Dobroljubov's influential essay, "Čto takoe oblomovščina?" ("What is Oblomovism?"), when he wrote (in 1879), "The author himself often perceives the idea – with the help of an acute critical interpreter such as, for example, Belinskij or Dobroljubov." [19]

Here the critic emerges as the intermediary between the artist and society. The artist functions as a sort of oracle, the meaning of whose pronouncements may be obscure to or mistakenly apprehended by the oracle himself. It is the critic who, as the interpreter of the oracle, plays the key role, interposes his interpretation of a work of art between it and the public, uses the work of art as a kind of raw material out of which the critic creates an expression of his own *Weltanschauung*. It has been asserted that Dobroljubov's criticism functions in this way, perhaps most frequently in the case of Ostrovskij's work, but also in

---

[17]   Corbet insists that Dobroljubov's interest in such relatively minor writers as Marko-Vovčok, Zadovskaja, Kokorev, and Slavutinskij is accounted for by his approval of their subject matter. See *op. cit.*, pp. 42-43.
[18]   Quoted in Lunačarskij and Lebedev-Poljanskij, *op. cit.*, II, p. 187.
[19]   Gončarov, *Sobranie sočinenij*, VIII, p. 70.

the case of Gončarov's *Oblomov* and Turgenev's *Nakanune* (*On the Eve*). Ždanov remarks that it is common to think of Katerina, the heroine of Ostrovskij's *Groza* (*The Storm*) as Dobroljubov's creation rather than Ostrovskij's (an opinion the origin of which he attributes to Pisarev).[20] Šelgunov goes so far as to write, "It has justly been remarked that Dobroljubov created Ostrovskij." [21]

Dobroljubov, however, does not confine himself to this one system of relationships between the critic, the artist, and the public. Lebedev-Poljanskij emphasizes Dobroljubov's concept of the artist as the leader of society.[22] On the other hand, Ivanov-Razumnik and Vorovskij, for example, emphasize Dobroljubov's idea that the artist simply formulates the questions raised by society as it develops.[23]

Several forces may be seen at work here. Like Belinskij, Dobroljubov saw both the artist and the critic as seeking the answers to social problems. The difficulty was this: Could the artist be trusted to find them? If he did, then he deserved the position of a leader of society. If not, then he must be content as a follower, and it was safer for society to follow the critic than the artist. It has been pointed out that Černyševskij suggested a class theory of literature. Lebedev-Poljanskij and Lavreckij find the same suggestion in Dobroljubov.[24] This concept was useful to discredit the artist as a leader of the whole of society, and it was in accord with a materialist view of man as the product of his *milieu*. Presumably the critic had emancipated himself from this class limitation.

Why were Dobroljubov's aesthetic pronouncements so obviously contradictory, inconsistent, and piecemeal? In part, these inconsistencies were inherited from his predecessors, Belinskij and Černyševskij. Further, like Černyševskij, Dobroljubov's principal focus of attention centered on social problems, though Dobroljubov left the direct handling of such questions to his mentor. It is important not to forget that in addition to being students of Feuerbach, Černyševskij and Dobroljubov were also influenced by the Utopian socialists, Saint-Simon, Louis Blanc, and Fourier, and politically they were revolutionary democrats,

[20]   Akademija nauk SSSR, *Istorija russkoj kritiki*, II, p. 115.
[21]   Šelgunov, *Sočinenija*, II, p. 691.
[22]   Lunačarskij and Lebedev-Poljanskij, *op. cit.*, II, p. 189.
[23]   Ivanov-Razumnik, *Istorija russkoj obščestvennoj mysli*, II, p. 40; Vorovskij, *Literaturnye očerki*, p. 24.
[24]   Lunačarskij and Lebedev-Poljanskij, *op. cit.*, II, p. 180; Lavreckij, *Belinskij, Černyševskij, Dobroljubov*, p. 258.

seeking to promote changes in the social order by such means as lay at their disposal. Like Belinskij at the end of his life, like his master Černyševskij, Dobroljubov was a socialist, but one in whom the revolutionary element was more pronounced than it was in Belinskij.[25] This revolutionary element helps to explain the attractiveness to Dobroljubov and the other revolutionary democrats of the didactic aspect of literature. They saw in "education" a lever by means of which social change might be effected.

Here the theurgic motif, the desire to change reality, already observable in Belinskij, expresses itself. This motif was reflected in Dobroljubov's attitude toward literature. As Lebedev-Poljanskij puts it, "He clearly acknowledged the organizing social function of ideology in general, of art and literature in particular. As an opponent of aesthetic criticism, as a social activist, he particularly emphasized this function." [26] But Dobroljubov's attitude on this point, as on so many others, is not consistent, a fact which has been pointed out by a variety of critics.[27]

Another influence which needs to be taken into account when considering Dobroljubov's literary criticism is the influence of the times. In the chapter on Černyševskij, the effect of the expectation of immediate political and social reforms was mentioned. As the Emancipation drew closer and closer, the need for a program of action became ever more imperative. Volynskij, a writer generally critical of the Belinskij school, writes: "There is no doubt that Dobroljubov's activity coincided with one of the most remarkable moments in Russian history, when all the forces of society, tense in the expectation of reform of the social order already set in movement by the first hints of a new epoch, endeavoured to solve the immediate historical problem." [28] At such a moment it is not to be wondered at that the search for the answers to social problems took precedence over other considerations.

[25] While there is no direct evidence that Dobroljubov engaged in illegal revolutionary activity, he may have been in close touch with active revolutionaries, and Ždanov believes that he assisted their propaganda and worked toward the foundation of a revolutionary party. Dobroljubov, *Sobranie sočinenij*, I, pp. xxxiii-xxxv.

[26] Lunačarskij and Lebedev-Poljanskij, *op. cit.*, II, p. 153. Cf. Lavreckij, *Èstetika Belinskogo*, pp. 349-350.

[27] For example, Lebedev-Poljanskij, *N. A. Dobroljubov*, p. 113; Lunačarskij and Lebedev-Poljanskij, *op. cit.*, II, p. 47.

[28] Volynskij, *Russkie kritiki*, p. 151. Cf. Kotljarevskij, "Iz istorii obščestvennogo nastroenija šestidesjatyx godov", p. 249.

Like his master Černyševskij, Dobroljubov has been accused of being the "destroyer of aesthetics". But, as was the case with Černyševskij, most of those who have studied Dobroljubov's criticism deny him the right to this questionable distinction. But it is true that Dobroljubov was more interested in the content of a work of art than its form. As a result, aesthetic analysis plays a relatively unimportant and isolated role in Dobroljubov's criticism. He regarded form simply as an external matter and not as an integral principle controlling the very organization of content. Though he did not label the pursuit of beauty in itself as socially harmful, he did not consider it socially useful. Like Černyševskij, Dobroljubov did not theoretically deny the validity of "aesthetic" criticism; he simply tended to consider such questions essentially irrelevant.

This relative neglect of and indifference to the aesthetic aspects of literature is at least in part attributable to Dobroljubov's hostility to the champions of "pure art". This attitude, as we have seen, had been adopted by Belinskij and by Černyševskij and was simply continued by Dobroljubov, who treated "aesthetic criticism" with contempt. This contempt for "aestheticism" does not mean that Dobroljubov was himself devoid of aesthetic taste, but the general effect of his literary criticism was to increase the emphasis upon the social function of literature and literary criticism.

Dobroljubov's significance in emphasizing the "publicistic" element in Russian literary criticism is rather widely acknowledged. His influence upon his immediate chronological successor, Pisarev, will be discussed in the next chapter. What about other aspects of his influence? Vengerov attributes to it the strong socio-political coloration of Russian literature from his time on and the tendency of Russian writers to assume (and to be granted) the role of socio-political leaders.[29] Volynskij attributes to Dobroljubov's influence a neglect of the aesthetic aspects of literature on the part of literary critics and a consequent decay of literary criticism, although he is willing to admit that such criticism may have played a social role.[30] Both phenomena are commonly acknowledged, but how much they are attributable specifically to Dobroljubov's influence, apart from the general influence of the school of literary criticism in which he, admittedly, played a conspicuous role, seems open to question.

[29]   Vengerov, *Očerki po istorii russkoj literatury*, pp. 59-60.
[30]   Volynskij, *op. cit.*, p. 251.

2

To Dostoevskij's work Dobroljubov devoted one essay. It appeared several months after Dostoevskij had published an article on Dobroljubov, and since, at least in part, Dobroljubov's essay is a rebuttal of Dostoevskij's position, it is necessary to discuss Dostoevskij's essay before proceeding to Dobroljubov's.

That Dostoevskij did not share the *Weltanschauung* common to Černyševskij and Dobroljubov is abundantly clear both from the journalistic articles published by Dostoevskij at this period in *Vremja* and *Èpoxa* and particulary in such later works as "Zapiski iz podpol'ja" ("Notes from Underground"), *Prestuplenie i nakazanie* (*Crime and Punishment*), and *Besy* (*The Devils*). Indeed, one wonders how much the effectiveness of these works is due to the urgency with which Dostoevskij felt it necessary to express his ideas with such force and clarity that the reading public could not be misled as to their meaning.[31]

Dostoevskij's differences of opinion with Dobroljubov (and, by implication, with Černyševskij also), especially on the question of literature, are expressed most fully and explicitly in his article, "G. -bov i vopros ob iskusstve" ("Mr. -bov and the Problem of Art") (Dobroljubov's articles in *Sovremennik* were signed -bov), which was published in the February number of *Vremja*, 1861. As we have seen in the previous chapter, Dostoevskij's personal contacts with Černyševskij were tenuous. According to the testimony of Dostoevskij's wife, Dobroljubov and Dostoevskij first met only at the end of September or the beginning of October, 1861, shortly before Dobroljubov's death; thus when Dostoevskij wrote his article, he did not know Dobroljubov personally, and contacts between the two men seem to have been even slighter than those btween Dostoevskij and Černyševskij. After the publication of Dostoevskij's article, when Katkov attacked Dobroljubov, Dostoevskij came to his defense,[32] and when Dobroljubov died, an obituary notice published in *Vremja* (and possibly written by Dostoevskij) spoke of him as "one of the most remarkable Russian writers" and "a brave, upright fighter for truth".[33] Kirpotin calls attention to the fact that in

[31] For a discussion of Dostoevskij's opposition to Dobroljubov, see *Protiv bezidejnosti v literature*, pp. 156-159.
[32] Akademija nauk SSSR, *Literaturnoe nasledstvo*, XXV-XXVI, p. 41.
[33] Quoted in Rejser, *N. A. Dobroljubov v vospominanijax sovremennikov*, p. 391.

1869, after Dobroljubov's death, Dostoevskij, in a letter to Straxov, expressed admiration for and approval of Dobroljubov's articles on Ostrovskij.[34]

Dostoevskij's essay on Dobroljubov appeared early in the relatively short life of the magazine *Vremja,* before the *tendencija* of the magazine was clearly defined either in the minds of the editors (Dostoevskij and his brother Mixail) or in the attitude toward it of the public. At first the magazine attempted to take up a middle ground between the Slavophile and Westernizer ideological camps, and the essay in question reflects this situation in its attempt to disassociate itself both from "aesthetic" literary criticism and that variety practiced by Černyševskij and Dobroljubov, to which Dostoevskij refers as "utilitarian".

In essence, Dostoevskij's essay is a defense of the independence of art. As Kirpotin points out, this was Belinskij's position, especially during the earlier part of his career as a critic. He also calls attention to the fact that in polemics with Katkov, Dostoevskij relies, in contrast, on the authority of Belinskij's position at the end of his career.[35] Dostoevskij writes, "We believe that art has its own complete organic life, and, consequently, fundamental and immutable laws for this life". Of these, "The first law of art is freedom of inspiration and creation". Consequently, "One should not prescribe to art goals and sympathies".[36] Why not? In the first place, we know very little about the way in which art acts on people. In the second place, if we insist that art be socially useful, how are we to be sure of what is beneficial and of what is harmful? This question strikes at the very root of the whole revolutionary democratic *Weltanschauung* and tends to undermine its authority.

In Dostoevskij's opinion, the "aesthetic" critics make the mistake of transgressing against the independence of literature by denying even the possibility of condemnatory literature, thus limiting the freedom of literature by denying to it a specific approach and subject matter. On the other hand, critics like Černyševskij and Dobroljubov underestimate the power of artistic quality. What they lose sight of is the fact that bad art is never good propaganda. This proposition, too, echoes Belinskij.[37] Dostoevskij undertakes to prove his case by a detailed analysis

---

34   Kirpotin, *Dostoevskij v šestidesjatye gody*, p. 218.
35   *Ibid.*, pp. 213-214, 218.
36   Dostoevskij, *Polnoe sobranie sočinenij*, XI, pp. 73, 52, 82.
37   Kirpotin, *op. cit.*, pp. 215-216. Cf. G. Solov'ev, *Èstetičeskie vzgljady N. A. Dobroljubova*, pp. 267-268.

of the short stories of Marko-Vovčok which Dobroljubov had reviewed in the *Sovremennik*, No. 9, 1860 ("Čerty dlja xarakteristiki russkogo prostonarod'ja"). Dostoevskij sums up his opinion of the book (which Dobroljubov had praised) by writing: "We attack Marko-Vovčok not at all because he writes with a *tendencija*. . . . We attack the author of stories of folk life precisely because he did not know how to do his work *well*, because he did it badly and thus harmed the work and did it no good." [38]

A proposition dear to Černyševskij and Dobroljubov was insistence that art be "true to life" and "contemporary". Dostoevskij considers this insistence out of place, for art is an organic part of man's life, and, as a result, art is always contemporary and true. This position is that once expressed by Belinskij: "Every man, and consequently every poet, experiences the inevitable influence of time and place." [39] Art may appear to be "untrue" and "uncontemporary", but this may be the fault of the reader, misled by desire for the achievement of immediate goals. Dostoevskij admits that a few artists do lose touch with reality, but he contends that those who seem to have done so may actually not have done so.

Dostoevskij's faith in man and his faith in art are indissolubly allied, for he writes: "The more fully art develops, the more normally it grows, the sooner it will find its genuine and *useful* road. And since its interests and goals are one with the goal of man, whom it serves and with whom it is indissolubly united, then the freer its development is, the more good it will bring to humanity." [40]

Though this essay is the most extended and coherent of Dostoevskij's statements in opposition to the critical standards championed by Černyševskij and Dobroljubov, it does not stand alone. In *Dnevnik pisatelja* (*Graždanin*, No. 13, 1873) Dostoevskij made another attack upon the position of the "utilitarian" school of criticism. In the interim of over ten years separating the two sets of remarks, his attitude had not altered: "I am terribly afraid of 'tendency' when it takes hold on a young artist, especially at an early stage of his career. And what do you think I am specifically afraid of? – Specifically, that the aim of the tendency is not going to be attained. Will a certain dear critic whom I had been reading of late and whom I do not wish to name

[38] Dostoevskij, *Polnoe sobranie sočinenij*, XI, p. 70.
[39] Belinskij, *Polnoe sobranie sočinenij* (1953-1959), VI, p. 284.
[40] Dostoevskij, *Polnoe sobranie sočinenij*, XI, p. 82. Družinin, in 1856, took a very similar position. See, *Sobranie sočinenij*, VII, p. 222.

at present – will he believe that every artistic creation, without a pre-conceived tendency, produced solely because of the artistic urge, dealing with a strictly neutral subject hinting at nothing 'tendentious' – will this critic believe that such a creation will prove more useful *for his own purposes* than, for instance, all songs of the shirt (not by Hood, but by our writers), even though it may on the surface resemble that which is denoted as 'satisfaction of idle curiosity'?" [41]

Dostoevskij's theoretical statements about art are thus consistently opposed to *tendencija* in literature. But let us take a look at his practice as a literary critic. We shall find that it is significantly similar to that of his opponents and plagued by the same inconsistencies. In addition to the more formal literary articles published in *Vremja* in 1861, Dostoevskij not infrequently turned to literary subjects in *Dnevnik pisatelja* (published in one form or another, 1873-1881). Here it is instructive to contrast Dostoevskij's handling of contemporary writers with the treatment he accords to writers of the past.

Dostoevskij's respect for artistic quality may explain the reverent tone with which he consistently refers to his great contemporaries. He invariably writes of Turgenev and Tolstoj in the most respectful terms, even when he is regretfully obliged to disagree with their ideas. His tone then is not so much angry as hurt that individuals possessed of such talents should use them in the service of ideas which Dostoevskij considers false. Take, for example, his remarks about Turgenev's *Nov'* (*Virgin Soil*). He is careful to say that, "The artistic merit of Turgenev's creations is unquestioned." But he continues immediately, "I shall only remark that on top of page 92 of the novel (see *Messenger of Europe*) there are fifteen or twenty lines in which, in my opinion, is condensed, as it were, the whole idea of the work, the author's view of his subject. It is to be regretted that this view is quite erroneous, and I profoundly disagree with it." [42] Tolstoj's *Anna Karenina,* particularly the last part, moved Dostoevskij to protest, but he concludes his remarks in a rue-fully respectful tone: "Men, such as the author of *Anna Karenina,* are teachers, while we are merely their pupils. What, then, do they teach us?" [43] (It is interesting to note here Dostoevskij's tacit acceptance of the idea, dear to Belinskij and to Černyševskij and Dobroljubov on occasion, of the writer as the teacher, the leader of society.)

On the other hand, what does Dostoevskij say about literary works

---

[41]   Dostoevskij, *Diary of a Writer*, I, p. 79.
[42]   *Ibid.*, II, p. 584.
[43]   *Ibid.*, p. 813.

of the past? He mentions only past literary works of which he approves, and it is instructive to see the grounds on which he bases his approval. For example, he writes, "All that is genuinely beautiful in Russian literature has been borrowed from the people. . . . Do recall *Oblomov* and Turgenev's *Gentlefolk's Nest*. Of course, here we are not dealing with the people; yet all that is lasting and beautiful in these types of Goncharov and Turgenev – all this is due to the fact that, through them, they established contact with the people." [44] Here the criterion of excellence seems to be the extent of the author's contact with the people, in short, the ideological content of the literature discussed.

In another essay Dostoevskij discusses Puškin, Lermontov, and Nekrasov. On what grounds does he praise them? Of Puškin he says, "The greatness of Pushkin . . . lay precisely in the fact that he . . . so soon *found* a firm path, *a great and keenly looked for outcome for us Russians, and indicated it.* This outcome was – populism – *the worship of the Russian people's truth."* Of Lermontov he writes, "The moment he touches upon the people, he is serene and lucid. He loves the Russian soldier, the Cossack, and he reveres the people", and a little further on he writes, "Had Lermontov lived, we should have had a great poet who would have acknowledged the people's truth." Of Nekrasov he writes, "Immortality, fully deserved immortality, belongs to Nekrasov, and I have already explained why: for his worship of the people's truth which, in him, was not a result of some kind of imitation, nor even of a fully conscious process – it was an urge, an irresistable impulse." [45] In these instances the criterion for eligibility to immortality seems to be acknowledgement of "the people's truth", again, an ideological consideration.

Most revealing is Dostoevskij's praise of Puškin's *The Songs of the Western Slavs.* Dostoevskij hailed this work as a masterpiece, and, after explaining that it was derived not from authentic sources but from a literary hoax perpetrated by Prosper Merimée, Dostoevskij finds it possible to write, "It stands to reason that no such songs exist in Serbia; the Servians have other songs, but this makes no difference: Pushkin's are all-Slavic, popular songs, which poured out of the Slavic heart, expressing the spirit of the Slavs, their image, their meaning, their customs, their history." [46] Here it seems quite clear that Dostoev-

---

[44]   *Ibid.,* I, p. 203.
[45]   *Ibid.,* II, pp. 939-944, *passim.*
[46]   *Ibid.,* pp. 596-597.

skij's critical judgment was determined by his sympathy for and interest in Pan-Slavism rather than by any other consideration. Again, the ideological factor proves to be the chief element in determining critical praise.

I trust that the quotations given have made it clear that Dostoevskij's critical estimate of past literature is dependent upon his evaluation of the ideological content of that literature, quite in "utilitarian" fashion. And his judgment of contemporary literature is determined in the same fashion, as we saw from his comments on *Nov'* and *Anna Karenina*. Such evaluation does not explicitly prescribe to a writer what ideas he should embody in his work, but, by implication, it does indicate what ideological content he must employ in order to receive the critic's praise.

Dostoevskij insists on a mystical faith in artistic instinct, for he writes, "Our literature precisely has the merit that, almost without exception, its best representatives, ahead of the intelligentsia – please note this point – bowed before the popular truth, and recognized the people's ideals as genuinely beautiful. In fact, literature was compelled to adopt them as standards, almost involuntarily. Verily, in this respect, it was prompted by artistic instinct rather than by free will." [47] This statement is quite in accord with Dostoevskij's expressed theoretical distrust of preconceived dictation, of *tendencija*, and an echo of Belinskij's "unconscious creativity", but, as we have seen, it is quite contradictory to his actual practice.

One striking factor emerges from the juxtaposition of Dostoevskij's praise of past writers, and that is the fact that the ideological content upon which praise is based varies from instance to instance. Now, contact with the people is the criterion; now, acknowledgement of the people's truth; now, evidences of Pan-Slavism. True, all of these ideas are related to a single complex in Dostoevskij's mind, but one cannot help suspecting that Dostoevskij simply turned to literature whenever he needed support for whatever idea he happened to be promulgating at the moment. That pattern, at least, is quite consistent.

Dostoevskij's procedure, in such cases, has numerous advantages. In every case, Dostoevskij asserts as fact the supposition that the established reputations rest squarely upon the idea in which he is interested. Such an assertion may pass unchallenged by the uncritical; thus an attack upon Dostoevskij's idea becomes confused with the issue

[47]   *Ibid.*, I, p. 203.

of an attack upon the established reputations in question. Dostoevskij thus uses established names as a bulwark behind which to operate, a polemical tactic used effectively by Pisarev, as we shall see in the next chapter.

Since Dostoevskij's ideas could not have been consciously shared by the writers appealed to for support, it becomes necessary for Dostoevskij to account for the presence of these ideas in their work. Now one sees the necessity for Dostoevskij's adherence to the doctrine of "freedom of inspiration and creation" and the efficacy of "artistic instinct". The presence of Dostoevskij's ideas in the work of earlier writers is explained as due to the operation of "artistic instinct" operating under conditions of "freedom of inspiration and creation". Thus "artistic instinct" rather than "free will" appears as a reliable key to truth, and the fact that writers in the past have achieved truth without recourse to "free will" and unhampered by *tendencija* is explicable on this basis. Essentially, this is the same argument used by Dobroljubov to explain the presence, in the work of writers of a hostile *tendencija*, of ideas he wishes to approve, except that he uses the term "unconscious creativity" instead of "artistic instinct", and the method is applied to contemporary writers rather than to writers in the past.

The difficulty with Dostoevskij's argument is that the truth of the work of the writers he discusses was discovered only subsequently; at the time when these works were written, it was not recognized. Is it not possible, then, that the artistic instinct operating in the present is now creating or exemplifying truths that will not be recognized until some future time? If so, how is one to judge contemporary literature, so far as its "truth" is concerned, if the truth may pass unrecognized in the present and be revealed only in the future? It thus becomes logically impossible to judge contemporary literary work, since valid judgments may depend upon criteria not yet recognized. But Dostoevskij was unable to deny himself the indulgence of criticizing contemporary writers when he did not agree with their ideas. Logically, he should have denied the existence of "artistic instinct" in their work, but, as we have seen, this he declined to do. Rather, he admitted their "artistic instinct", but denied the validity of their ideology. Can it be that in the case of contemporary literature, "artistic instinct" has failed as an infallible guide to truth? Or has "artistic instinct" been rendered unnecessary by the discovery of immutable truth?

One thing of two: either "artistic instinct" is an infallible guide to truth (in the present as well as in the past), or it is fallible (in the past as well as in the present). The first view invalidates Dostoevskij's objections to *Nov'* and *Anna Karenina* (since he does not deny the possession of "artistic instinct" to the authors of these works). The second view deprives Dostoevskij of whatever support for his ideas he can find in an appeal to earlier (or indeed any) literary production. To admit that "artistic instinct" may lead to either correct or erroneous conclusions also invalidates such an appeal. And if Dostoevskij's discovery of truth eliminates the need of "artistic instinct" as a means of arriving at the truth, what becomes of the need for "freedom of artistic inspiration and creation"?

Dostoevskij was faced with the same problems as the "utilitarian" critics whom he opposed. Like them, he wanted literature to promulgate what he considered to be the truth. Very much in their fashion, he tried to reinterpret the literature of the past as they reinterpreted contemporary literature. He, too, wanted to influence his contemporary fellow writers, so he withheld praise from writers whose *tendencija* he disapproved, and, again like them, he subordinated aesthetic to ideological considerations.

3

Dobroljubov's article on Dostoevskij's work, "Zabytye ljudi" ("Downtrodden People"), was occasioned, in part, by the appearance in 1860 of a two-volume collected edition of Dostoevskij's works and, further, by the publication in *Vremja* (Nos. I-VII, 1861) of *Unižennye i oskorblennye* (*The Scorned and Insulted*).[48] (Černyševskij had already called attention both to the periodical and to Dostoevskij's novel.) Possibly the essay does not rank as one of the handful of Dobroljubov's most influential articles, but it falls not far behind them in importance, and Aničkov points out the fact that Dobroljubov's essay on Dostoevskij is thematically closely related to his articles on Ostrovskij and Turgenev.[49]

The polemical aspects of Dobroljubov's essay need to be borne in mind. It is a response to Dostoevskij's article, and at the same time a continuation of his attack upon the Russian social order. It will be remembered that Dostoevskij reproached Dobroljubov with underestimating the "aesthetic" aspects of works of literature. Dobroljubov

---

[48]   It appeared on 13 December 1861 in the issue of *Sovremennik* for September. See Rejser, *Letopis*, p. 309.

[49]   Dobroljubov, *Polnoe sobranie sočinenij*, V, pp. 7-8.

chose to counter-attack by an analysis of Dostoevskij's work which denied its aesthetic quality but demonstrated its usefulness, from a "utilitarian" point of view, in raising social questions. This was argument *ad hominem* with a vengeance. The essay is, accordingly, divided into two sections, in the first of which Dobroljubov attacks the position of the "aesthetic" critics (among whom he includes Dostoevskij) and in the second, the Russian social order.

Dobroljubov's own attitude toward literature is clearly stated in the first section of the essay: "An author may make no contribution to art, take no step forward in the history of literature, strictly speaking, but nevertheless be remarkable to us because of the ruling *tendencija* and idea of his work. Let him not satisfy artistic demands; let him, another time, miss his mark and express himself badly; we pay no attention to this and we are, nevertheless, ready to discuss him much and long if only the idea of his work is somehow important to society." [50] This attitude toward literature is precisely that to which Dostoevskij objected. Dobroljubov tries to demonstrate that Dostoevskij's novel is worthless by "aesthetic" standards. If this attempt is convincing and yet, however, the novel must be acknowledged as somehow valuable and significant, then the standard which has been applied to it is discredited and not the novel. Dobroljubov's frequently quoted remark that *Unižennye i oskorblennye* is "beneath aesthetic criticism" is ironic and directed rather against the position of "aesthetic" critics than against the novel.[51]

That Dobroljubov by no means considered Dostoevskij's novel contemptible is clear when, near the beginning of his essay, he writes, "Mr. Dostoevskij's novel so far represents the most important literary event of the current year", though he adds, "But try to apply to it the rules of a strictly aesthetic criticism!" [52] Dostoevskij's novel is treated

---

[50]   Dobroljubov, *Sočinenija*, III, pp. 514-515.
[51]   *Ibid.*, p. 513. The polemical aspect of Dobroljubov's essay seems often to have been overlooked or given inadequate weight, a situation which explains the fact that the view that Dobroljubov had a low opinion of Dostoevskij's artistic powers is not infrequently encountered. Indubitably, Dobroljubov considered Dostoevskij's work inferior to that of Ostrovskij, Turgenev, and Gončarov, but if Dobroljubov was unwilling to place Dostoevskij in the very front rank of contemporary Russian writers, this does not mean that he necessarily assigned him a position far to their rear. Egorov remarks on Dobroljubov's fondness for turning the weapons of his ideological opponents against them ("Dobroljubov – polemist", p. 169), and Derkač calls attention to this aspect of Dobroljubov's essay. See Leningradskij universitet, *Dobroljubov*, p. 105, note 10.
[52]   Dobroljubov, *Sočinenija*, III, p. 502.

simply as a convenient example of the deplorable aesthetic level of contemporary literature and by no means the worst.

Dobroljubov sums up his general opinion of the novel by saying, "In the novel are very many convincing, well finished details; the hero of the novel, though somewhat melodramatic, comes through not badly in places; the character of little Nelli is depicted decidedly well; the character of the old man, Ixmenev, is also drawn very convincingly and naturally. All this gives the novel the right to public attention, what with the general lack of good stories at present, but even all this does not raise it enough to make it possible to apply universal artistic requirements to all its particulars and make it an object of detailed aesthetic analysis." [53] Let us now take a look at some of the objections raised by Dobroljubov against Dostoevskij's novel on "aesthetic" grounds, bearing always in mind the ironic background against which they are raised.

First, Dobroljubov objects to Dostoevskij's handling of the device of narration in the first person. Because of the organization of the plot of the novel, the narrator should be a central figure; due to his intimate relationship to the principal characters, he can scarcely have been indifferent to the events which he records, but his own reactions are not described; under the circumstances, this fact gives a false and artificial tone to the book, For this reason, Dobroljubov concludes that Dostoevskij has made a clumsy and inept use of the device of first person narration.

Second, Dobroljubov objects to the division of plot interest, which is shared between the adventures of Nataša and those of little Nelli. Since Prince Valkovskij is a key figure in both stories, one might logically look to him as a unifying element, but Dobroljubov finds him, as depicted by Dostoevskij, inadequate to this function.

Third, Dobroljubov objects that the motivation of the various characters is never elucidated. This was the cause of his dissatisfaction with Dostoevskij's handling of the narrator, Ivan Petrovič, and Dobroljubov finds the same defect in Dostoevskij's handling of Nataša and of Prince Valkovskij.

Fourth, Dobroljubov remarks in Dostoevskij's work a tendency to repeat certain character types. He points out similarities between the heroine of Dostoevskij's unfinished novel, *Netočka Nezvanova*, the hero in his story "Malen'kij geroj" ("The Little Hero"), and Nelli in

[53]   *Ibid.*, p. 504.

Unižennye i oskosblennye; between Goljadkin in "Dvojnik", the musician Efimov in *Netočka*, and Foma Fomič in *Selo Stepančikovo*; between Bykov in *Bednye ljudi*, the hero of "Xozjajka", Petr Aleksandrovič in *Netočka*, and Prince Valkovskij in *Unižennye i oskorblennye*; between Varvara Dobroselova, the heroine of *Bednye ljudi*, Nasten'ka in *Selo Stepančikovo*, and Nataša. (In the second part of his essay, as we shall see, Dobroljubov makes another and more influential classification of Dostoevskij's characters into types.) Dobroljubov goes on to comment: "This poverty of images, this necessity to repeat himself, this inability to work over each character even enough to impart to it appropriate means of external expression – all this indicates, on the one hand, insufficient variety in the author's stock of observations, and, on the other, speaks directly against the artistic wholeness and completeness of his creations." [54]

After thus demonstrating Dostoevskij's inadequacies from the aesthetic point of view and after referring to obvious personal references in the novel, Dobroljubov comments: "Mr. Dostoevskij obviously looks on his work as all us average people do – not as an indestructible monument for posterity, but simply as journalistic labor." [55] So much for the negative side of Dobroljubov's argument. If Dostoevskij's work is unsatisfactory from an "aesthetic" point of view, has it other and more valid claims on our esteem?

For Dobroljubov, as for Belinskij, Dostoevskij's importance as a writer grew out of his "humanitarianism", his championship of the notion of innate universal human worth. For Belinskij, as we have seen, the "humanitarian" aspect of literature was socially important in that it fostered in the reading public a sense of human dignity. Dobroljubov carried this line of thought one step further. An aroused sense of human dignity led inevitably to protest against whatever hindered or prevented the realization of this ideal. As Dobroljubov saw the situation, what made impossible the realization of this ideal in the Russia of his day was the duly constituted social order. The implications of Dobroljubov's position were clearly (though, due to the restrictions imposed by the censorship, covertly) subversive.

For Černyševskij, as we have seen, the supreme value by which all things were to be measured was the ideal of man as he *ought to be*. Further, a man *would* be what he *ought to be* if he were not prevented by inimicable external circumstances. What did Dobroljubov find in

[54]   *Ibid.*, pp. 512-513.
[55]   *Ibid.*, p. 514.

Dostoevskij's work when he approached it from this point of view? What is the ideal of man as he *ought to be* presented in Dostoevskij's work? " 'Every man ought to be a man and conduct himself toward others as one man to another' – this is the ideal which has taken shape in the soul of the author." This was an ideal to which Dobroljubov, as a faithful disciple of Černyševskij, could subscribe. The pathos of Dostoevskij's work lies in its insistence upon the fact that this ideal is not realized. "In Dostoevskij's work we find one general characteristic, more or less noticeable in everything he has written: this is anguish over the human being who acknowledges himself as not strong enough or, in the final analysis, even as not having the right to be a real human being, a complete and independent man, standing on his own two feet." [56] By insisting upon the existence of the ideal of universal human dignity and worth as something fundamentally inalienable from human nature, by showing that the realization of this ideal is frustrated, Dostoevskij's works, in Dobroljubov's opinion, make a protest against this state of affairs. According to this line of reasoning, to show man as he *ought to be* and at the same time to stress that he is *not* what he *ought to be* necessarily implies protest against whatever prevents man from being what he *ought to be* (in this case, the social order), and stimulates an impulse to alter the conditions responsible for such a situation. Thus Dostoevskij's work was neatly fitted into Černyševskij's and Dobroljubov's *Weltanschauung*.

For Dobroljubov, the paramount importance of Dostoevskij's work lay in the fact that it seemed to him to raise the social question with inescapable urgency. The question is put by Dobroljubov in the following form: "What is the root of his incomprehensible dissonance between what ought to be, in a natural, rational state of affairs, and what we actually find?" [57] Dobroljubov writes of Dostoevskij, "He puts the question, and no reader, after reading his stories, can ignore it." However, in Dobroljubov's opinion, a truly great writer not only puts questions but also supplies answers. "With powerful talents, the very act of creation so penetrates the very depths of the truth of life that sometimes, from the simple putting of facts and relationships by an artist, the solution flows of itself." [58] Of Dostoevskij's work, this is not true; therefore, in Dobroljubov's opinion, his work requires supplementary commentary. But, if Dostoevskij fails to answer the question

---

[56]   *Ibid.*, p. 516.
[57]   *Ibid.*, p. 520.
[58]   *Ibid.*, pp. 516-517.

he raises, neither does Dobroljubov. He simply remarks: "In any case, you, the reader, would be naive to expect from me detailed enlightenment on this subject." [59] This seems a clear reference to the limitations imposed by the censorship on the expression of ideas in the Russia of that time. If the conditions of censorship make it impossible to answer the social question raised by Dostoevskij's work, then it seems unfair to reproach him for failing to accomplish the impossible. We are led back again, by implication, to the motif of protest. Dostoevskij is not so much to be condemned for not having created a more perfect work of art; rather, a protest against the conditions which made it impossible for him to write a better work is registered. One is led to the conclusion that Dostoevskij's work, imperfect as it may be (in terms of what it *ought to be*), is still as good as it *can* be, given the conditions under which it was produced. Thus what seems to be an objection (or reservation) as to Dostoevskij's work turns into praise of Dostoevskij for having achieved as adequate a work of art as possible and a protest against social conditions which precluded the possibility of creating something more fully satisfactory.

Let us see how Dobroljubov develops his view of Dostoevskij's work as social protest. As we have seen, this aspect of Dostoevskij's work grows out of his "humanitarian" ideal: "Every man ought to be a man and conduct himself toward others as one man to another." This is Dostoevskij's ideal, as Dobroljubov sees it. But what do we find in Dostoevskij's work? "In varied aspects and situations Mr. Dostoevskij sets before us lack of respect of a human being for himself and lack of respect for a human being on the part of others." On the basis of this general observation, Dobroljubov groups Dostoevskij's characters into two main types: the meek and the obdurate. Members of the first group react by striving to accept the situation in which they find themselves; members of the second group react by frustrated rebellion. Dobroljubov distinguishes yet a third group, which he relates to the first type: "Between these two extremes stands yet another category of people whom it is possible, if you like, to relate more to the first type; these are people who, having lost a broad sense of their human dignity but having exchanged it for some narrow fictitious conventional dignity, have become attached to this fiction and carefully defend it." [60] Representatives of the first type are traced through Makar

<hr/>

[59] *Ibid.*, p. 547.
[60] *Ibid.*, pp. 519-521. This typology is still recognized. See for example, Simmons, *Dostoevski*.

Alekseič in *Bednye ljudi,* Goljadkin in "Dvojnik", "G. Proxarčin", and "Slaboe serdce" ("A Faint Heart"). After a study of four "meek" characters, Dobroljubov reaches the conclusion that, try as they may, in the last analysis, they do not and cannot contentedly accept and reconcile themselves to the humiliating circumstances in which they find themselves. Dobroljubov next directs his attention to two representatives of the second type, characters who are frankly and openly discontented and unhappy in the position forced upon them by society. These are Nelli and Ixmenev in *Unižennye i oskorblennye.* Dobroljubov points out that they are both helpless and utterly unable to defend themselves, to alter their situation in any way.

Thus, as demonstrated in Dostoevskij's work, as interpreted by Dobroljubov, the organization of society not only fails to satisfy the human needs of individuals who accept it (as illustrated by the characters in *Bednye ljudi,* "Dvojnik", "G. Proxarčin", and "Slaboe serdce") but also effectively frustrates those who (like Nelli and Ixmenev) are discontent. If the truth of the picture of life presented by Dostoevskij (as interpreted by Dobroljubov) is admitted, then Dobroljubov suggests two alternatives: Either something is wrong with man, or something is wrong with society. Which alternative Dobroljubov accepts is clear when he writes: "Moralists have insisted that social discontent is a result of the corruption of mankind and of the obfuscation of his mind; others, on the contrary, have cried out that the theory of a would-be ideal organization consisting of the de-humanization of man is contrary to the real demands of human nature and therefore should be repudiated as unsatisfactory and give way to another, acknowledging all the rights of personality and the principle of infinite development, infinite advance; i.e., progress, in contrast to stagnation." [61]

For Dobroljubov, as for Belinskij, the chief significance of Dostoevskij's work lay, as we have just demonstrated, in its "humanitarianism." Thus Dobroljubov's attitude toward Dostoevskij's work is based squarely upon Belinskij's. Indeed, Dobroljubov emphasizes this fact by referring to Belinskij, summarizing and approving his opinion of *Bednye ljudi* in the first pages of his essay. Like Belinskij, Dobroljubov emphasizes the influence of Gogol' as the fountainhead of the humanitarian stream in Russian literature, a stream in which Dostoevskij's work is one of the currents. In addition to the influence of Gogol', Dobroljubov discerns in Dostoevskij's work also the influence of Belinskij himself. The

[61]   Dobroljubov, *Sočinenija,* III, p. 527.

humanitarian ideal which Dobroljubov discerns in Dostoevskij's work
he traces back to the end of the eighteenth century and the influence
of Rousseau's ideas in Russia; however, he regards Gogol' as responsible for the introduction of these ideas into Russian literature. In
contrast to Belinskij, Dobroljubov does not mention foreign influences
on Dostoevskij, but he does point out one similarity between the work
of Dostoevskij and that of Turgenev: after noting the indecisiveness of
the narrator's relationship to the heroine of *Unižennye i oskorblennye*,
Dobroljubov points out that as a literary type the narrator is rather
like the hero of Dostoevskij's own earlier work, *Belye noči* (*White
Nights*), and that the type appeared first in Turgenev's work and had
been repeated there in the hero of *Nakanune* (*On the Eve*). Dobroljubov also points to an autobiographical element in the narrator of
Unižennye i oskorblennye. Like Dostoevskij, he is an author, and his
first work is markedly similar to Dostoevskij's *Bednye ljudi*.

Belinskij had objected to certain crudities in Dostoevskij's literary
technique, and Dobroljubov complains of Dostoevskij's handling of
first-person narrative in *Unižennye i oskorblennye*. Belinskij had complained that the character of the heroine of *Bednye ljudi* was not fully
realized. Dobroljubov echoes this opinion when he discusses the type
to which he assigns the heroine of this novel when he writes, "All of
them are very wise and good girls . . . but in reality very colorless. The
author knows how to put them in very interesting situations, but that
is all he does for them." [62] Dobroljubov follows Belinskij, too, in his
opinion that the characters in Dostoevskij's stories and novels speak
in the same language as the author. Like Belinskij, Dobroljubov points
out a melodramatic tendency in Dostoevskij's work, and he seems to
share Belinskij's poor opinion of insanity as a suitable subject for
literary composition. Dobroljubov's treatment of "Dvojnik", however,
presents an interesting contrast to Belinskij's attitude toward the story.

Belinskij, it will be remembered, could make nothing of "Dvojnik".
Dobroljubov devotes considerable attention to it. As a youth, Dobroljubov kept a record of what he read, and from this source we know that
he first read "Dvojnik" on 19 February 1850. (Dobroljubov was then
fourteen.) His comment, at that time, was as follows: "Filth! The
character of Goljadkin could not be more artificial, the plot, more
stupid; tiresome to read. . . . The devil knows what to make of it." [63]
On 31 May 1850, however, he reread the story and arrived at a more

[62]   *Ibid.*, p. 512.
[63]   Quoted in Rejser, *Letopis*, p. 29.

favorable conclusion: "I reread 'Dvojnik' and it seemed by no means so nasty as before. I understand, now, that Goljadkin is insane. In parts, particularly good." [64] That Dobroljubov was at this time aware of Belinskij's reaction to the story seems doubtful. The earliest record of Dobroljubov's having read anything of Belinskij's dates 7 February 1852, almost two years later, and then it was Belinskij's essay on Kol'cov prefaced to a volume of his poetry.[65] Dobroljubov seems to have begun to study Belinskij's work seriously only in the winter of 1854-1855, when he had access to works of Belinskij's printed in London.[66]

When Dobroljubov returned to the story in 1861, his attitude toward it was ambivalent. On the one hand, he speaks of "leafing through the story (I confess I was unable to get through all of it)",[67] and he does not insist that Dostoevskij has handled his subject well. Like Belinskij, he complains that the story is long drawn out and objects to its fantastic coloration. On the other hand, he discusses the story quite as seriously and in as great detail as others of Dostoevskij's works. Did he hesitate to acknowledge interest in a story so generally unpopular with readers, or was he displaying deference to Belinskij's estimate of the story?

Dostoevskij himself seems to have adopted a relatively low critical estimate of the story. In *Dnevnik pisatelja* for November, 1877, he wrote of it: "Most decidedly, I did not succeed with that novel; however, its idea was rather lucid, and I have never expressed in my writing anything more serious. Still, as far as form was concerned, I failed utterly. Fifteen years later, I made considerable improvements in it for the then 'Complete Collection' of my works (presumably the edition Dobroljubov reviewed); however, also at that time I came to the conclusion that in this work I had not succeeded at all, and were I now to expound and express this idea, I should adopt an altogether different form. But in 1846, I failed to find it, and was unable to master the novel." [68] However, he defended himself against the charge of fantasticality frequently levelled against the story. His defense rests upon the proposition that truth is stranger than fiction.

An idea which Dostoevskij several times expressed was the opinion that actual life was often fantastic. For example, "True events, depicted

---

[64] *Ibid.*, p. 30.
[65] *Ibid.*, p. 42.
[66] *Ibid.*, p. 97. Dobroljubov's diaries, unfortunately incompletely preserved, give no help in determining with certainty just when and how he became acquainted with Belinskij's work.
[67] Dobroljubov, *Sočinenija*, III, p. 531.
[68] Dostoevskij, *Diary of a Writer*, II, p. 883.

with all the exclusiveness of their occurrence, nearly always assume a fantastic, almost incredible character." [69] Elsewhere we find: "Do you know that no matter what you might write or depict, no matter what you might record in a belletristic work, you would never be equal to reality? No matter what you might delineate, it would always be weaker than actual life. You might think that in some work you have reached the maximum of comicalness in this or that phenomenon of life, that you have caught its most ugly aspect – not at all. Reality will forthwith reveal to you such a phase along similar lines that you have never suspected, and one that exceeds everything your own observation and imagination was able to create!" [70] And in his introduction to the story "Krotkaja" ("The Meek One"), Dostoevskij remarks, "Now – about the story itself. I called it 'fantastic', although I consider it real in the highest degree." [71] Though none of these remarks refers specifically to "Dvojnik", one senses behind these protestations a defense against the charge of fantasticality levelled at Dostoevskij from the time of Belinskij's remarks on "Dvojnik" on.

How much Dobroljubov's estimate of Dostoevskij is indebted to Belinskij is quite clear. His notion of the basic importance of Dostoevskij's work, its "humanitarian" significance, is simply an extension of Belinskij's opinion, and he echoes Belinskij even on relatively minor points, as we have seen. In only one important point does he run counter to Belinskij, in his estimate of "Dvojnik", and we have seen with what diffidence and reservations he expressed his opinion.

Dobroljubov's article on Dostoevskij's work, developing and extending the point of view toward it expressed first by Belinskij, set the tone and approach to Dostoevskij's work long dominant in Russian literary criticism, and in general, Dobroljubov's opinion is still influential in the attitude of Soviet critics toward Dostoevskij. Objections to Dobroljubov's article have, however, been raised.

In the first place, Dobroljubov's article was written at a time when Dostoevskij's talent had not yet reached maturity, before he had written that group of major works beginning with *Prestuplenie i nakazanie*; thus it is based on but a portion of the corpus of Dostoevskij's work, and, at that, on relatively minor works.[72] In the second place, Dobrol-

---

[69]   *Ibid.*, I, p. 90.
[70]   *Ibid.*, p. 468.
[71]   *Ibid.*, p. 491.
[72]   Vvedenskij, *Literaturnye xarakteristiki*, p. 93. For Mixajlovskij's views on this point, see Chapter VI.

jubov approached Dostoevskij's work from the point of view of seeking support from it for his own views and using it for his own ends, thus ignoring, minimizing, or distorting whatever could not be utilized in this fashion.[73] In the third place, Volynskij emphasizes the differences in temperament and *Weltanschauung* existing between the two men and insists that for this reason it was impossible for Dobroljubov to understand Dostoevskij and to interpret his work sympathetically.[74]

Dobroljubov's essay on Dostoevskij provides a striking example of the critical treatment accorded by Dobroljubov to writers who did not share his views. By the time Dobroljubov wrote his essay, it must have been abundantly clear to him, especially after Dostoevskij's essay, "G.-bov i vopros ob iskusstve", that Dostoevskij did not share the *Weltanschauung* common to Černyševskij and Dobroljubov, that *Vremja* and the *Sovremennik* differed about more than "those questions about which there can be a difference of opinion in good society" (as Černyševskij had put it when he noted the appearance of *Vremja*). Instead of frankly admitting this situation, Dobroljubov accuses Dostoevskij of lacking sufficient artistic talent to comprehend the significance of what he himself has created. Presumably, if Dostoevskij had had greater artistic powers, he would have seen his material as Dobroljubov saw it. Thus the critic assumes a position of superiority to the artist and attempts to lead him in the desired direction by simultaneously enlightening him and brandishing the carrot of potential critical approval. At the same time, he influences public opinion by, in effect, rewriting the work under review and creating in the mind of the reading public an image of it more powerful than that of the work itself. Instead of revealing the work to the reading public, the critic interposes, between the work and the public, his own creation, thus usurping part of the creative function of the writer, an act justified by the fact that, in Dobroljubov's opinion, the writer is misleading the public. The paramount issue is that the public be led in the proper direction, and if the writer cannot or will not do so, the critic must and will. We shall see Pisarev applying the same technique for the same purposes in his analysis of Dostoevskij's Raskol'nikov.

---

[73]   Dobroljubov, *Polnoe sobranie sočinenij*, V, p. 8; Egorov, "O forme literaturno-kritičeskix statej N. A. Dobroljubova", p. 195.
[74]   Volynskij, *op. cit.*, p. 231. Rozanov asserts that almost all of Dobroljubov's critical estimates were wrong for this reason. See *Literaturnye očerki*, p. 95.

V

DMITRIJ IVANOVIČ PISAREV (1840-1868)

1

The death of Dobroljubov deprived the *Sovremennik* of its principal literary critic and one of its most influential contributors. Černyševskij, then directing the magazine, was faced with the problem of finding a suitable replacement for his friend and protégé. Among the possible candidates to whom he turned was Dmitrij Ivanovič Pisarev, then barely twenty-one years old, a young man who had begun his career as a literary critic about three years previously in *Rassvet* (*Daybreak*), a women's magazine which had begun to appear in January, 1859. After working for this periodical for a little over a year, in 1860 Pisarev began to publish in *Russkoe slovo* (*The Russian Word*), a magazine which, under the leadership of Blagosvetlov, was soon to contend with the *Sovremennik* for position as the leading radical periodical. In November of 1861, the month in which Dobroljubov died, Černyševskij approached Pisarev and asked him to join the staff of the *Sovremennik,* according to a letter written by Pisarev's mother and published by the *Sovremennik* in 1865.[1] Pisarev must have been aware of the letter, if he did not dictate it. The precise function in which Pisarev was asked to serve is not specified in the letter in question, but Pisarev's published work, both in *Rassvet* and the *Russkoe slovo,* had been in the field of literary criticism, and it seems likely that Pisarev was asked to continue this activity in the *Sovremennik*. In any case, the offer was refused.

Who was this young man who rejected what would, on the face of it, appear to have been a flattering offer from one of the acknowledged leaders of the intelligentsia to join the staff of the most prominent radical periodical of the day? Dmitrij Ivanovič Pisarev had been born into an aristocratic family of deteriorating financial position on 2 (14) October 1840. The social background from which he derived was thus

[1] March, Part II, p. 219.

different from that of Belinskij, Černyševskij, and Dobroljubov. After completing the course in a gymnasium in Peterburg, he entered the university there in 1856, and, like Dobroljubov, he began to publish before his graduation in 1861.[2]

Just why Pisarev rejected Černyševskij's offer is not altogether clear, but a number of considerations may explain Pisarev's refusal. In the first place, Pisarev had been, from the first, rather hostile to Dobroljubov and the *Sovremennik*.[3] This attitude is perhaps attributable to the personal influence of the Majkovs, a family circle into which Pisarev had been introduced in 1858 and where he met such writers as Pisemskij and Gončarov, who were associated with the *Otečestvennye zapiski* (*Fatherland Notes*) (then a more moderate periodical and an ideological opponent of the *Sovremennik*). Pisarev had maintained this attitude in his articles in the *Russkoe slovo*. The relationship between the two periodicals was uneasy. On the one hand, they joined forces in opposition to the more conservative periodical press, while on the other, they contended against each other for radical leadership. This ambivalent attitude seems to have been Pisarev's own as well as the official policy of the *Russkoe slovo* and its editor, Blagosvetlov. Furthermore, at the very moment when he was approached by Černyševskij, Pisarev must already have submitted to the *Russkoe slovo* an article, "Ženskie tipy v romanax i povestjax Pisemskogo, Turgeneva i Gončarova" ("Feminine Types in the Novels and Stories of Pisemskij, Turgenev, and Gončarov"), containing a veiled attack on Dobroljubov which Černyševskij could scarcely be expected to relish when it appeared in print. Under these circumstances, Pisarev may well have felt reluctant to accept Černyševskij's offer. Also to be considered was the question of Pisarev's loyalty to Blagosvetlov (a loyalty which subsequently wavered and collapsed but which was still firm at this time), not to mention the fact that at just about this time Pisarev was beginning to make his influence felt among the general public as well as beginning to be recognized as at least one of the ideological leaders of the *Russkoe slovo*. Pisarev may well have preferred to remain on the staff of a journal with which his growing reputation was already identified and where his leadership was coming to be acknowledged rather than to transfer to another, however distinguished, where he would have had to compete with established contributors and to contend for leadership

---

[2]   Except where otherwise noted, the treatment of Pisarev's biography and ideological development follows Coquart, *Dmitri Pisarev*.

[3]   Pisarev, *Sočinenija* (1904-1907), III, pp. 58-59.

with so formidable an opponent as Černyševskij himself. Also, his personal relations with Černyševskij were uncomfortable, thanks to the latter's social tactlessness, so there were numerous grounds for Pisarev's declining to join the staff of the *Sovremennik.*

Some months later, in May of 1862, a mysterious epidemic of fires broke out in Peterburg. The government contended that these were the work of revolutionaries and used the pretext to resort to repressive measures, including, in June, the temporary suspension of both the *Sovremennik* and the *Russkoe slovo.* Although the general tenor of Pisarev's thinking, in contrast to that of Černyševskij and the other leading radicals, inclined toward social evolution rather than political revolution, Pisarev, apparently in an access of exasperation, wrote an appeal for immediate revolt intended as part of a tract destined for clandestine publication.[4] Unfortunately, the publisher was denounced and arrested; the incriminating manuscript was discovered; and Pisarev himself was arrested on 2 July. After at first denying authorship of the compromising manuscript, Pisarev eventually confessed and was condemned to imprisonment, from which he was not released until 18 November 1866. During the four years he spent in prison, Pisarev continued to write for and to publish in the *Russkoe slovo* (after publication of the periodical was resumed in 1863), and his articles of this period were his most brilliant and influential.

The world into which Pisarev emerged after his sojourn in prison was quite different from that which he had left more than four years earlier. The government, after the liberal gesture of the liberation of the serfs in 1861, had soon taken fright and become more repressive as the result of a series of events: first, the Peterburg fires of 1862, already mentioned; second, the Polish Insurrection in 1863; third, the attempted assassination of Alexander II on 4 April 1866 by Karakozov. The official reaction to the attempt upon the tsar's life was a prompt and energetic increase of repressive measures, including the suppression of both the *Sovremennik* and the *Russkoe slovo,* which had been in chronic difficulties with the censor. Two of Pisarev's articles, intended for publication in the *Russkoe slovo,* thus appeared in the first volume of a sort of miscellany, *Luč (The Ray),* which Blagosvetlov attempted to carry on as a successor to the *Russkoe slovo,* but the second volume was confiscated before it could appear.

---

[4] The article was considered sufficiently inflammatory by the tsarist censorship to prevent its publication until after the Revolution of 1917. See Kovalev, "D. I. Pisarev i carskaja cenzura", p. 198.

Thus, after four years in prison, Pisarev emerged into a repressive political atmosphere strongly in contrast to the political optimism which characterized the period culminating in and immediately following the emancipation of the serfs. Further, there was the problem of finding an organ in which he could continue to publish. Blagosvetlov, through the use of a *prête-nom*, returned to the publishing field with a new periodical, *Delo* (*The Deed*), which appeared in November, 1866. Though his personal relationship with Blagosvetlov had deteriorated, Pisarev collaborated, for a time, in this new venture, though with considerable reluctance, but he needed an income, and there was no other organ in which he could publish.

Meanwhile, Nekrasov, publisher of the now defunct *Sovremennik*, had succeeded in gaining control of the *Otečestvennye zapiski*, and at the end of 1867 Pisarev was invited to collaborate on the staff of this periodical. At about this time, Pisarev broke with Blagosvetlov and joined Nekrasov, though Skabičevskij held the role of principal critic on the periodical and Pisarev played only a minor role, seldom signing the articles which he contributed, and his name did not appear on the mast-head as one of the collaborators. What position he might eventually have been able to make for himself in the new magazine was a problem never to be resolved. On 4 July 1868, Pisarev was drowned, in circumstances which provoked rumors of suicide among his contemporaries.

Biographers of Pisarev and students of his work, both foreign and Russian, pre-Soviet and Soviet, have claimed for him a position as a central figure in the intellectual life of Russia during the period when he was active. This claim has been seconded by scholars with a more general interest in the period, particularly pre-Soviet and emigré Russian scholars and foreigners. In general, Soviet scholars (except for those devoting themselves especially to the study of Pisarev's work) tend to ignore or minimize the significance of his contribution. As an ideological leader of the period, Pisarev shares honors with Černyševskij and Dobroljubov; indeed, his work is almost inconceivable without theirs as a foundation. Though Pisarev's attitude toward both men was customarily reserved and even, on occasion, hostile, he was very strongly influenced by them. As we study Pisarev's *Weltanschauung*, we shall find frequent echoes of Černyševskij's and Dobroljubov's ideas, reproduced sometimes faithfully and sometimes in distortion, as well as ideas and intellectual positions peculiar to Pisarev alone.

Pisarev's *Weltanschauung* was by no means coherent and consistent.

Indeed, in Pisarev's thinking, dissonances and inconsistencies are, perhaps, more obvious than in the thinking of the other Russian critics previously studied. As with Belinskij and Dobroljubov, the excuse for this confusion of ideas is attributed by Pisarev's apologists in part to the times and in part to the conditions under which he was obliged to work. In part it was premeditated and conscious; Pisarev wrote: "There can be nothing more disastrous for the student of nature than to have a general outlook on the universe." [5] Nevertheless, when Pisarev's work is reviewed as a whole, certain leading themes emerge, sometimes coalescing into coherent clusters and sometimes clashing. Even at the end of his life, after his release from prison when he was trying to find his way in a new political atmosphere, the ensemble of his ideas remained characteristic and recognizable.

What, then, are some of the leading themes of Pisarev's thought? In the first place, Pisarev was a socialist and a democrat, faiths which he shared with Černyševskij, Dobroljubov, and, in general, the whole westernizing wing of the Russian intelligentsia of his time. Pisarev's attitude toward socialism, however, had certain characteristics which distinguish it from that of his contemporaries. Pisarev shared neither Gercen's faith in a federal socialism based on the peasant nor Černyševskij's belief that in the *mir* lay seeds that could grow into a social order which would satisfy Russia's needs. Rather, he shared Blagosvetlov's view that the masses needed the leadership of an elite dedicated to the task of educating and rousing them. Perhaps more important was the fact that while Černyševskij and Dobroljubov were political revolutionaries, Pisarev was essentially, except for the unfortunate episode which led to his arrest and imprisonment, a believer in political evolution.[6] Such an attitude is compatible with the determinism which marked Pisarev's thinking as well as with the political implications of the evolutionary theory of Darwin, whose convert and propagandist Pisarev became. Pisarev's political ideas also reflect an impressively wide acquaintance with Western European political writers. Coquart detects in Pisarev's articles echoes of Humboldt, Fourier, Robert Owen, Lassalle, and Proudhon. He was rather less influenced by the ideas of

[5]   Quoted in Masaryk, *Spirit of Russia*, II, p. 71.
[6]   Koz'min, "Painjati D. I. Pisareva", pp. 244-245. For a contrary opinion, see Meščerjakov, "Èvoljucija mirosozercanie D. I. Pisareva". Cf. Borščevskij, *Ščedrin i Dostoevskij*, p. 371, Recent Soviet criticism frequently presents Pisarev as a revolutionary, but Ballod, the principal in the affair which led to Pisarev's imprisonment, denied this, at least so far as Pisarev's early career is concerned. See "Zametka o dele D. I. Pisareva", p. 54.

Hegel and Feuerbach than Belinskij, Černyševskij, and Dobroljubov.[7]

In the second place, Pisarev was a mechanistic materialist and a determinist, a follower of Büchner, Vogt, and Moleschott. The ideas of these men had influenced Černyševskij and Dobroljubov and the *Weltanschauung* of many others of Pisarev's generation. It is Coquart's thesis that Büchner's *Stoff und Kraft* was especially significant in the case of Pisarev. From Büchner Pisarev adopted a number of leading ideas: in the first place, materialism, with its attendant hostility to idealism in all of its manifestations; second, determinism and allied with it an absolute faith in science as the force which was capable of resolving all human problems together with a conviction of the necessity of propagating the physical and natural sciences; third, egoism; and fourth, a belief that morality is based on social needs. One of the contradictions which plagued Pisarev was inherited from Büchner: How is one to reconcile individual egoism with social utility?[8] Reenforcing the influence of Büchner and the other German materialists was that of the English historian Buckle, an influence which Pisarev shared with many other Russians of his generation. The source of Buckle's attractiveness was his idea of linking history to the natural sciences, of coordinating the physical and moral worlds in a single system whose universal laws were yet to be discovered. Pisarev's faith in the natural sciences was inspired originally by Büchner, but it was reenforced by the influence of Auguste Comte. Pisarev's absolute faith in science finds expression as early as his articles in *Rassvet,* and his efforts in favor of the natural sciences were not only ardent and consistent but eminently successful, for Mixajlovskij, writing toward the end of the nineteenth century, declared, "C'est à [Pisarev] ... que nous devons le culte extrême des sciences naturelles."[9] A good deal of the intensity and effectiveness of Pisarev's campaign in favor of the natural sciences was the result of his linking a faith in science with his desire for social and political change. He declared that an increase in the number of individuals whose thought and action were firmly grounded in the natural sciences would inevitably lead to the expeditious amelioration of social and political institutions: thus a concentrated effort should be directed toward the creation of such an elite.

---

[7]   Kružkov, "Filosofskie vzgljady D. I. Pisareva", pp. 102-104.
[8]   Coquart, *op. cit.*, p. 421. For a contrasting opinion, see Stanis, *Osnovnye čerty mirovozzrenija D. I. Pisareva*, pp. 50-52.
[9]   Mixajlovskij, "Le mouvement littéraire en Russie", p. 94. Cf. Stanis, *op. cit.*, pp. 58-59.

In third place and closely related to Pisarev's faith in the natural sciences and materialism was his advocacy of utilitarianism, a cast of thought which he was by no means unique in upholding in the Russia of his day, though he was, perhaps, readier than others to follow the doctrine to extreme conclusions and to accept it as a fundamental moral standard. Indubitably, Pisarev's utilitarianism is in line with the general shift in interest from philosophical idealism to materialism, and it owes a good deal, specifically, to Černyševskij. So far as non-Russian thinkers were concerned, Coquart believes that John Stuart Mill exercised a greater influence upon Russian thought at this period than Jeremy Bentham, and he detects in Pisarev's thought a strong influence deriving from Saint-Simon, especially in the case of Pisarev's ideas on the social organization of labor.[10]

In the fourth place, Pisarev was an ardent believer in individualism, in self-development, in egoism, a faith which he shared with Blagosvetlov.[11] Like his devotion to socialism, mechanistic materialism, and utilitarianism, his belief in individualism was widely shared. This faith in individualism was nurtured by Pisarev's early contacts with the Majkov Circle, in which the idea of individual self-development played an important role, and it is echoed in Pisarev's early articles for *Rassvet*. It was reenforced by Černyševskij's and Dobroljubov's "rational egoism", which owed a good deal to the English utilitarians. As developed by Pisarev, it became a powerful destructive tool, a vital weapon in the arsenal of his nihilism.

A fifth element in Pisarev's *Weltanschauung* is his nihilism, his relentless, adroit, persistent, and effective negative criticism. The beginnings of this sort of criticism are to be found in the work of Belinskij. Černyševskij and Dobroljubov made their contributions toward developing it, and another influence was that of Gercen. Curiously enough, an important influence upon Pisarev's nihilism is that of Turgenev, or rather that of the character of Bazarov in Turgenev's novel, *Otcy i deti* (*Fathers and Sons*). Instead of interpreting Bazarov as a calumny on the younger generation, Pisarev rose to Bazarov's defense and adopted him as a personal ideal.[12] Another important purely literary influence upon Pisarev was that of Raxmetov, the hero of Černyšev-

---

[10] Coquart, *op. cit.*, pp. 423-424. Cf. Pisarev, *Izbrannye filosofskie i obščestvenno-političeskie stat'i*, p. 10.
[11] Kuznecov, *Žurnal "Russkoe slovo"*, p. 48.
[12] See Bel'čikov, "Bazarov v ponimanii Pisareva".

skij's novel, *Čto delat'*? (*What is to be Done*?). A component of Pisarev's nihilism, and one which it will be necessary to consider in some detail, was his notorious hostility to art. As we shall see, Pisarev's anti-aestheticism was complex in its sources and complex in its services to ideas which Pisarev held dear.

As a result of the preceding cursory summary of the principal themes in Pisarev's thinking, certain conflicts become obvious. As the most important of these, Coquart sees two: the conflict between mechanistic determinism and individualism and reconciliation of the interests of the individual with those of society. In neither case was Pisarev able to reach a satisfactory resolution.

Mechanistic determinism and individualism imply quite different interpretations of history. Mechanistic determinism holds that events succeed one another in a rigidly linked chain of cause and effect. In this case, since the present and the future are already determined by the unalterable past, such a system admits no possibility of altering the already predetermined course of history. But belief in individualism implies faith that man is not powerless to alter the course of history and the development of social institutions. At first Pisarev espoused an extreme and thoroughgoing determinism, but he soon saw the difficulties of such a position and vacillated. In his article, "Populjarizatory otricatel'nyx doktrin" ("Vulgarizers of Negative Doctrines"), he retreated considerably. He now took the position that progress was not automatic and that a significant role was played by the individual. He thus enunciated a relative rather than an absolute determinism, suggesting an interplay between determinism and human will. But Pisarev was unable to maintain this position. In 1867, in two articles published almost simultaneously, he took almost perfectly opposed positions. In discussing Pope Gregory VII, he reached the conclusion that Gregory is an example of the intervention of an individual in the course of history. But in his articles on Dostoevskij's *Prestuplenie i nakazanie* (*Crime and Punishment*), he reverted to strict determinism. (As we shall see, there were polemical reasons which may explain his position in the latter case.) Thus Pisarev was never able to reconcile determinism and individualism. Coquart remarks, "Pisarev adhère sans réserve au dogme du déterminisme absolu, le faisant coexister avec son individualisme ... Mais il les juxtapose, il ne les combine pas." [13]

If Pisarev was unable to reconcile the claims of determinism and

---

[13]   Coquart, *op. cit.*, p. 160.

individualism, neither was he able to reconcile the claims of society
with those of the individual. At the beginning of his career, Pisarev
preached individualistic hedonism. It was in this sense that he understood Černyševskij's rational egoism. For Pisarev, the emancipation of
the individual meant the freeing of the individual from social and moral
restraints. In prison Pisarev discovered altruism. This revelation forced
a re-evaluation of his ideas on individualism. As a result, it became
the duty of the individual to serve the needs of society. This new attitude of Pisarev's toward the relationship of the individual to society
is expounded in "Realisty" ("Realists"), written in June and July,
1864, and appearing in the *Russkoe slovo* under the title, "Nerazre-
šennyj vopros" ("An Unsettled Question") in September, October, and
November of the same year. Did not this new position mean a surrender
on the part of the individual, a submission of his own proper ends to
those of society? By no means, according to Pisarev. He contended
that the interest of the individual coincided with that of society
and that, so far as individuals were concerned, "the more profound
their egoism becomes, the stronger becomes their love of humanity."
At this point, Coquart asks, "Est-ce là lever une antinomie ou l'esqui-
ver?" [14]

Coquart also points up another fascinating paradox in Pisarev's
work: "Comme écrivain . . ., Pisarev vit nur une contradiction. . . .
D'un côté, rabaissant violemment tout ce qui est *esthétique,* il professe
la plus dédaigneuse indifférence pour la presentation littéraire; selon
lui, il n'y a pas lieu de se préoccuper spécialement de la forme à propos
d'un livre, et le style ne prête à aucun remorque dès l'instant qu'il rend
exactement et correctment ce qu'il y a à rendre. D'un autre côté
cependant, il écrit avec gout et même avec art." [15]

Glaring and obvious as the contradictions and unresolved conflicts
of ideas in Pisarev's thinking are, they did not redound to his discredit
nor serve to limit his influence. On the contrary, they were part and
parcel of the confusions of his time, and the vigor with which he
expressed them accounts, at least in part, for his popularity and influence. In this respect Pisarev is strongly reminiscent of Belinskij in
his aspect as a mirror of the intellectual preoccupations of his time as
well as an influential ideologue.

[14]   *Ibid.*, p. 428.
[15]   *Ibid.*, p. 415.

2

Pisarev's attack upon art was not only, as we have seen, one of the most notoriously scandalous facets of his activity; it has also a direct bearing upon his attitude toward Dostoevskij's work. Therefore, it becomes necessary to consider this aspect of Pisarev's ideas in some detail. If Pisarev's *Weltanschauung* was incoherent and contradictory, then it is not surprising that his aesthetics share these same defects. As a recent Soviet student of Pisarev points out, part of the difficulty resides in Pisarev's loose and fluid use of the term: "Pisarev extends the meaning of aesthetics so far that the word becomes a synonym for every kind of inertia and reaction in general – not only in art but also in life . . . . Elsewhere, he gives a narrower and more specific definition – 'that criticism which prefers form to content'. Finally, Pisarev speaks of aesthetics as a specific kind of attitude to the world determined not by critical analysis but by the principle of irresponsible personal taste. But, of course, in all these cases, aesthetics stands as a single word representing different ideas." [16]

As with his other ideas, Pisarev's views on aesthetics were significantly conditioned by the situation in which he worked. Furthermore, aesthetic theory was by no means a central preoccupation with Pisarev (any more than it was with Černyševskij or Dobroljubov), and this fact, in part, explains its piecemeal characteristics. Also, Pisarev's theoretical ideas about art and his attitude toward it experienced a considerable evolution. Since Pisarev's critical articles devoted to Dostoevskij's work came late in his career ("Pogibšie i pogibajuščie" ["Those Who Have Perished and Those Who Are Perishing"]) devoted to *Zapiski iz mertvogo doma* [*Memoirs from the House of the Dead*], was published in *Luč*, I, 1866, and "Bor'ba za žizn' " [The Fight for Life"], which discusses *Prestuplenie i nakazanie,* was Pisarev's final critical article), it is the final form of his ideas about art that interests us most here.

At the beginning of his career, Pisarev was by no means hostile to art or even to aesthetics. In one of his early articles for *Rassvet* (a

---

[16] Plotkin, *Pisarev i literaturno-obščestvennoe dviženie*, p. 353. Also *D. I. Pisarev, žizn' i dejatel'nost*, pp. 146-147. Masaryk complains of the same imprecision in Pisarev's use of such terms as *utilitarianism, materialism*, and *positivism*. See *op. cit.,* II, p. 57.

review of an article on the influence of art in education), Pisarev approved an aesthetic education as conducive to harmony between duty and inclination, judgment and feeling. The thesis is superficial, but at least it is indicative of no early anti-aesthetic bias.

The opening gun in Pisarev's crusade against art in general and *belles lettres* in particular, which was to reach its climax in 1864-1865, was fired by Pisarev in an article which appeared in the *Russkoe slovo* for November,1861, "Pisemskij, Turgenev, i Gončarov". Here, for the first time, Pisarev enunciated his purely utilitarian concept of the function of literature and at the same time ridiculed objectivity as an ideal, a shot aimed in Dobroljubov's direction.

A further step in the development of Pisarev's position took place in 1864 in two articles: "Cvety nevinnogo jumora" ("Flowers of Innocent Humor") (February, 1864) and "Motivy russkoj dramy" ("Themes of the Russian Drama") (March, 1864). It is important to keep in mind the polemical aspect of these articles. Černyševskij was no longer at the helm of the *Sovremennik*. Pisarev and Zajcev were sceptical of the orthodoxy of the political ideas of Saltykov-Ščedrin, his successor, and when he permitted himself criticism of Černyševskij's novel *Čto delat'?* both Zajcev and Pisarev rose in defense of Černyševskij, a defense which took the form of a counter-attack against Ščedrin and the *Sovremennik*, which, it was maintained, had renounced the heritage of Černyševskij and Dobroljubov, a heritage which (by implication) only the *Russkoe slovo* now remained to champion. In this quarrel Dostoevskij also involved himself.[17]

Since Zajcev began the campaign (in an article which took exception to Ščedrin's gibes at Dostoevskij's *Zapiski iz mertvogo doma*),[18] and took a conspicuous role in its subsequent development, it may be appropriate, at this point, to summarize his career and to define his relationship to Pisarev. Like Dobroljubov and Pisarev, Zajcev's career as a literary critic began early (in Zajcev's case, at the age of twenty). Since he joined the staff of the *Russkoe slovo* only after Pisarev's imprisonment, the two men did not meet until after Pisarev's release from prison in 1866. However, a sort of instantaneous sympathy and mutual understanding sprang up between them, and the crusade against art was a joint undertaking. Though Pisarev had laid the foundations

---

[17] For extensive accounts of these polemics, see Koz'min, "Raskol v nigilistax"; Borščevskij, *op. cit.*, pp. 359-390; Pospelov, *Èpoxa rascveta kritičeskogo realizma*, pp. 216-222; Kuznecov, *Žurnal "Russkoe slovo"*, pp. 276-321.
[18] *Kušelov, op. cit.*, p. 294.

for the attack upon art as early as 1861 and had become increasingly hostile as time went on, it may be questioned whether he would have gone as far as he eventually did in his final assault had he not been egged on by Zajcev. It is certain, for example, that Pisarev's second article on Puškin ("Puškin i Belinskij", *Russkoe slovo,* June 1865) was written at Zajcev's instigation. Zajcev went rather farther than Pisarev in his anti-aestheticism and he possessed considerable gifts as a polemicist, but he contributed nothing new to the theories enunciated by Pisarev, and his role is a subordinate one, though by no means negligible.[19]

Once begun, Pisarev's campaign, originally directed against Ščedrin and the *Sovremennik,* soon roused a more traditional opponent, the *Otečestvennye zapiski,* and new sallies were directed at this adversary. This new polemic helps to make clear one aspect of Pisarev's and Zajcev's joint attack upon aesthetics, upon "pure art". This position was, indeed, dear to the conservatives, and the attack upon it was simply another episode in the general assault against conservative positions. The most important of Pisarev's articles attacking art was his "Realisty" (1864), though the battle over aesthetics continued to rage for some time after its publication.

In "Realisty" the determining interest is social, the problem posed by the existence of the hungry and the naked. From this point of view purely aesthetic activity is dismissed as socially irrelevant. Pisarev does not go so far here as to suggest that the poet would be more profitably occupied if he devoted his energies to the manufacture of shoes rather than of verses, but he does demand that the poet use his gift in the service of society. Pisarev distinguishes two groups of poets: valiant fighters and contemptible parasites. It is impossible for the former to remain aloof to the sufferings of mankind, and they are to be honored for having effectively championed salutary notions.

Having sketched in the background against which Pisarev's ideas about art were expressed as well as having taken a glance at these ideas themselves, it may be worthwhile to recall the rising tide of anti-aestheticism, perceptible in the work of Belinskij, beginning to flow in the work of Černyševskij and Dobroljubov, and reaching full flood in the articles of Pisarev and Zajcev and to try to establish Pisarev's place in the tradition of literary criticism going back to Belinskij.

Pisarev considered himself as the heir to and the continuator of this

[19]   Coquart, *op. cit.,* pp. 253-254.

Russian critical tradition. This position has, in general, been granted
to Pisarev, both by his opponents and by his supporters, though often
with reservations. Though there is general (if uneasy) agreement that
the critics with whom we have been concerned (Belinskij, Černyševskij,
Dobroljubov, and Pisarev) are mutually related and genuinely members
of the same school, it is not easy to establish direct, convincing, and
satisfactory evidence of this relationship. In part, the difficulty is due
to the fact that each of the separate bodies of individual criticism with
which it is necessary to deal is complex, inconsistent, and often in flux.
Further, additional confusion may be attributable to the fact that later
critics have been intent upon using those with whom we are concerned
to establish some thesis of their own. Vengerov, for example, presents
a neat schematization of the relationship of these critics which is attractive in its simplicity and clarity (and which has a certain validity)
but which attains these qualities at the expense of completely over-
looking Pisarev's final critical position. This distortion may be attributed to Vengerov's desire to present the intellectual history of the
period as a struggle between individualism and anti-individualism, and
it is, in its way, typical of the fashion in which Russian critics are given
to dealing with the work of their predecessors.[20]

In any case, we know that Pisarev became acquainted with Belinskij's work in 1860. Plotkin points out several aspects in which
Pisarev's work is related to Belinskij's at the end of the latter's career:
hostility toward art as an end in itself, an insistence that "life" is more
important than "art", a linking of art with social phenomena.[21]

Pisarev's attitude toward Belinskij was determined by polemical considerations. As part of his campaign to discredit "aesthetics" (as an
attitude toward art which considered form more important than content), it was tactically desirable to demolish Puškin's literary reputation,
since the corpus of Puškin's work was used as an infallible touchstone
by the defenders of "aesthetics". The veneration of Puškin was a cult
whose adepts included not only the partisans of "aesthetics" but also
such leaders of radical thought as Černyševskij and Dobroljubov. True,
these latter tended to prefer Gogol' to Puškin, but they refrained from
denigrating Puškin, possibly restrained by veneration for Belinskij,
whose appreciations of Puškin had done much to found the cult. Gen-

[20] Vengerov, *Očerki po istorii russkoj literatury*, pp. 69-70.
[21] Plotkin, *Pisarev*, pp. 340-341. Also *D. I. Pisarev, žizn' i dejatel'nost'*, pp.
145-146. Cf. Volynskij, *Russkie kritiki*, pp. 31-32; Kaun and Simmons, *Slavic
Studies*, pp. 143-145.

eral acknowledgement of Puškin's prestige made him a valuable ally for the "aesthetic" critics.

The tactical problem for Pisarev was, on the one hand, to demolish Puškin's literary reputation, while, on the other, to dissociate Puškin's literary reputation from that of Belinskij so as to demolish the one without damaging the other, to attack the "aesthetic" critics without alienating that portion of the Russian reading public which followed Černyševskij and Dobroljubov in granting Puškin a position of prestige and authority. This delicate operation Pisarev sought to accomplish by distinguishing two aspects of Belinskij's criticism: one aspect in which he appears as an "aesthetician" and another, Belinskij's "real" position, in which he appears as the predecessor of the "realists". Thus Belinskij's prestige was not only saved from damage but also turned to account.

Pisarev's most important discussion of the work of Černyševskij is contained in his article, "Razrušenie èstetiki" ("The Destruction of Aesthetics") (*Russkoe slovo*, May, 1865). The article is clearly polemical, and it is important to understand the setting in which it made its appearance. The specific occasion for the article was the direct question, posed in an article by Antonovič which appeared in the February, 1865, number of *Sovremennik*. Pisarev was asked whether or not he subscribed to the conception of art developed by Černyševskij in his dissertation. As Coquart points out, the question was a trap. To deny Černyševskij's position would have deprived Pisarev of the protection of Černyševskij's authority and compromised him in the eyes of that very considerable portion of the intelligentsia which idolized Černyševskij. To accept Černyševskij's position, as interpreted by Antonovič, would have meant committing himself to a position which would have denied him freedom of action. Pisarev chose to deny not Černyševskij's position but Antonovič's interpretation of it and to claim Černyševskij as the legitimate originator of Pisarev's own position. This polemical maneuver served several purposes. In the first place, Pisarev sought to secure for his own ideas the still powerful prestige and authority of Černyševskij. In the second place, it served to discomfit the *Sovremennik* as a journal with pretentions to leading radical thought and one which had joined Pisarev's opponents in attacking him. In the third place, it continued Pisarev's difference of opinion with Antonovič, which had begun over the interpretation of Turgenev's *Otcy i deti,* a novel which Antonovič had attacked and which Pisarev had warmly defended.

Was not Černyševskij's an aesthetic doctrine, anti-idealist, materialist, democratic, but undeniably aesthetic? Antonovič had asked. This conclusion Pisarev emphatically denied on the basis of a passing remark of Černyševskij's, the sense of which he either patently misunderstood or flagrantly misinterpreted. Such was Pisarev's version of his debt to Černyševskij, but what do others make of the relationship between the two? There seem to be a number of genuine and conspicuous debts.

In the first place, the two men shared a general tendency. Černyševskij's principal interest lay not in art but elsewhere, and his attitude toward the question of art was determined by his other interests. Thus Pisarev shared with the later Belinskij, Černyševskij, and Dobroljubov a tendency to place art in a subordinate position, to make it subservient to other, social interests.

In the second place, several of Pisarev's most striking and characteristic positions are simply further developments of ideas expressed first by Černyševskij. When Černyševskij maintained that the source of beauty was not art but life itself and that what was beautiful was what was interesting, he obviously introduced an extra-aesthetic standard by which art was to be judged. Pisarev carried this process one step further by maintaining that what was "interesting" was what was "useful". Černyševskij had made an effort to define the "interesting" with inconclusive results. Pisarev, ever impatient of strict definitions, was more subjective in determining the "useful" than Černyševskij had been in his use of the term "interesting". Pisarev's criterion is borrowed from the social sciences, but its applicability elsewhere was not questioned by Pisarev. Furthermore, once having accepted Černyševskij's position that life is superior to art, which is, at best, only an inferior copy, it was logical to argue that art was dispensable. Pisarev's extreme hostility to the non-verbal arts was determined by his inability to see, logically, how these arts could act upon human consciousness, and for this reason Pisarev consigned them to the category of "pure" or "useless" art. Černyševskij's appreciation of the non-verbal arts suffered from the same limitation, though he expressed himself less categorically than Pisarev upon this point.

In the third place, Pisarev sometimes simply borrowed Černyševskij's ideas. Much of the theoretical ammunition Pisarev employed in order to demolish the pretentions of aesthetics – for example, the demonstration of the impermanence of aesthetic standards – was taken over directly from Černyševskij.

Pisarev has been accused of caricaturing Černyševskij's ideas, and

certainly he developed them in a one-sided fashion, however this
fashion be interpreted. For example, Plexanov sees Pisarev as developing non-materialist, "idealistic", elements of Černyševskij's ideas.
Četunova, on the other hand, accuses Pisarev of failing to see (as
Černyševskij did) that art is a legitimate expression of man's thirst for
what is perfect, faultless, "ideal". Kirpotin accuses Pisarev of often
carrying an historical approach to literary phenomena so far he falls
into subjectivism.[22]

As was the case with Černyševskij, it has been denied, on occasion,
that Pisarev was the "destroyer of aesthetics". It has been maintained
that, again like Černyševskij, Pisarev was not so much interested in
destroying art as in founding it anew. This is, perhaps, true, in the
sense that instead of basing art on the "beautiful" or the "interesting",
Pisarev sought to base it on the "useful". Coquart, however, reaches
the conclusion that Pisarev's contribution to aesthetics was purely
destructive.[23]

Pisarev's debt to Dobroljubov is as clear and strong as his debt to
Černyševskij. Pisarev's critical principles and practice were squarely
based upon Dobroljubov's example. If Pisarev, on occasion, found
fault with Dobroljubov, it will be remembered that the relationship of
Pisarev to the *Sovremennik* and its contributors was always touchy.
Furthermore, Pisarev undoubtedly considered himself as Dobroljubov's
rival, and so long as Dubroljubov was alive, Pisarev was unwilling to
heighten Dobroljubov's already considerable reputation. However, it is
significant that when Pisarev does find fault with Dobroljubov, it is
often because the latter had not applied his own principles with sufficient rigor and consistency, a defect which Pisarev readily undertook
to remedy. Thus, in spite of minor differences between the two, Pisarev
is usually conceded to be Dobroljubov's successor, both in terms of
continuing the main lines of Dobroljubov's criticism and in terms of
succeeding to his prestige.[24]

As we have seen, Dobroljubov had developed the essay of literary

[22] Plexanov, *N. G. Černyševskij*, pp. 261-262; Četunova, "Čto razrušil 'nigilist'
Pisarev?", pp. 12-13; Lunačarskij and Lebedev-Poljanskij, *Očerki po istorii russkoj
kritiki*, II, p. 227. But Kuznecov sees Pisarev as maintaining Černyševskij's basic
principles. See *op. cit.*, p. 324.

[23] Coquart, *op. cit.*, pp. 261-262. Cf. Lunačarskij and Lebedev-Poljanskij, *op.
cit.*, p. 226; Ivanov-Razumnik, *Istorija russkoj obščestvennoj mysli*, II, pp. 34,
51; Vengerov, *op. cit.*, p. 58; Mixajlovskij, *op. cit.*, p. 49; Kuznecov, *op. cit.*,
p. 332.

[24] For a discussion of Pisarev as an opponent of Dobroljubov, see Koz'min,
"Ras'kol v nigilistax".

criticism "*à propos*". The genre was further developed by Pisarev. When Pisarev dealt with apolitical works, he tried to view them from an angle which permitted him to point a social moral. When he dealt with works written from a point of view he conceived to be similar to his own, he emphasized similarities between the ideas expounded in these works and his own. His attitude toward works written by those whom he considered to be his political adversaries was purely polemical. In Pisarev's work the publicistic element is even more pronounced and persistent than in that of his predecessors.

In comparing the work of Pisarev with that of Černyševskij and Dobroljubov, two further factors are often mentioned; the fact that the activity of the latter two was confined to the period preceding and immediately succeeding the liberation of the serfs in 1861, whereas Pisarev's activity continued into a period in which the political atmosphere had changed, when, on the one hand, the government showed evidences of regretting the liberal gesture of the liberation and, on the other, the intelligentsia had split into warring camps of liberals and radicals, and the fact that Pisarev's social derivation was quite different from that of the other two, a factor emphasized by Mixajlovskij, who considered Pisarev an example not of the *raznočinec* (like Belinskij, Černyševskij, and Dobroljubov) but of a new social type, the *kajuščijsja dvorjanin* (the "repentant nobleman").

Pisarev's attitude toward literature, his conception of the function of the writer and the literary critic, is clearly related to his political position. As we have seen, Pisarev was, except for a relatively brief episode, an evolutionary rather than a revolutionary in politics. He shared with the other leaders of the radical wing of the Russian intelligentsia a desire for and a belief in the necessity of social and political change; he differed from them as to the means by which he believed this change was best to be wrought. Instead of basing his hopes on the prospect of a political revolution and directing his efforts toward this end, he evolved and expounded a belief in the efficacy of science to achieve this goal. The very first step, as Pisarev analyzed the problem, was the creation of an intellectual elite, thoroughly grounded in the natural sciences. The expectation that social and political change could be achieved in this way seems naive or, at best, over-sanguine, and this aspect of the matter did not escape Pisarev, who sought to over-ride the objection by advancing the principal of the economy of intellectual forces. In order to achieve the desired result, it would be necessary to concentrate all intellectual activity on a single problem,

to direct everything toward the achievement of a single goal. Therefore, on the one hand, Pisarev devoted himself to propaganda in favor
of science and, as a corollary, attacked any interest which competed
with it. Insofar as art (including literature) represented an interest in
competition with science for man's attention, it must be attacked, its
pretentions demolished, its seductions exposed.

Pisarev's socio-political position thus explains the savageness of his
attack upon art; he felt that art competed with science, and as a rival
to science, art was intolerable. However, an exception to the general
indictment against art was made in the case of literature reduced to
the status of a serviceable handmaiden. Literary criticism, if it were
to survive, had to be subordinated, like everything else, to a single
interest, and Pisarev saw himself as not so much a literary critic as
rather the banner-bearer of a socio-political program.

Viewed synthetically, Pisarev's assault upon aesthetics developed
along two lines. One prong of the attack was a frontal assault upon
the theoretical foundations of aesthetics; the other consisted of an
attempt to establish a new and extra-aesthetic foundation for literature,
the only form of art which Pisarev was prepared to permit. In an
attempt to demonstrate the impossibility of arriving at general laws of
aesthetics, Pisarev took two lines of argument: the one, historical, the
other, theoretical. On the one hand (taking a lead from Černyševskij),
Pisarev attempted to show, by an appeal to history, that aesthetic
criteria actually did change, and if this were true, then what permanent
and unchanging foundations for aesthetics were possible? On the other
hand, as the measure of aesthetic experience, Pisarev (again following
Černyševskij) insisted upon individual taste (as in philosophy he insisted upon individual intuition as the criterion of truth). How was a
science to be built upon such a foundation? At this point in his development, early in his career, Pisarev saw literature as a means for advancing his primary interest – the emancipation of the individual. The
function of the critic was simply to transmit to the reader his own
subjective and personal reaction.

As we have seen, in prison the fundamental basis of Pisarev's
thinking altered. As a result of this change, of his substitution of the
good of the majority in place of the emancipation of the individual as
a goal, he found new grounds for his attack upon aesthetics, an attack
which became more violent and sweeping, as well as a new conception
of the function of literature and of literary criticism.[25] From his new

[25] Kružkov denies a basic shift in Pisarev's ideas after release from prison but

point of view he rejected, and not only rejected but ridiculed, the individualistic and subjective literary criticism which he had previously preached and practised. If individual taste is rejected as an aesthetic criterion, some other must take its place, and for Pisarev the new criterion was the idea of the general good. From this position, Pisarev simply denied the contributions of art to the general good and thus disposed not only of aesthetic questions but also of art itself.

Pisarev's new criticism was justified on ethical and humanitarian grounds. So long as the problems of poverty and hunger remain unsolved, how could any honorable individual concern himself with any others? asked Pisarev. Yet another objection rested on Pisarev's theory of the economy of intellectual forces. The solution of the immediate practical problems facing Russia could be accomplished only at the price of concentrating effort and attention on this single goal, and any distraction was obstructionist and immoral, as well as illogical. Pisarev's criterion of value became more narrowly utilitarian than Černyševskij's or Dobroljubov's and limited to immediate and practical applications.

Yet another objection to art rested upon Pisarev's notion that a taste for art ran contrary to man's natural propensities (an idea which seems to be a further development of Černyševskij's proposition that a healthy man is satisfied with what is good instead of demanding what is perfect, and it is an obvious corollary of utilitarianism, which sees man as primarily interested in satisfying his material needs); thus art represents some perversion of man's fundamental nature. Art is attacked not so much on a class basis, as a toy of the privileged, but as an artificial cultural excrescence.

There are several interesting aspects of this new position of Pisarev's. In the first place, it is perhaps the culminating point in the displacement of interest from abstract questions to immediate and pressing social problems which marks the shift from idealism to realism. In the second place, it is typical of the extremism of Pisarev's thought. In the third place, the idea of moral duty comes to the fore, and this is responsible for the moralizing tone of so much of Pisarev's writing.

From his general condemnation of art as frivolous, irrelevant, and immoral, Pisarev was willing to exclude only literature, but not literature in general, only specific varieties of literature. Since, in his opinion, the natural sciences could contribute most to the general good, through

---

emphasizes a change from expectation of speedy revolution to a faith in enlightenment, work, and the creation of an intellectual elite. See Pisarev, *Izbrannye filosofskie*, pp. 10-13.

the operation of the principle of the economy of intellectual forces, art must serve the ends of science.

Since the function of literature is to serve science, the question as to how it may best perform this function arises. For Pisarev, literature and literary criticism had common goals and served common functions. Their value was either educational or propagandistic. The educational value of literature consisted of the fact that it could serve as a substitute for real life (an echo of Černyševskij and Dobroljubov). As a vehicle of propaganda, literature was to guide and form public opinion. (Here literature is given the function originally assigned by Belinskij to literary criticism, to act as the mentor of society.)

Theoretically, both literature and literary criticism play the same subordinate role. Actually, however, as Černyševskij and Dobroljubov had discovered, literature is less suited to the role than literary criticism. Consequently, criticism emerges as a stronger force than literature itself, as it had already tended to do in Černyševskij's and Dobroljubov's critical practice, and the critic supersedes the author as a leader of social thought. The desire to exercise ideological leadership is perfectly clear in Pisarev's criticism, and he attributed the origin of this function of literary criticism to Dobroljubov.

The standard applied to a work of literature is extra-aesthetic (as it was in Černyševskij's and Dobroljubov's criticism): a work of literature is judged as to whether or not it coincides with a predetermined *Weltanschauung*, that of the critic. It will be remembered that in his polemic with Dobroljubov, Dostoevskij had pointed out the difficulty of guaranteeing the usefulness, the genuine utility of the critic's *Weltanschauung*. Pisarev simply assumed that his subjective evaluation was the only one possible.

The only thing that counted in a literary work, so far as Pisarev was concerned, was the matter. This attitude was rooted in Pisarev's criticism as early as his first reviews in *Rassvet*, in which, because the magazine was intended for a feminine audience (at that time very inadequately educated), it was necessary to discuss the subject dealt with in a book under review as well as the book itself in relation to that subject. Dobroljubov had proceeded upon this principle as a rule of method, and Pisarev accepted it unquestioningly as an axiom. Pisarev, however, pushed on further than Dobroljubov was usually willing to do, being ever ready to look at a work of art as so much raw material, disregarding the interpretation of its author, and drawing from it whatever conclusion he liked. This difference can be clearly seen by comparing the way in which Dobroljubov and Pisarev handled such writers as Gončarov and Ostrovskij.[26]

Obviously, the theoretical aspect of literature did not greatly interest Pisarev, and there are crying inconsistencies between his theory and his critical practice. In theory, in contrast to his predecessors, Pisarev contended that artistic creativity was a conscious process only. This contention justisfied Pisarev's demand that the writer adopt a conscious attitude toward social phenomena, which, especially in a period of social conflict, should be the principal subject matter of art, since in this way art could best serve humanity. So far, so good: this portion of Pisarev's theory is coherent and consistent. The difficulty arose when Pisarev attempted to apply this principle to the literary work of his period, little of which fulfilled his theoretical prescriptions.

Pisarev (like Černyševskij and Dobroljubov) was thus faced with the problem of converting work which did not fit his formula into grist for his mill. This he did by falling back on the theory of unconscious creativity (which Černyševskij and Dobroljubov had used in the same way). This theory enabled Pisarev to discuss writers whose work showed no discernible social attitude and even those whose attitude was different from his own, though not so much so as to produce works which could not be equated with real life, an accusation used to dispose of writers whose social point of view was too obviously inimicable to his own. Inconsistent as it was with Pisarev's theory, this position permitted him to discuss the subject matter of a literary work, regardless of the subjective intention of the author, and to draw his own conclusions. A work of literature thus becomes so much raw material, a substitute for life itself, and the interpretation of its significance falls to the lot of the critic.

In spite of his extremely doctrinaire utilitarian attitude toward literature, like his predecessors, Belinskij, Černyševskij, and Dobroljubov, Pisarev was endowed with considerable literary taste. This facet of his talent doubtless helps to explain his popularity and influence. Indubitably more important were his achievements as a literary stylist. Indeed, Volynskij, who thoroughly disagreed with Pisarev's criticism, explains Pisarev's success mainly on this ground, and Evgenij Solov'ev writes: "Turn to any page in Pisarev's works and read it. You will find, first of all, a striking model of the Russian language, which appears before you in its full beauty and power. His equal in power and expressiveness

---

[26] Coquart, *op. cit.*, pp. 122, 236.

of style I find only in Gercen. No one was able, like Pisarev, to make the literary language approximate colloquial language and to do it without impertinent and unnecessary innovations." [27]

During Pisarev's lifetime, in spite of his great influence and popularity (especially among the young), he was by no means accepted by all. His name was anathema in conservative circles, and his extremism caused many of the liberals to regard him with reserve. (Turgenev was a notable exception.[28]) Later the *narodniki* (Populists) were unsympathetic to his ideas. Only the Marxists found in his work elements which they were able to use and to develop further. But in spite of an inevitable reaction against Pisarev's *Weltanschauung* (due in part to the excesses of those who proclaimed themselves his disciples), his influence was enduring. Coquart justly remarks: "Pisarev a su aider à s'affirmer des idées naissantes et leur donner l'essor. Parfois même il les imposa sous une forme qui les marquait ineffaçablement comme venant de lui", and he traces Pisarev's influence on Russian writers as diverse as Lavrov, Kropotkin, Bakunin, Nečaev, and Tkačev.[29] Others have detected Pisarev's influence on Grigor'ev, Mixajlov, Gleb Uspenskij, and Lev Tolstoj.[30]

3

Pisarev discussed Dostoevskij's work in two articles. The first of these, "Pogibšie i pogibajuščie" ("Those Who Have Perished and Those Who are Perishing"), appeared in 1866, in the first volume of *Luč* (*The Ray*), a miscellany organized by Blagosvetlov in an attempt to carry on the work of the suppressed *Russkoe slovo*. This essay discusses Dostoevskij's *Zapiski iz mertvogo doma* (*Memoirs from the House of the Dead*) together with the *Očerki bursy* (*Seminary Sketches*) of Nikolaj Gerasimovič Pomjalovskij. Pisarev's second essay, dealing with Dostoevskij's *Prestuplenie i nakazanie* (*Crime and Punishment*), appeared in two installments. The first, entitled "Budničnye storony žizni"

---

[27]   Pisarev, *Sočinenija* (1894), VI, p. xi. Cf. Volynskij, *op. cit.*, p. 31; Vengerov, *op. cit.*, p. 69; Protopopov, "Dobroljubov", p. 288. Indeed, Kazanovič attributes Pisarev's influence principally to his literary talent. See "D. I. Pisarev posle kreposti", p. 628.
[28]   Kazanovič, "Turgenev. Perepiska s D. I. Pisarevym".
[29]   Coquart, *op. cit.*, pp. 433, 435-437, 445-447.
[30]   For Pisarev's influence on Grigor'ev, see Masaryk, *op. cit.*, I, p. 381. On Mixajlov, Gleb Uspenskij, and Tolstoj, see Ovsjaniko-Kulikovskij, *Istorija russkoj literatury*, IV, pp. 133, 176-177; V, pp. 349-350.

("Every-day Aspects of Life"), was published in *Delo* (*The Deed*) in the number for May, 1867, and the second appeared in the same journal in 1868 (after Pisarev's death) under the title "Bor'ba za suščestvovanie" ("The Fight for Survival"). The two installments were published in Pisarev's *Sočinenija* (*Works*) in an altered version at the end of 1868 under the title "Bor'ba za žizn'" ("The Fight for Life").

According to the testimony of Pisarev's mother, in 1860 Pisarev had read Dotsoevskij's story, "Djadjuškin son" ("Uncle's Dream"), which he wanted to turn into a play, and in 1861 *Selo stepančikovo* (*Stepančikovo Village*, published in English translation as *A Friend of the Family*), which he also enjoyed.[31] In articles published previous to those dealing specifically with Dostoevskij, Pisarev had mentioned him in passing. For example, in "Realisty" ("Realists") (1864) Pisarev classed Dostoevskij together with Gogol', Belinskij, Nekrasov, Turgenev, and Dobroljubov as "very remarkable and conscientious writers", and he followed Belinskij in relating Dostoevskij to Gogol'.[32]

In general, Dostoevskij's *Zapiski iz mertvogo doma* had been accorded a warm reception by left-wing critics, and Pisarev added his voice to the chorus. In form, "Pogibšie i pogibajuščie" is presented as a comparative study of two social institutions, the seminaries and the Siberian prisons. In this respect, the essay is typical of Pisarev's method, derived from Dobroljubov, in which works of art are equated with reality and used simply as a short-cut for dealing with reality. The essay may well have been suggested to Pisarev by a passage in which Pomjalovskij himself compares the seminarists and Dostoevskij's convicts. The passage occurs in the third of Pomjalovskij's sketches, which had appeared originally in the issue of *Sovremennik* for April, 1863, an issue which also contained the second part of Černyševskij's *Čto delat'?*, which Pisarev must have read. In any case, almost three years later, in January of 1866, Blagosvetlov delivered the two books to Pisarev in prison, apparently at Pisarev's request. Pomjalovskij's book, having appeared in 1865, was relatively recent; Dostoevskij's had been published as a book in 1862 (after having previously appeared in *Vremja* in 1861-1862). Pisarev must have requested the two together because he already had his article in mind.

A natural consequence of the comparison between the seminaries and the prisons, as posed by Pisarev, was the question: Who is better off, the seminarist or the convict? Pisarev's answer to this question was

---

[31] Koz'min, "Pis'ma D. I. Pisareva", pp. 249-250.
[32] Pisarev, *Sočinenija* (1909-1911), IV, pp. 143, 122.

decisive: "To hold out against the seminary must be, in any case, much more difficult than to remain uncontaminated in the House of the Dead." [33] Far from being an impartial and objective comparison, Pisarev's essay is actually a transparently veiled polemical attack upon the seminaries, ostensibly, and, by implication, upon the conditions of Russian life reflected in them. The condemnatory motive is clear. At any rate, it was clear enough to the censor for him to recommend that Pisarev be prosecuted on the basis of the essay in question.[34] Another disingenuous aspect of the essay is the sophism involved in the attempt to represent the seminaries as typical examples of Russian education. Highly as Pisarev prized education, he had scant respect for Russian educational institutions as they existed in his day, a fact which his essay, "Sxolastiki xix veka" ("Nineteenth Century Scholastics") makes abundantly clear. As clear as the condemnatory aspect of the essay is its emphasis on Pisarev's notion that poverty was the dominant factor in Russian life.

So far as *Zapiski iz mertvogo doma* is concerned, aside from its utility as a stick with which to beat the seminaries, Pisarev saw the value of the book as lying in its insistence upon the human qualities displayed by the convicts. In "Realisty" Pisarev had remarked, "We by no means demand of novelists that they necessarily describe the sufferings of the poor or point out to us the human being in the criminal",[35] (an echo of the humanitarian motif dear to Belinskij), but it is not hard to see that it was the fulfillment of the latter prescription which constituted the source of a considerable portion of Pisarev's sympathy for Dostoevskij's book, for Pisarev writes:

To speak of the human virtues of convicts is at present not only necessary but even dangerous to a certain degree. If you say that a convict is not a savage beast and not a filthy vermin, that in him the best instincts of human nature are not dead, that he is capable of standing up on his feet and beginning a new life, then the stern sages, the solid moralists and impeccable *censores morum* consider themselves wounded to the quick: they think that you are placing them on the same plane as despicable convicts; they shout at the top of their lungs that you degrade virtue and glorify vice; they accuse you of conniving at theft, of inciting murder and trying to undermine the authority of the law which punished the destroyer of another's goods and another's life.[36]

[33]   Pisarev, *Sočinenija* (1904-1907), V, p. 276.
[34]   Pisarev, *Izbrannye sočinenija*, II, p. 610.
[35]   Pisarev, *Sočinenija* (1909-1911), IV, p. 127.
[36]   Pisarev, *Sočinenija* (1904-1907), V, p. 307.

Another element in Dostoevskij's book which interested Pisarev particularly was its practical implications. Again in "Realisty", Pisarev remarks, "We want the creations of the poet to delineate for us, cleanly and clearly, those aspects of human life which we need to know in order to ponder soundly and to act." [37] Dostoevskij's book reveals, according to Pisarev, the fundamental requirement for a genuine improvement of the convicts' lot. Pisarev writes, "The House of the Dead, described by Dostoevskij, contains within itself the promise of its improvement. This promise will fulfill itself and the morality of the prisoners improve if only they are given the possibility of carrying on their own work, boldly and openly." [38] Throughout Pisarev's writing, respect for work is explicit. In reference to Pisarev's attitude on this point, Evgenij Solov'ev wrote, "The principal source of satisfaction should be labor, work, but only when harmony exists between the personality and the work." [39] It was this harmony that Pisarev desired for the convicts.

As we know, Pisarev was fond of finding justification for his own ideas in works supposedly opposed to them. For example, this tactic is observable in his discussion of the character of Bazarov in Turgenev's *Otcy i deti*. In "Realisty", speaking of Bazarov, Pisarev writes:

I take precisely this image, precisely that one which you consider a caricature or an exposé. I analyze each feature of this image; I take each of Turgenev's words at its face value; I give ear, thus, to the most powerful and the wisest enemy of contemporary realism – an enemy who 'nevertheless is not accustomed to lie'; and from all the evidence of this enemy I am unable to elicit a single feature which actually would make realists people who are stupid, dishonorable, immoral, and injurious to society or to the well-being of separate individuals.[40]

The same treatment is meted out to Dostoevskij. The passage is extended, but it is so characteristic of Pisarev's procedures that it is worth reproducing in full:

'I remember', says Dostoevskij, 'how one day a brigand, drunk (it was possible on occasion to get drunk during imprisonment), began to recount how he murdered a five-year-old boy; how he enticed him at first with a toy, led him away into an empty shed, and there murdered him. The whole barrack, which had laughed at his jokes up to then, cried as a single man and the brigand was forced to shut up; the barrack cried out not from indig-

---

[37] Pisarev, *Sočinenija* (1909-1911), IV, p. 104.
[38] Pisarev, *Sočinenija* (1904-1907), V, pp. 311-312.
[39] *Ibid.*, VI, p. 54.
[40] Pisarev, *Sočinenija* (1909-1911), IV, p. 97.

nation, but just so, because it was *unnecessary* to talk *about that*, because to talk *about that* was not acceptable.' The fact is remarkable, but the explanation added by the author explains exactly nothing and decidedly does not stand up under criticism. How does the author know that the barrack cried out *not from indignation*? And what sort of reason is expressed by the words *just so*? And if the story of the brigand in no way aroused indignation and disgust, then why was it *unnecessary* and *not acceptable* to speak of such subjects? To these questions the author again answers: *just so*, but who is satisfied with that sort of an answer? It seems to me that the barrack cried out precisely out of indignation, because, in the first place, the murder of a helpless child and, in the second place, the naked braggadocio seemed to it utterly disgusting. The auditors felt that this braggadocio deeply offended their humanity. For whom, said they, does this ass take us, if he thinks we will relish such abominations? Dostoevskij supposes that 'to talk *about that* is not acceptable'. That is, about what, precisely? About what kind of a *that*? If by the word *that* Dostoevskij implies murder in general, then he is mistaken and contradicts himself. In the same volume Lučka tells his comrades very circumstantially how he murdered an angry assistant commandant, and everyone listened to him and nobody cried out at him. This means that it is possible to talk of murder, and it means that the cry of the barrack in the first instance was directed not against an infringement of convict etiquette but against the repulsiveness of the brigand's effusion.[41]

Thus Pisarev re-interprets the facts as given by Dostoevskij.

Pisarev preached independence of mind in approaching the classics. He writes, "Nothing so powerfully broadens the whole horizon of our conceptions of nature and human life as a close acquaintance with humanity's greatest minds, no matter with what realm of knowledge or creation the activity of these first-class representatives of our species concerns itself. But, in the first place, on becoming acquainted with these titans, it is necessary without fail to preserve, in relationship to them, the full independence of one's own ideas, otherwise one is apt to take for pure gold even what constitutes a dirty blot in the works of a titan." [42] If such an attitude toward admitted classics is to be practised, what objection can there possibly be to practising it also upon Dostoevskij's work?

Pisarev's second essay on Dostoevskij's work, "Bor'ba za žizn'," is devoted exclusively to a consideration of Dostoevskij's *Prestuplenie i nakazanie*. According to a letter written by Pisarev's mother to Dostoevskij in 1878, ten years after Pisarev's death, Pisarev became acquainted with the book upon being freed from prison. The effect of the book upon Pisarev was so intense that the reading was interrupted at the

---

41   Pisarev, *Sočinenija* (1904-1907), V, p. 308.
42   Pisarev, *Sočinenija* (1909-1911), IV, p. 118.

suggestion of Pisarev's physician and resumed only after Pisarev's nerves were steadier. Even then, one passage in the book reduced Pisarev to tears.[43] Apparently this novel, like *Bednye ljudi,* was capable of eliciting tears from readers endowed with the requisite sensibilities.

When Pisarev came to write about the novel, however, his attitude toward the book was colored by polemical considerations. Shortly before the publication of Pisarev's essay, in February, March, and April of 1867, there appeared in the *Otečestvennye zapiski* an essay by N. Straxov, a collaborator on Dostoevskij's magazines *Vremja* and *Èpoxa.* Straxov's essay attempted to demonstrate that Raskol'nikov's theories were responsible for his crime and that life itself discredited his theories, which Straxov attributed directly to the influence of Černyševskij, Dobroljubov, and Pisarev.[44]

Straxov's article was a polemical attack, and it is typical of Pisarev's verve that he should choose to counter-attack over the same terrain. The method used by Pisarev is one already familiar: that of dissociating the subject matter of the book from the interpretation given it by the author and using that subject matter as so much raw material from which to draw his own conclusions. Zonin points out that this procedure is inconsistent with Pisarev's earlier position, taken in "Pisemskij, Turgenev, i Gončarov", in which he states that author and work cannot be dissociated.[45] Needless to say, after analyzing the content of the novel, Pisarev arrives at conclusions very different from those attributed to Dostoevskij by Straxov.

Pisarev begins by making his attitude perfectly clear:

In setting out to analyze the new novel of Dostoevskij, I warn the reader in advance that I have no business whatsoever with the personal convictions of the author, which, perhaps, run counter to my own personal convictions, nor with the general tenor of his work, to which, perhaps, I am not altogether sympathetic, nor even with those ideas which the author, perhaps, tried to exemplify in his work and which may seem utterly worthless to me. I am very little interested in the question as to what party and to what shade of opinion Dostoevskij belongs, what ideas or interests he wishes to serve with his pen, and even what means he considers permissible in conflict with his literary or other opponents whatsoever. I concentrate attention only on those phenomena of social life which are depicted in the novel: if these phenomena are observed truly, if the raw facts constituting the basic plot of the novel are completely credible, if there are in the novel neither libels on

[43] Koz'min, "Pis'ma D. I. Pisareva", p. 250.
[44] For extracts from Straxov's article, see Zamotin, *F. M. Dostoevskij v russkoj kritiki,* I, pp. 96-102.
[45] Zonin, "Obščestvennye tendencii", pp. 144-145.

life nor false and artificial touching up of the colors, if, in a word, in the novel living people bearing the stamp of real social conditions act and suffer, struggle and err, love and hate, then I regard the novel as I would regard a credible account of something that actually happened; I shall look into and ponder over these occurrences, trying to understand in what way they flow one out of another, trying to explain to myself how much they are dependent upon the general conditions of life, and at the same time I set aside utterly the personal viewpoint of the narrator, who may transmit the facts very truly and circumstantially and explain them in a fashion unsatisfactory to the highest degree.[46]

Pisarev professes to see in Dostoevskij's novel an indictment of poverty. The connection between poverty and crime had already been pointed out in "Realisty": "[Statistics] shows in figures the link between poverty and crime." [47] Since this linkage is the basis of Pisarev's approach to the novel, it is not astonishing that Pisarev should devote his analysis to the events leading up to the crime and treat the rest of the novel in cursory fashion.

In order to indict poverty as the real villain in *Prestuplenie i nakazanie,* Pisarev attempts to establish several points. In the first place, Pisarev seeks to establish the fact that Raskol'nikov's is a typical rather than a special case. Pisarev writes, "One may even say that the majority of the crimes against property come about, in general, in the same way as Raskol'nikov's crime came about. The most common cause of theft, robbery, and brigandage is poverty; this is known to everyone who is at all familiar with criminal statistics." In one respect, however, Pisarev is willing to admit that Raskol'nikov's case is distinguished from others. He writes, "The crime described in Dostoevskij's novel stands out from the ranks of ordinary crimes only because its hero is not an illiterate wretch, utterly undeveloped in mental and moral respects, but a student capable of analyzing all the movements of his own soul in the finest detail, able to create whole elaborate theories for the justification of his acts, and preserving the fine and many-sided sensitivity and moral delicacy of a highly developed human being in the midst of his most savage errors." Nevertheless, this peculiarity does not invalidate the typicality of Raskol'nikov's situation, for Pisarev remarks, "Raskol'nikov commits his crime not at all *in the way* in which an illiterate wretch would have committed it; but he commits it *for the same reason* as any illiterate wretch would have

---

[46]   Pisarev, *Sočinenija* (1904-1909), VI, pp. 343-344.
[47]   Pisarev, *Sočinenija* (1909-1911), IV, p. 154. Fridlender points out that this position disagrees with that of Zajcev. See *Realizm Dostoevskogo*, p. 153.

committed it. Poverty in both cases is the principal inciting circumstance." [48]

Two more questions remain to be disposed of. First, is Raskol'nikov insane? (As some early critics of the novel maintained.) Second, are the theories elaborated by Raskol'nikov responsible for his crime? It is easy to see why Pisarev is anxious to dispose of the question of Raskol'nikov's sanity. If Raskol'nikov is insane, then his insanity, not his poverty, is responsible for his crime. Predictably, Pisarev rejects the idea that Raskol'nikov is insane: "Every thought and every action of Raskol'nikov, especially up to the commission of the murder, is motivated most satisfactorily. We see in each separate instance why and for what reason he took this or another step." As for the influence of Raskol'nikov's ideas on the consummation of the crime, Pisarev has this to say: "The crime was committed not because Raskol'nikov convinced himself, by means of various philophizings, of its lawfulness, reasonableness, and necessity. On the contrary, Raskol'nikov began to philosophize along these lines and convinced himself only because circumstances incited him to crime." [49]

But it was not enough for Pisarev simply to dismiss Raskol'nikov's theories as the rationalizations of a desperate man. In order to refute the accusation that Raskol'nikov's ideas in any way represented a legitimate reflection of radical ideology, Pisarev attempted to show that Raskol'nikov's idea that superior men are exceptions to the general law was not in accord with radical doctrine, and Pisarev attacks the validity of this idea. In reference to superior men Pisarev writes, "Not one of these personalities, however much a genius he may be, had a reasonable pretext, in the name of this future or in the name of his genius, to permit himself such actions as damage other people and, in consequence, are to be considered as not permissible to ordinary mortals", and though Pisarev traces the origin and growth of Raskol'nikov's criminal project, he is careful to point out that he does not approve: "Raskol'nikov simply did not think through and solve his problem." [50]

So far as Raskol'nikov's conduct after the crime is concerned, Pisarev dismisses it as follows: "To follow those processes of thought

[48] Pisarev, *Sočinenija* (1904-1907), VI, pp. 347-348. Coquart traces the idea that most criminals are not responsible for their crimes back to Büchner. See *op. cit.*, p. 421. Van der Eng points out the same motif in Černyševskij's *Čto delat?* See *Dostoevskij romancier*, p. 31.
[49] Pisarev, *Sočinenija* (1904-1907), VI, pp. 350-351, 392.
[50] *Ibid.*, pp. 382, 372.

which elicit such actions and in general to explain these actions by any thought processes whatsoever, accessible and comprehensible to a healthy man, – of this I see no possibility. Here one can only say that the man went crazy with fear and arrived at some kind of somnambulism during which he both walked and talked and apparently even thought. Whether or not such a psychic condition exists and whether or not it is accurately described in Dostoevskij's novel – about this let the physicians judge, if these questions seem to them worthy of attentive study." [51] Here we find an echo of Belinskij's contempt for Dostoevskij's interest in abnormal psychology, an attitude echoed also Pisarev's "Realisty".[52]

So far as the attitude of the reader toward Raskol'nikov is concerned, Pisarev points to two possibilities: "The reader may either despise and detest Raskol'nikov as a noxious and contemptible wretch for whom there is and should be no place in society; or the reader can look on him with respectful sympathy as an unfortunate man who collapsed into the mire under the intolerable oppression of such severe and invincibly hostile conditions as might break even a very strong will and muddle even a very clear head." Needless to say, it is the second, humanitarian viewpoint which Pisarev espouses, and this attitude places Pisarev firmly in the humanitarian tradition descended from Belinskij. Pisarev writes, "Place in Raskol'nikov's position any other man of ordinary dimensions who developed differently and looked at things with different eyes, and you will see that the same result is produced. An intolerable position will nourish in him that same illness, and all his thoughts will lead in the same pernicious and dangerous direction." [53]

As we have seen, the two parts of Pisarev's essay first appeared in *Delo* in May, 1867, and in 1868. Pavlenkov had begun a collected edition of Pisarev's works, the first volume of which appeared in an edition of 3,000 copies in March, 1866. At the end of 1868, the essay appeared in volume IX of Pavlenkov's edition in a version significantly different from that of its original appearance in *Delo*. In a note, Pavlenkov remarks that the title, "Bor'ba za žizn", was that of the original manuscript, and the inference is that his text follows the original version. The differences between the two versions are not enormous, but they may throw some light on Pisarev's attitude toward

[51]   *Ibid.*, p. 404.
[52]   Pisarev, *Sočinenija* (1909-1911), IV, p. 119.
[53]   Pisarev, *Sočinenija* (1904-1907), VI, pp. 353-354, 364.

the novel. The text given in Pavlenkov's edition is longer than that which appeared in *Delo*. Aside from changes involving only a few words, the additions serve to emphasize Pisarev's principal arguments: that poverty is the cause of crime, that free will is an illusion and that Raskol'nikov is not a free agent. At the same time, the beginning of the second part of the essay as it appeared in *Delo*, an encomium of Dostoevskij's talent, is cut.[54] This cut improves the unity of the text, since nothing else in it relates to Dostoevskij's talent. The history of the second half of the article is obscure. Permission to publish it was originally refused by the censor, and though Pisarev did not feel entitled to withdraw it after his break with Blagosvetlov, neither did he care to re-write it.[55] Since the essay appeared only after Pisarev's death, the changes in the text may be due to another hand. B. I. Esin contends that they are attributable to Blagosvetlov, who made them in order to get the essay approved by the censor.[56]

How successfuly did Pisarev refute the contention that Raskol'nikov's ideas are a reflection of radical ideology? The answer to this question, even today, is apt to depend upon the *Weltanschauung* of the individual answering it. It is generally agreed, nowadays, that Dostoevskij's intention in writing the novel approximated that attributed to him by Straxov. The question is whether or not Dostoevskij succeeded in his intention, whether or not one sees Raskol'nikov as a product (though only one of many possibilities) of the ideas of Černyševskij, Dobroljubov, and Pisarev. Even the suggestion that the ideas of these men could in any way countenance crime outraged Pisarev and continues to outrage those who consider themselves the legitimate ideological descendents of these men. Recent Soviet critics, for example, accept Pisarev's defense as valid.[57] On the other hand, those (both Russians and non-Russians) whose ideology permits them to entertain the unpleasant possibility that Dostoevskij was not only correct but persuasively demonstrated his correctness are not convinced.[58] Coquart

---

[54] Pisarev, *Izbrannye sočinenija*, II, pp. 497-542, 613. Cf. *Sočinenija* (1955-1956), IV, pp. 451-452.
[55] See Pisarev's letter to M. A. Markovič, Piksanov and Cexnovicer, *Šestidesjatye gody*, pp. 157-158.
[56] Moskovskij gosudarstvennyj universitet, *Iz istorii russkoj žurnalistiki*, p. 220.
[57] Belkin, *F. M. Dostoevskij v russkoj kritike*, p. xxi. Cf. Akademija nauk SSSR, *Istorija russkoj literatury*, VIII, Part I, pp. 270-271. Fridlender, however, admits the relationship of Raskol'nikov's ideas to his crime but labels the ideas as "individualistic and bourgeois-anarchistic". See *op. cit.*, p. 149.
[58] For examples, see Vvedenskij, *Literaturnye xarakteristiki*, pp. 96-97; Ovsjaniko-

points out an embarrassing stumbling-block to a serious acceptance of Pisarev's contention that the idea that geniuses are subject to the laws of history like everyone else represented his own position. In "Italjancy" ("The Italians"), an essay published almost simultaneously with the first half of his essay on *Prestuplenie i nakazanie,* Pisarev argues that Pope Gregory VII was able to intervene, personally, in the course of history.[59] The positions taken in the two essays are diametrically opposed, so that the argument of the one tends to be cancelled out by the argument of the other. Coquart feels that Dostoevskij not only successfully established a causal relationship between Raskol'nikov's theories and his crime but that, despite the fact that Raskol'nikov was scarcely a typical follower of Černyševskij, Dobroljubov, and Pisarev, Raskol'nikov's ideas do represent one possible development of theirs.[60]

It is perhaps worth noting, as a side-light, that in 1878, ten years after Pisarev's death, Pisarev's mother, apparently at the request of Dostoevskij's wife, who had written to Mme. Pisareva that Dostoevskij "loved and esteemed" her son and would like something of his, wrote to Dostoevskij, sending him four letters and a photograph of her son, a file which was discovered in the Dostoevskij archive.[61] In a deposition made after his arrest, Pisarev declared that he was acquainted with F. M. and M. M. Dostoevskij, whom he had met through Count Kušelov-Bezborodko,[62] but traces of a personal relationship between Pisarev and Dostoevskij are meagre.

Kulikovskij, *op. cit.,* III, pp. 64-65; Van der Eng, *op. cit.,* pp. 34-35; Wellek, *A History of Modern Criticism,* IV, p. 263.

[59]   Pisarev, *Sočinenija* (1904-1907), VI, p. 115.
[60]   Coquart, *op. cit.,* pp. 404-405.
[61]   Koz'min, "Pis'ma D. I. Pisareva", pp. 248-249.
[62]   Lemke, *Političeskie processy,* p. 560.

NIKOLAJ KONSTANTINOVIČ MIXAJLOVSKIJ (1842-1904)

1

During Pisarev's lifetime, he cooperated with the writers associated with the *Sovremennik* in a common opposition to common adversaries, simultaneously contending (for a time successfully) for leadership of the radical intelligentsia. The radicals were thus temporarily split, and the fraction which acknowledged Pisarev as its leader, usually known as the nihilists, enjoyed a relatively brief ascendancy. Once Pisarev's leadership was lost, however, nihilism began to lose ground, and its influence dwindled into relative insignificance by the end of the seventies.

Meanwhile, that fraction of the radical intelligentsia led originally by Černyševskij and Dobroljubov and grouped around the *Sovremennik,* now led by Nekrasov and Saltykov-Ščedrin and regrouped around the reoriented *Otečestvennye zapiski,* reestablished its leadership.[1] This relatively loosely-knit group is usually referred to as the *narodniki* (Populists). The chief theoreticians of *narodničestvo* (Populism) were Petr Lavrovič Lavrov and Nikolaj Konstantinovič Mixajlovskij. During the course of its career, *narodničestvo* experienced a considerable evolution, but the movement had basic coherence.

Narodničestvo proposed a synthesis between the ideas of individual and social development attempted already by Pisarev. With these it combined the mystique of the *narod* (folk). This faith in the peculiar virtues and destiny of the Russian people which *narodničestvo* shared with the Slavophiles (though in a rather different form) found expres-

---

[1] Recent Soviet writers have attempted to install Saltykov-Ščedrin as the successor to Belinskij, Černyševskij, and Dobroljubov. For example, see Akademija xudožestv SSSR, *Očerki marksistsko-leninskoj èstetiki,* pp. 47-50. For a Soviet discussion of the struggle between the *narodniki* and the Marxists over the succession to Černyševskij and Dobroljubov, see Gorodeckij, "O sozdanii istorii russkoj literaturnoj kritiki", p. 325.

sion in economic and literary studies of peasant life and was one facet of the messianism prominent in Russian thought of the period (an element which links *narodničestvo* to the ideas of such men as Fedorov, Vladimir Solov'ev, and Dostoevskij). To this amalgam it added the morally attractive idea of personal self-sacrifice, so that the result was the proposition that the individual could find personal salvation (a theme developed by Pisarev's followers) in dedicated service, in one form or another, to the *narod*.

Such earlier leaders of the Russian radical movement as Belinskij, Černyševskij, and Dobroljubov had been typical *raznočincy,* that is to say, representatives of social classes other than the aristocracy. Typical of the *narodniki* was a rather different mentality, that of the *kajuščijsja dvorjanin* (penitent nobleman), who renounced the historical privileges of his class and sought to expiate past social wrongs in dedicated self-sacrifice to the *narod*. For the *kajuščijsja dvorjanin,* the social problem was put in personal, ethical terms: "The aroused conscience of the penitent nobleman demanded an immediate solution to the personal, ethical problem, an answer to the question: How am I to live worthily in order to repay my debt to the people?" [2] The term *kajuščijsja dvorjanin* (variously rendered in English as "penitent nobleman", "conscience-stricken nobleman", and "aristocrat doing penance") was coined (or at least given currency) by Mixajlovskij, who instanced Pisarev as an example of the type, and the term has been applied to Mixajlovskij himself as well as to Lavrov, Nekrasov, Lev Tolstoj, Kropotkin, and Sof'ja Perovskaja.[3]

Originally social rather than political in its orientation, *narodničestvo* first encouraged an attempt to bridge the abyss separating the intelligentsia from the peasants. About 1872, countless young Russian idealists "went to the people"; that is, left the cities and tried to work as teachers and what we would now call social workers among the peasants. Disillusionment as to the practicality of effecting a rapid social revolution by this means was not long in coming. By 1878 this phase of the *narodnik* movement was over.

The moral drawn from this failure was the need for a shift of emphasis from social to political action. As a result, *narodničestvo* shifted its support from the political party *Zemlja i volja* (Land and Will) to *Narodnaja volja* (The People's Will), from social to political activity.

---

[2] Ovsjaniko-Kulikovskij, *Istorija russkoj literatury*, III, p. 60.
[3] Bjalyj specifically denies the importance of the *kajuščijsja dvorjanin* as a social phenomenon. See Akademija nauk SSSR, *Istorija russkoj kritiki*, II, p. 335.

This new phase of *narodničestvo* gained strength until 1881, when the assassination of Alexander II caused the government to put a stop to the revolutionary movement. In 1884 the *Otečestvennye zapiski* was suppressed, and the loss of its principal organ was a blow from which *narodničestvo* never fully recovered, though it did experience a certain renaissance in the nineties.

The suppression of the *Otečestvennye zapiski* not only put an end to the ascendancy of *narodničestvo* but also marked the end of an epoch in Russian intellectual history, the period usually referred to as the seventies. In the immediately succeeding years there was little radical intellectual activity; active revolutionaries were in prison or abroad, Tolstoj's doctrine of non-resistance to evil enjoyed considerable popularity, and Russia stagnated in the atmosphere described in Čexov's stories. Mixajlovskij's estimate of the situation, published abroad in 1894, is perhaps worth quoting: "Le situation de la société russe est, à l'heure qu'il est, bien triste. Le triomphe de la réaction, en l'année 1881, a amené une sorte de désenchantement à l'égard de nos anciennes idoles. D'autre part, le travail de la génération précédente semble tout à fait perdu pour la génération actuelle. Les periodiques, les livres, où rayonnait l'ame russe de l'époque liberale, sont prohibés et ne sont plus accessibles au public. La génération présente est sans idéal; elle n'a même pas où le chercher." [4]

Though the suppression of the *Otečestvennye zapiski* destroyed the semi-official organ of *narodničestvo,* its contributors eventually found places in other periodicals, and in the course of time a new organ, *Russkoe bogatstvo* (*Russian Wealth*), was created. But in the nineties *narodničestvo* was already fighting a rearguard action against assorted opponents. Tolstoj's ideas continued to be influential, and a new intellectual current, much less politically oriented than *narodničestvo*, began to absorb the attention of a significant portion of the intelligentsia. This broad and ill-defined movement assimilated "decadent" and other "modernist" trends. It refurbished the bespattered banner of "art for art's sake", joined the Western European symbolist movement, and displayed an interest in the philosophical ideas of such different men as Dostoevskij, Vladimir Solov'ev, and Friedrich Nietzsche. At the same time, a vigorous and eventually triumphant contender for leadership of the radical wing of Russian political opinion appeared in the Marxists. Indeed, this rivalry was more significant than that of the

---

[4]   Mixajlovskij, "Le mouvement littéraire en Russie", p. 187.

revolutionary democrats and the nihilists in the sixties. Ivanov-Razumnik, writing before the Russian revolution of 1917, refers to it as the "second schism" of the Russian intelligentsia.[5] (The "first schism", of course, was the break between the Westernizers and the Slavophiles in the forties.)

2

No satisfactory biography of Mixajlovskij is in existence, nor is one likely to be written, since his private papers were destroyed before he died.[6] He was born on 15 November 1842, and, like Pisarev, came of an aristocratic family of modest means. After attending the gymnasium, he was sent to the Mining Academy, but he did not complete the course there, having been expelled for leading a student demonstration.[7] Like Belinskij, like Dobroljubov and Pisarev, Mixajlovskij began his career as a journalist at an early age, in Mixajlovskij's case, eighteen. Like Pisarev, he published his first article (on Gončarov) in *Rassvet* (in the spring of 1860). By this time Pisarev was no longer working for the periodical, and the two men did not meet at that time. They met but once, casually, several years later in the office of *Delo*, shortly before the break between Pisarev and Blagosvetlov. Mixajlovskij became acquainted with Zajcev when both were working on the *Knižnyj vestnik (Book Bulletin)* in the early 60's.[8]

As a young man, Mixajlovskij fell briefly under Pisarev's spell, but in his mature work, Mixajlovskij was a consistent opponent of nihilism. Of more importance in Mixajlovskij's development was the influence of N. D. Nožin, a biologist who died prematurely at the age of twenty-three in 1866. Another significant personal influence was that of Eliseev, whom Mixajlovskij met in 1862 and with whom he was to be associated on the *Otečestvennye zapiski*.

After contributing to various periodicals (*Knižnyj vestnik, Glasnyj sud', Nedelja, Nevskij sbornik, Sovremennoe obozrenije*), in December, 1868, his first article appeared in the *Otečestvennye zapiski*, and he soon became a regular contributor. In 1878, after the death of Nekrasov, he became co-editor, together with Saltykov-Ščedrin.[9] He was

---

[5]   Ivanov-Razumnik, *Istorija russkoj obščestvennoj mysli*, II, p. 319.
[6]   Billington, *Mikhailovsky and Russian Populism*, p. vii.
[7]   Billington, "The Intelligentsia and the Religion of Humanity", p. 809.
[8]   Billington, *Mikhailovsky*, p. 22.
[9]   Leningradskij gosudarstvennyj universitet, *Očerki po istorii russkoj žurnalistiki i kritiki*, II, p. 275.

also, at this time, on friendly terms with Šelgunov. With his work for the *Otečestvennye zapiski*, Mixajlovskij established himself not only as a sociologist and journalist but also as an influential literary critic.

At the beginning of the seventies, Mixajlovskij shared a position of ideological preeminence with Petr Lavrovič Lavrov. Lavrov was born in 1823, thus belonging to an earlier generation than Mixajlovskij. In 1862 he joined *Zemlja i volja*, though he played no prominent part in the activities of the group. In 1866 he was arrested and in 1867 exiled to Vologda, where he wrote his *Istoričeskie pis'ma* (*Historical Letters*) which were published first in *Nedelja* (*The Week*) (1868-1869) and then as a book (1870). He left Russia and reached Paris in 1870. From 1873 to 1876 he was the editor of the emigré revolutionary periodical *Vpered* (*Forward*). For some years thereafter, Lavrov was not active in emigré revolutionary affairs, but after the assassination of Alexander II, he returned to revolutionary activity, and from 1883 to 1886 he was co-editor of the *Vestnik narodnoj voli* (*Bulletin of the People's Will*). He died in Paris in 1900.[10]

Lavrov's *Istoričeskie pis'ma* together with Mixajlovskij's "Čto takoe progress?" ("What is Progress?") (1869) exercised a determining influence upon the *Weltanschauung* of the seventies. But, as we have seen, in 1870 Lavrov left Russia and from then on influenced Russian thought only through emigré publications. In contrast, Mixajlovskij remained in Russia, continued to publish in the legal press, and thus reached a wider public. In 1873 Lavrov invited Mixajlovskij to join him in emigration and to collaborate on *Vpered*.[11] Mixajlovskij's decision to remain in Russia was probably the crucial one in his career, and he stayed at his post. Much of the respect which he enjoyed and the influence which he wielded stemmed from this decision.

Mixajlovskij supported the social orientation of *narodničestvo* at the beginning of the seventies. Later he joined the swing toward a political orientation of the movement. Mixajlovskij occasionally wrote for the clandestine press, especially at the end of the seventies, and it is perhaps significant that in 1882 he was deputed by Lavrov to take part in negotiations between *Narodnaja volja* and the government, but the extent of his association with the active revolutionary movement is obscure. In January, 1883, Mixajlovskij was arrested and exiled from Peterburg.[12] That he collaborated with active revolutionaries at

[10]   Masaryk, *The Spirit of Russia*, II, pp. 115-117.
[11]   *Ibid.*, p. 163.
[12]   Leningradskij gosudarstvennyj universitet, *op. cit.*, II, p. 309.

least as late as 1897-1898 is proved by his literary contributions to the Peterburg *Rabočij vestnik* (*Labor Herald*).[13]

When the *Otečestvennye zapiski* was suppressed, Mixajlovskij published in such periodicals as the *Severnyj vestnik* (*The Northern Messenger*) (particularly during the period 1885-1888) and the *Russkaja mysl'* (*Russian Thought*) (1889-1895) until a new rallying point for the *narodniki* was found in the *Russkoe bogatstvo*. Of this periodical Mixajlovskij was at first officially a stockholder (1892) and only in 1897 was he recognized as co-editor, together with V. G. Korolenko.[14] Mixajlovskij's voice remained a respected force down to the end of his life, on the eve of the revolution of 1905. His death, on 28 January 1904, was mourned by partisans and opponents alike.

Mixajlovskij's name has been linked, in various ways, with those of Belinskij, Černyševskij, Dobroljubov, and Pisarev. As Ivanov-Razumnik once succinctly put it: " 'Belinskij begat Černyševskij; Černyševskij begat Dobroljubov; Dobroljubov begat Pisarev'. Thus the historian Pogodin once wryly jibed at the men of the sixties; to this genealogy one might add, 'And Pisarev begat Mixajlovskij'." [15] Such a genealogy is justified on several grounds. In the first place, Mixajlovskij was, in general, the continuator of the ideals and attitudes of his predecessors. He was also their successor as a leader of public opinion.[16] When one considers the length of his activity, over forty years, during much of which time Mixajlovskij occupied a position of considerable eminence, in contrast to the relatively brief, though meteorically brilliant, careers of his predecessors, Mixajlovskij's contribution to, as well as his influence upon, Russian social life may well have been greater.

---

[13]   Billington, "The Intelligentsia", p. 817, note. Bjalyj states flatly that Mixajlovskij was a member of no revolutionary party but that he was in contact with revolutionaries. See Mixajlovskij, *Literaturno-kritičeskie stat'i*, pp. 5-6. Cf. Akademija nauk SSSR, *op. cit.*, II, p. 344. Masaryk and Ivanov-Razumnik see him principally as the theoretician of the revolutionary movement. See Masaryk, *op. cit.*, II, p. 160, and Ivanov-Razumnik, *op. cit.*, II, p. 106. Cf. Struve, *Patriotica*, pp. 398-402; Rusanov, " 'Politika' N. K. Mixajlovskogo".
[14]   Zapadova, *Istorija russkoj žurnalistiki XVIII-XIX vekov*, p. 460. Cf. *Iz istorii russkoj žurnalistiki vtoroj poloviny XIX v.*, p. 67, note 12.
[15]   Ivanov-Razumnik, *Literatura i obščestvennost'*, p. 2. Cf. *Istorija Rossii v xix v.*, VII, p. 40. Elsewhere he gives a different genealogy: Gercen – Černyševskij – Lavrov – Mixajlovskij. See *Istorija*, II, p. 131. In the one case, he seems to be indicating a succession of leaders of public opinion; in the other, an ideological succession.
[16]   For minority opinions, see Struve, *op. cit.*, p. 416; Ovsjaniko-Kulikovskij, *op. cit.*, V, p. 421. For a typical Soviet view, see Stepanov, *Filosofskie i sociologičeskie vozzrenija V. G. Belinskogo*, pp. 353-354.

If we have no satisfactory biography of Mixajlovskij, neither have we a completely satisfactory exposition of his *Weltanschauung*.[17] The study of Mixajlovskij's ideas is made difficult by the very diversity of his interests and activities: he was a journalist, a sociologist, a political ideologue, a literary critic. Furthermore, he never wrote a book containing the systematic elaboration of a specific theme. His ideas were thus expressed piecemeal, often in the course of criticizing someone else's work. However, it is possible to gain some notion of the general development of his ideas and to outline their salient features.

Since Mixajlovskij began his career in the sixties, when the influence of Pisarev was at its apogee, it was only natural that Mixajlovskij should have been influenced by Pisarev's ideas, but Mixajlovskij soon became a determined and consistent opponent of nihilism. Ivanov-Razumnik attributes to Pisarev's influence Mixajlovskij's interest in individualism, but he contends that by the beginning of the seventies, Mixajlovskij had achieved intellectual independence.[18] Vengerov sees Mixajlovskij principally as a theoretician in reaction to Pisarev's extremism and links him with Černyševskij and Lavrov, while Kirpotin sees Pisarev as a link in the chain, leading ideologically from the views of Černyševskij to those of Mixajlovskij and Lavrov.[19] Ivanov-Razumnik stresses the influence of Černyševskij's politico-economic ideas upon Mixajlovskij.[20] The influences of Belinskij and Gercen upon Mixajlovskij have also been noted.[21] So far as his contemporary compatriots were concerned, the most important influence was indubitably that of Lavrov.

In addition to Russian influences, Mixajlovskij was strongly influenced by Western European thought, a factor which Masaryk emphasizes perhaps more strongly than anyone else. The influences of Hume, Mill, Spencer, Comte, Proudhon, Louis Blanc, Marx, Darwin, Rousseau, Feuerbach, Dühring, and Lange have been traced in Mixajlovskij's work.[22]

[17]   The best available study of Mixajlovskij's ideas is Billington, *Mikhailovsky*.
[18]   Ivanov-Razumnik, *Literature i obščestvennost'*, p. 2. Pisarev's biographer takes a rather different view. See Coquart, *Dmitri Pisarev*, p. 434.
[19]   Vengerov, *Očerki po istorii russkoj literatury*, p. 87; Lunačarskij and Lebedev-Poljanskij, *Očerki po istorii russkoj kritiki*, II, pp. 240-241. Cf. the notes to Pisarev, *Izbrannye sočinenija*, II, p. 594.
[20]   Ivanov-Razumnik, *Literatura i obščestvennost'*, p. 14.
[21]   Masaryk, *op. cit.*, II, pp. 140, 181.
[22]   *Ibid.*, pp. 136-140, 144, 151, 157; Billington, *Mikhailovsky*, pp. vi, 64, 69; Akademija nauk SSSR, *op. cit.*, II, pp. 333-334; Billington, "The Intelligentsia", pp. 813-815, particularly for the influence of Comte.

Like Belinskij, like Černyševskij and Dobroljubov, like Pisarev, Mixajlovskij was a socialist. Like the socialism of his predecessors, Mixajlovskij's had a strong subjective ethical basis,[23] but Mixajlovskij's socialism had features which distinguish it from that of his predecessors. They were able to combine faith in socialism and a faith in progress linked to belief in a vague historical determinism which was expected to bring socialism into existence eventually (though precisely how was never clear). When Marx and his followers produced a deterministic theory of history which claimed to show how this process must inevitably proceed, Mixajlovskij rejected the theory (though he accepted others of Marx's ideas – his criticism of the capitalist economic system, for example). Though Mixajlovskij had faith in progress and admitted that history was subject to laws, he insisted on more scope than Marxism permitted for the play of free will in the politico-moral field, where human desire is one factor among many which must be considered, and he based his faith in the eventual triumph of socialism on ethical rather than historical grounds, as the Marxists did.[24] Mixajlovskij saw the interests of the individual and society as mutually opposed, and he rejected the primacy of social ends. For Mixajlovskij the supreme value was always the individual, and his evaluation of society depended upon its amenability to the interests of the individual as Mixajlovskij conceived them. If he asked for sacrifice of the individual to society, this was a personal expiation of inherited social guilt, and the sacrifice was to be made in the name of a society for which the individual was a supreme value, not to social organization as an end in itself.

One respect in which Mixajlovskij differed from the rest of the *narodniki* should be mentioned. Though he shared their faith in the *narod,* he identified the *narod* with the broad mass of working people rather than exclusively with the peasants, as a majority of the *narodniki* tended to do, and he insisted on enlightened service to the people's interest rather than acceptance of the people's opinions based, frequently, upon prejudice and inadequate information.

If Mixajlovskij's biography and his general *Weltanschauung* have

---

[23]   Billington emphasizes the religious element in Mixajlovskij's activity and ideology. See *Mikhailovsky,* pp. 120 ff.
[24]   Mendel, "N. K. Mikhailovsky", p. 334. For Soviet criticism of Mixajlovskij's ideas on this score, see Kirpotin's notes in Pisarev, *Izbrannye,* II, p. 594; Mixajlovskij, *Literaturno-kritičeskie stat'i,* pp. 8 ff.; Akademija nauk SSSR, *op. cit.,* II, pp. 350-351; Leningradskij gosudarstvennyj universitet, *op. cit.,* II, pp. 419-422. Cf. Veresaev, "N. K. Mixajlovskij", for Mixajlovskij's struggle with the Marxists.

been inadequately studied, his principles and practice as a literary critic have received even less attention.[25] Though he considered himself the heir to Belinskij, Černyševskij, Dobroljubov, and Pisarev, he wrote very little about them.[26] An analysis of the content of his *Sočinenlja* (*Works*) (S.-Peterburg, 1896-1897) shows that during the early part of his career on the *Otečestyennye zapiski* (1869-1871), his writing was mostly concerned with the scholarly work of other men, discussed from the point of view of propagating his own ideas. From 1872 on, Mixajlovskij kept up a running commentary (under various titles) on Russian life and letters. It is this work that Vengerov characterizes as "A response to literally everything of interest to Russian society, as much in the sphere of scientific thought as in the sphere of practical life and current literary events." [27] In Mixajlovskij's criticism, the "publicistic" tendency of Russian literary criticism reaches its fullest expression.

As Rusanov sensibly points out, one's attitude toward Mixajlovskij's literary criticism depends upon one's definition. "If the word 'literary' is a synonym for the exclusively artistic, the purely aesthetic, then Nikolaj Konstantinovič was not that kind of a critic. Indeed, in this sense, neither was Dobroljubov. But if by literary criticism you understand not only that criticism which studies strictly the creative methods of a given artist and his artistic temperament but also that which reveals the fundamental idea of a given work (whether conscious or unconscious), makes clear the social and personal elements in the development of one or another author, then Mixajlovskij should of right be placed in the first rank of literary critics." [28]

In Mixajlovskij's opinion, the artist was one who speaks both for himself and for others. The wider the circle for which he is the spokesman, the greater his significance. Since the writer is always the spokesman for some group, Mixajlovskij denied the possibility of the existence of "pure" art, thus maintaining a tradition of hostility to "art for art's sake" going back to Belinskij. Later, when "naturalism" appeared, Mixajlovskij also opposed it.

[25]   Billington, for example, rather curtly dismisses Mixajlovskij's literary criticism. See *Mikhailovsky*, p. vii. The best discussions of Mixajlovskij's literary criticism are to be found in Masaryk, *op. cit.*, II, p. 181, and Akademija nauk SSSR, *op. cit.*, II, p. 329-354.
[26]   Korolenko records the fact that Mixajlovskij kept a bust of Belinskij on his desk. "Nikolaj Konstantinovič Mixajlovskij", p. 293.
[27]   Vengerov, *op. cit.*, p. 86.
[28]   Ovsjaniko-Kulikovskij, *op. cit.*, IV, p. 127.

Since the artist always spoke for some social group, it was the business of the critic to point out to the reader the group for which the writer was acting as spokesman and to judge the value of the work in terms of its contribution to the interests of the individual, the criterion by which Mixajlovskij also judged social phenomena. Such was the function of the literary critic as Mixajlovskij saw it, but in his practice, he did not confine himself solely to a consideration of the socio-ideological content of works of art. For example, he complained of lack of measure in the works of Grigorovič and Leskov (especially the latter), and he objected to the sermonizing which he detected in the work of Gogol', Tolstoj, and Dostoevskij. Though Mixajlovskij's preoccupation with the ideological content and social utility of works of literature led him to suggest that Grigorovič, in spite of his artistic deficiencies, had been a more influential social force than Turgenev, Mirskij, who had scant respect for many aspects of Mixajlovskij's criticism, granted him genuine critical acumen.[29] No one has praise for Mixajlovskij's literary style.

As the "decadent" literary movement gained momentum, Mixajlovskij's literary criticism came under attack by such champions of the new movement as Merežkovskij and Volynskij, the latter of whom denied Mixajlovskij any critical flair. Later, Aničkov characterized his aesthetics as "an aesthetics without aesthetics."[30]

3

Mixajlovskij's career was a long one, and he turned his attention to Dostoevskij's work on more than one occasion. Under these circumstances, one might expect some evolution in Mixajlovskij's attitude toward Dostoevskij, but instead, it is remarkably consistent. In 1902 Mixajlovskij was able to write: "Returning *en passant* to Dostoevskij now, twenty years later, I take back nothing of what I wrote then."[31]

Mixajlovskij's first significant article on Dostoevskij's work, "Iz literaturnyx i žurnal'nyx zametok 1873 goda, II" ("From Literary and Magazine Notes for 1873, II"), appeared in February, 1873, in the *Otečestvennye zapiski*. It was devoted to a discussion of Dostoevskij's

---

[29]   Mirskij, *Contemporary Russian Literature*, p. 45.
[30]   Volynskij, *Kniga velikogo gneva*, pp. 137-138; Aničkov, "Očerk razvitija èstetičeskix učenij", p. 187.
[31]   Mixajlovskij, *Poslednie sočinenija*, II, p. 270.

novel, *Besy* (*The Devils*, perhaps better known in English translation as *The Possessed*). Next, after an interval of some seven years, came a cycle of four essays, of which the most important was Mixajlovskij's best known study of Dostoevskij's work, "Žestokij talant" ("A Cruel Talent"). The first of the cycle, "Literaturnye zametki 1880 g., VII" ("Literary Notes for 1880, VII"), was prompted by Dostoevskij's Puškin speech; it was published in the *Otečestvennye zapiski* in September, 1880, followed in February, 1881, by an article "O Pisemskom i Dostoevskom" ("Concerning Pisemskij and Dostoevskij"), evoked by the public response to Dostoevskij's funeral, an article which was capped at an interval of a little more than a year by "Žestokij talant", published in September and October, 1882. The coda to this cycle, "Pis'ma postoronnego v redakciju 'Otečestvennyx zapisok', X" ("Letters of an Outsider to the Editors of the *Otečestvennye zapiski, X*") is Mixajlovskij's review, published in January, 1884, of the official biography of Dostoevskij by O. Miller and N. N. Straxov, which had appeared in 1883.

Thereafter, having had his say on the subject, Mixajlovskij returned to Dostoevskij's work only casually. In order to illustrate Mixajlovskij's later attitude to Dostoevskij's work, two additional essays, both dating from 1894, will be discussed briefly. These consist of a survey of the current state of Russian letters intended for European consumption and published in the *Revue des revues* in January and February, 1894, "Le mouvement littéraire en Russie", and "Raskol'nikov Dostoevskogo" ("Dostoevskij's Raskol'nikov"), published in Russia in July of the same year.

Pisarev's essay on *Prestuplenie i nakazanie* had appeared in 1867 and 1868. Mixajlovskij's first article on Dostoevskij's work, a discussion of *Besy*, was published in 1873. During this interval Dostoevskij had published *Idiot* (*The Idiot*), *Večnyj muž* (*The Eternal Husband*), and *Besy* (first serially in Katkov's *Russkij vestnik,* 1871-1872, and as a book in 1873). Furthermore, late in 1872, Dostoevskij had agreed to become the editor of Prince Meščerskij's *Graždanin* (*The Citizen*), to which he began, in January, 1873, to contribute *Dnevnik pisatelja* (*The Diary of a Writer*). Four installments of this had appeared before Mixajlovskij's article, and references to all of them are to be found in it.

After the publication of Dostoevskij's *Prestuplenie i nakazanie,* Pisarev had risen to the defense of the political left against the implications of that novel. Now, after the publication of *Besy*, which had been labelled reactionary as soon as the first chapters appeared, Mixajlovskij took up his pen in the same cause. With the publication of this novel and Dostoevskij's acceptance of the editorship of *Graždanin,* which already had a well-established reputation as a weekly organ of reactionary political opinion, there could be no question but that Dostoevskij's political position, ambiguous after his return from Siberia but increasingly anti-radical as time went on, was now openly and, apparently, confirmedly anti-progressive. Mixajlovskij's article is, in consequence, more frankly polemical than Pisarev's. The essay is ostensibly based on *Prestuplenie i nakazanie, Besy,* and the four installments of *Dnevnik pisatelja* which had appeared up to this time, but *Prestuplenie i nakazanie* is scarcely mentioned, and the importance of the essay lies in its linking *Besy* with the *Dnevnik pisatelja,* Dostoevskij's activities as a novelist with his journalism.

The essay begins on a note of dissatisfaction with Dostoevskij, ostensibly because he had consented to become the editor of so unimportant a periodical as *Graždanin,* but the real point at issue is to call attention to Dostoevskij's overt affiliation with a publication whose reputation was already well known. Dostoevskij is attacked on two fronts, as an artist and as an ideologue. The less important of these is the first. Mixajlovskij here demonstrates his solidarity with Dobroljubov and Pisarev by considering content more significant than form, but he does not dismiss aesthetic considerations as irrelevant.

The attack upon Dostoevskij as an artist is taken up first. Dostoevskij's talent and power are admitted and, indeed, emphasized. This was a point on which Mixajlovskij was never to waver. But Mixajlovskij raises the question as to of what kind is Dostoevskij's talent, a problem which he was not to settle to his satisfaction until he had written "Žestokij talant". In this first essay, Mixalovskij defines Dostoevskij's talent as psychiatric. By this Mixajlovskij is careful to point out that he does not mean that Dostoevskij correctly depicts aberrations of the intellect and will, but that though "his favorite heroes hang on at the limits dividing sanity from insanity, normal from abnormal states of will, either people in an excited condition or monomaniac, able to compose and expound extremely cerebral theories",[32] they are not insane. (It will be remembered that Pisarev took the same position as regards Raskol'nikov.) Given a talent of this sort, what subjects are suitable to it? Mixajlovskij suggests romantic historical subjects or contemporary subjects such as the Russian schismatic sects, monastic life, and spiritualism. Here it is not difficult to detect an echo of Belin-

[32] Mixajlovskij, *Sočinenija,* I, p. 844.

skij's (and Pisarev's) distaste for and distrust of Dostoevskij's interest in the romantic, the irrational, the abnormal.

Has Dostoevskij chosen such subjects? Mixajlovskij asks. The answer is in the negative. What, then, are the subjects he has chosen? So far as the plot of *Besy* is concerned, Mixajlovskij points out the similarity between it and the actual Nečaev case. Is this suitable material for the exercise of a novelist's talents? Mixajlovskij's answer is resolutely in the negative: "The Nečaev affair is to so great an extent and in all respects monstrous that it cannot serve as the subject for a novel with more or less wide significance.[33] But if a subject of this sort is to be treated, Mixajlovskij demands that it be treated realistically. How has Dostoevskij handled this material?

Mixajlovskij distinguishes three principal groups of characters in the novel: first, a group representing contemporary youth. These are minor, background figures, not suitable to Dostoevskij's talents, clumsily depicted and neither thought out nor felt through. Second, there are stock figures in Russian literature, given a fresh treatment by Dostoevskij. In the main, these are successfully handled, though there is some exaggeration, especially in the case of Stepan Trofimovič Verxovenskij and the author Karmazinov. A third group of characters is typical of Dostoevskij. This group includes Stavrogin, Šatov, Petr Verxovenskij, Kirilov, and Šigalev. All of them exist on the borderline between the normal and the abnormal, all lead eccentric lives, all express odd ideas.

Do such characters have any place in a novel of this sort? Mixajlovskij's opinion is that they do not: not that they are impossible, but that they are not typical, and typicality is the touchstone of artistic truth. Furthermore, the ideas expressed by these atypical characters are also atypical and out of place. How, then, is one to account for the presence of these atypical characters with their atypical ideas in a novel to which they are inappropriate? Their source lies not in the situation depicted in the novel, but in the author, in Dostoevskij.

For proof of this contention, Mixajlovskij turns to the *Dnevnik pistatelja* in which Dostoevskij is speaking for himself directly and not through the medium of a character in a novel, and he finds that the *Dnevnik pisatelja* is a sort of commentary to *Besy,* that the ideas expressed in the diary have already been expressed by characters in *Besy.* For example, Stravrogin is related to the peasant in *Dnevnik pisatelja* who destroyed the host, and both are cited as illustrations of

[33] *Ibid.,* p. 851.

Dostoevskij's notion that Russians are tempted by extremes. In both cases, this disposition to indulge in extreme behaviour takes the form of committing sin, not so much because the sin is, in itself, attractive, as the condition of sinfulness. The difference between Stavrogin and the peasant is that whereas the peasant atones for his sin and in atonement finds peace, Stavrogin is unable to do this. Thus material from the *Dnevnik pisatelja* serves to clarify *Besy*. Furthermore, by use of the *Dnevnik pisatelja*, Šatov is identified as the spokesman of Dostoevskij's ideas. Both express a similarly nationalistic conception of God. By use of the same method, the figure of Kirilov is related to Nekrasov and Gercen, though Mixajlovskij professes to find incomprehensible the relevance of this relationship.

By what methods does Dostoevskij express these ideas, through the medium of the novel as a form? Mixajlovskij detects two: either Dostoevskij selects some psychological subject, such as, typically, a sense of sinfulness and a desire for expiation, and shows it in action or he uses his characters as mouthpieces for the expression of his own ideas. The first method can be effective, in Mixajlovskij's opinion, and he cites Balzac as an example of an artist who has used this method successfully. Unfortunately, Dostoevskij does not confine himself to this method but makes all of his characters mouthpieces for his ideas, more or less, and, in consequence, simply swamps them under the weight of his ideas. As examples, Mixajlovskij cites Ljamšin and Petr Verxovenskij.

Since Dostoevskij uses his subjects to solve moral problems to which he gives a mystical solution, we are led to a consideration of these problems as posed by Dostoevskij and to his solutions for them, to a consideration of Dostoevskij as an ideologue, the problem which concerns Mixajlovskij most. As Mixajlovskij points out, Dostoevskij clearly intends the novel as a sort of allegory. As Mixajlovskij interprets the allegory, the sick man possessed of devils is Russia; the devils represent a loss of the distinction between good and evil; the herd of swine are those Russians who have lost a sense of their national identity while preserving only the Russian propensity for indulging in negation and destruction but lacking the desire for or the capacity to find expiation for their sins through suffering, thus bringing themselves to destruction, like the swine who dashed over the cliff and were drowned. By means of a comparison of the ideas expressed by Šatov in *Besy* and by Dostoevskij himself directly in the *Dnevnik pisatelja,* Mixajlovskij summarizes Dostoevskij's principal idea as follows: a peculiarly Russian truth, a folk sense of good and evil, developed on Russian soil. The reforms of Peter the Great divided Russians into two groups: the educated minority, who lost the Russian sense of good and evil, and the uneducated majority, who were relatively less affected. In time the educated minority was unable to understand or to communicate with the majority and together with a strictly national, folk sense of good and evil, lost all sense of good and evil. Some of the educated minority seek this lost sense, but since they are cut off from the Russian folk, they are unable to find it and perish.

After outlining Dostoevskij's main thesis, Mixajlovskij embarks upon a criticism of it. He suggests the Slavophile coloration of this system of ideas and remarks that the idea of a strictly national understanding of good and evil is scarcely compatible with the customary universalistic interpretation of Christianity. Furthermore, Mixajlovskij points out that Dostoevskij himself is unable to hold consistently even to his own interpretation of a "folk" sense of good and evil.

So far as the idea of a "folk" truth, a "folk" sense of good and evil is concerned, Mixajlovskij objects that folk ideas on this subject are varied and inconsistent, and he substantiates this contention by references to Afanas'ev. Since this is the case, what is one to do? In Mixajlovskij's opinion one can only either choose that part of the "folk" truth consonant with general ideas on the subject and attempt to counteract that part which is inconsistent with these, or simply attribute one's own ideals to the folk and ignore what is not consonant with them. Mixajlovskij accuses Dostoevskij of having taken the latter course. He denies categorically that a desire for suffering is a Russian national "folk" trait, and he criticizes Dostoevskij's position as one which counsels passivity for the educated minority. He contrasts Dostoevskij's interpretation of the position of the educated minority with his own, that the educated minority owes a debt to the majority and seeks to discharge its debt in seeking social reform, not in its own interest but in that of the majority.

In addition to the principal points outlined already, there are several minor points of interest in the essay. That Mixajlovskij views aesthetic considerations as of secondary importance is abundantly clear. In the first place, he denies that he is attempting a serious critical study of Dostoevskij, though he suggests that such a study would be interesting, thus anticipating his later article, "Žestokij talant". In the second place, his tone when treating of aesthetic considerations is deprecatory and faintly apologetic.

The significance of this article is threefold: (1) it established Mixaj-lovskij as an ideological opponent of Dostoevskij, one highly suspicious and critical of the irrational elements in his thinking, while acknowledging Dostoevskij's talent and power; (2) it links Dostoevskij's work as a novelist with his work as a publicist; (3) it points to the strongly subjective element in Dostoevskij's *Weltanschauung*.

Though Mixajlovskij had firmly criticized *Besy,* it is Kirpotin's opinion that he still hoped to lure Dostoevskij to the *narodnik* banner, that Dostoevskij was attracted by Mixajlovskij's presentation of *narodničestvo,* and that the influence of Mixajlovskij's ideas may be detected in Dostoevskij's novel, *Podrostok* (*A Raw Youth*). Dolinin detects the influence of Mixajlovskij's and Lavrov's ideas upon the thinking of Ivan Karamazov.[34]

Mixajlovskij's second article dealing with Dostoevskij was occasioned by the furore generated by Dostoevskij's speech, delivered during the ceremonies incident to the unveiling of the Puškin monument in Moscow. Dostoevskij spoke on 8 June 1880, and his speech provoked a phenomenal, if exceedingly short-lived, impression. For a moment, ideological differences between Westernizers and Slavophiles seemed reconciled, as Dostoevskij intended.[35] The influence of Belinsky's ideas upon this speech is marked. Dostoevskij's praise of Puškin echoes Belinsky's, particularly in the contention that Puškin was uniquely able to understand other times and cultures, and Dostoevskij's emphasis upon the brotherhood of man is also reminiscent of Belinskij. However, no sooner had the speech appeared in print in a Moscow daily newspaper owned by Katkov, whose reactionary political position was notorious, than reaction set in and the speech was vehemently attacked by the Westernizers. Among these attacks was an article by Professor Gradovskij, "Mečty i dejstviteľ'nost'" ("Dreams and Reality"), published in *Golos* (*The Voice*) (No. 174, 1880). When Dostoevskij himself published his speech in the *Dnevnik pisatelja* for August, 1880, he accompanied it with a preface and appended a lengthy defense of his views, especially against the interpretation given them by Gradovskij. (Though Dostoevskij began his *Dnevnik pisatelja* as a contribution to Prince Meščerskij's *Graždanin,* he did not long remain connected with

[34] Kirpotin, *Dostoevskij i Belinskij,* pp. 189-191, 194-196, 206; Dolinin, *F. M. Dostoevskij, materialy i issledovanija,* p. 68; Dolinin, *Poslednye romany Dostoevskogo,* pp. 9-13; Akademija nauk SSSR, *Literaturnoe nasledstvo,* LXXVII, pp. 64, 73, 94, 125, 450, 452, 465, 482.
[35] For a lively first-hand report of the occasion, see Gleb Uspenskij, *Polnoe sobranie sočinenij,* VI, pp. 579-613.

this publication. His last contribution appeared in it in January, 1874, and in March of the same year he formally resigned as editor. In 1876 he began to publish the *Dnevnik pisatelja* as a separate periodical. It appeared regularly through 1876 and 1877, but there was only one issue in 1880 and one in 1881, the year in which Dostoevskij died.)

Mixajlovskij's article appeared in "Literaturnye zametki" ("Literary Notes") in the *Otečestvennye zapiski* for September, 1880. Only about half of the article is devoted to Dostoevskij and then to him only as an ideologue rather than as a literary artist, so the article is of minor significance to the purposes of this study. In addition to Dostoevskij's speech, Mixajlovskij discusses Dostoevskij's polemic with Gradovskij, and almost half of the article is devoted to a plea for the importance of guarantees of the inviolability of personal freedom.

Mixajlovskij makes fun of Dostoevskij's conception of Russian universality, accuses him of evasiveness in his polemic with Professor Gradovskij and childishness. Mixajlovskij also refers to *Besy* and to his previous discussion of it. The article adds nothing important to the views Mixajlovskij had already expressed and serves merely to underline his continued ideological opposition to Dostoevskij's socio-political ideas, though Mixajlovskij again acknowledges Dostoevskij's talent.

When Mixajlovskij next wrote of Dostoevskij, his article was again occasional in the sense that it was elicited by a public event which aroused widespread interest and comment, this time, Dostoevskij's obsequies. These were, indeed, extraordinary and quite unprecedented in the Russia of that day.[36] Dostoevskij died on 28 January 1881; Mixajlovskij's article "O Pisemskom i Dostoevskom" ("Concerning Pisemskij and Dostoevskij") appeared as an installment of "Zapiski sovremennika" ("Notes of a Contemporary") in the *Otečestvennye zapiski* for February. The Russian novelist Pisemskij had died in Moscow a few days before Dostoevskij in Peterburg, and both the title of Mixajlovskij's article and its opening paragraph lead the reader to expect a necrology devoted equally to the two writers. Relatively little attention, however, is accorded to Pisemskij; rather, Mixajlovskij attempts in this article to objectify the reflections prompted by the extraordinary funeral honors accorded to Dostoevskij. Mixajlovskij found the public reaction on this occasion disturbing, since he felt that the sense of the event was open to misinterpretation.

As an example of confusion regarding the significance of Dostoev-

---

[36] For accounts in English, see Troyat, *Firebrand*, pp. 436-438; and Aimée Dostoevsky, *Fyodor Dostoevsky*, pp. 275-284.

skij's ideas, Mixajlovskij cites the one-sided interpretation of them given by A. F. Koni, a distinguished jurist, in a speech delivered at an annual meeting of the Society of Jurisprudence on 2 February, in which Koni discusses the relevance of Dostoevskij's work to the problems of jurisprudence.[37] Mixajlovskij emphasizes the one-sidedness of Koni's speech. It was precisely this one-sidedness, this attempt to exploit certain aspects of Dostoevskij's thought at the expense of others, that disturbed Mixajlovskij. "If there actually is a central point at which all can join hands, then point it out, hiding nothing and distorting nothing." [38] In Mixajlovskij's opinion, such a point had not yet been discovered, and because of confusion as to Dostoevskij's significance, Mixajlovskij attempts, in this article, to make clear his attitude toward Dostoevskij.

The article is thus, in a sense, a prelude to "Žestokij talant", Mixajlovskij's most important article on Dostoevskij. For example, he comes very close to using the term "cruel talent" with reference to Dostoevskij, and most of the ideas later to be developed at greater length are enunciated. The main lines of Mixajlovskij's attitude toward Dostoevskij are already clear, and his intention to return to them at a later date is clearly expressed. At the same time, Mixajlovskij's references to his remarks on *Besy* indicate that his attitude toward Dostoevskij had only been clarified and confirmed by time.

Like Mixajlovskij's earlier article, this one is designed to combat the influence of Dostoevskij as an ideologue. On the one hand, Mixajlovskij denies that Dostoevskij's influence was significant. On the other, he pays tribute to his work as a real force, due to the artistic power of his novels and stories. There is thus a certain inconsistency in Mixajlovskij's estimate of Dostoevskij's influence as an ideologue. It would seem that, as an ideological opponent, Mixajlovskij was unwilling to concede any influence to Dostoevskij's ideas. At the same time, both tacitly by devoting so much effort to combating them and overtly by admitting at least their potential influence, Mixajlovskij pays Dostoevskij the tribute of treating him as a serious ideological opponent. In this article, Mixajlovskij pays what is perhaps his strongest tribute to Dostoevskij as an author by writing, "Dostoevskij is one of the most powerful figures in Russian literature during the whole period of its existence." [39]

[37]   For the text of this speech, see Koni, *Za poslednye gody*, pp. 474-489.
[38]   Mixajlovskij, *Sočinenija*, V, p. 414.
[39]   *Ibid.*

Early in his essay, Mixajlovskij reminds the reader of Belinskij's prophecy of a brilliant future for Dostoevskij. Later he turns to that essay of Dobroljubov's on Dostoevskij which has already been studied. It is clear that by these references Mixajlovskij intended to place himself in line of succession from these earlier critics. It is interesting that he does not mention Pisarev, though, as we shall see, there are echoes of Pisarev in Mixajlovskij's attitude toward Dostoevskij. Mixajlovskij commends Dobroljubov's essay, but he goes on to point out that it was written in 1861, twenty years before Dostoevskij's death, and that the judgments expressed in it now stand in need of some revision. In his estimate of Dostoevskij, Dobroljubov had made, in Mixajlovskij's opinion, two errors: he had underrated Dostoevskij's talent and over-rated the "healthiness" of his *tendencija*.

Mixajlovskij admits and repeats Dobroljubov's strictures against Dostoevskij as a stylist: unnecessary unevenness in exposition, lack of a sense of aesthetic proportion, unconvincing characters, the fact that all of the characters speak the same language as the author. However, Mixajlovskij contends that, while remaining the weakest of the major Russian novelists from the point of view of construction, Dostoevskij, by dint of perseverance, accustomed the reading public to tolerance of his defects as a stylist and at the same time grew significantly as a portrayer of internal, spiritual states. Dobroljubov's essay appeared before Dostoevskij had published *Prestuplenie i nakazanie* (which Mixajlovskij regarded as Dostoevskij's best book after *Zapiski iz mertvogo doma*) and the other major works which succeeded it, so, taking this fact into consideration, Mixajlovskij feels that Dobroljubov's estimate of Dostoevskij was justified at the time he wrote it, though not as a final estimate.

As Mixajlovskij points out, Dobroljubov understood Dostoevskij's *tendencija* to be humanitarian; that is, directed toward arousing sympathy for the oppressed and implying protest against conditions permitting such oppression. While Mixajlovskij admits that this is the tone of Dostoevskij's early novels, *Bednye ljudi* and *Unižennye i oskorblennye* and points out that this strain persists even in *Brat'ja Karamazovy* (*The Brothers Karamazov*), he insists that from the beginning it was peculiarly tainted with an opposite element, a cruel feeling almost of jubilation at man's humiliation, an element which grew in importance and eventually became dominant as Dostoevskij's work progressed.

In Mixajlovskij's opinion this shift in emphasis was brought about by a conflict between sympathy for the oppressed and a rejection of social change which alone could relieve the sufferers. As Mixajlovskij analyzes the situation, if there are the oppressed, then there are oppressors, and how is one to react to them? One may demand retribution; one may exhort them on moral grounds; one may say, "Father, forgive them, for they know not what they do." But these are purely personal reactions. It is possible, also, to transfer the problem to a social context in which (at least, theoretically) it is possible to make oppression impossible. According to Mixajlovskij, the social approach to the problem does not invalidate the personal one, though Dostoevskij was unable to accept this point of view.

In Dostoevskij's early work there are no individual oppressors but only the established order. If there are no responsible individual oppressors but only a responsible social order, then it would seem obvious (at least to Mixajlovskij and to those who shared his point of view) that protest against the social order and an attempt to change it were in order. But this position Dostoevskij was unable to take. As a moralist, Dostoevskij needed to protest; but he was prevented from protesting against the established social order because he accepted it.

Since Dostoevskij was unable to accept the necessity for social change, he displaced the hatred which one might expect to be directed at an oppressive social order to those guilty of revolt against the established order. Mixajlovskij points to Dostoevskij's treatment of Raskol'nikov as an example. In contrast to Raskol'nikov stands Sonja Marmeladova, who accepts everything and protests only against the satanic pride and daring of Raskol'nikov. She seeks to become even more humble; she seeks suffering. She incorporates Dostoevskij's ideal, an ideal which he came to believe was not only his, but God's, and the Russian people's.

After *Prestuplenie i nakazanie,* Dostoevskij sought humility, a sense of sin, a consciousness of one's own lack of importance, and when he found the contrary, he grew angry. His enemies came to be those who sought to spare suffering, especially through social reorganization, because they transferred the problem from personal to social ground. Of these there are to be found three types in Dostoevskij's work, and he treats each differently. Dostoevskij equates respect for the established order with belief in God. Thus those who repudiate the established order (and struggle against it) commit morally reprehensible acts. Those who abandon the struggle and repent are sent either to penal servitude or to a father confessor (Raskol'nikov, Dmitrij Karamazov,

Vlas). If they persist in revolt against God, the established order, and suffering, then they commit suicide (Svidrigajlov, Stavrogin, Kirilov, Smerdjakov). If they complacently reject the established order without struggling against it, Dostoevskij treats them as simple scoundrels (Rakitin). Such, according to Mixajlovskij's analysis, are the varied fates accorded by Dostoevskij to those who reject the established order.

The crux of Mixajlovskij's attitude toward Dostoevskij lies in the difference in the attitudes of the two men toward human suffering. Dedicated as he was to the idea of social change, morally dependent upon a humanitarian impulse to decrease the sum total of human suffering insofar as possible, Mixajlovskij was intolerant of Dostoevskij's acceptance of human suffering. Such acceptance undermined the whole moral basis of Mixajlovskij's position. In an attempt to turn the tables, morally, Mixajlovskij pointed out in Dostoevskij an element of what we would nowadays call sadism, a pleasure derived from the contemplation of the suffering of others. "In Dostoevskij's exceptional talent was one characteristic which gave him a special power, a quality which I cannot describe otherwise than as a cruelty of talent." [40]

As a further unattractive trait, in addition to a propensity toward sadism, Mixajlovskij points out a strain of malice in Dostoevskij's work. As evidence, Mixajlovskij points to Dostoevskij's portrait of Rakitin [41] and the portrait of Turgenev in the figure of Karmazinov in *Besy,* and Dostoevskij is accused of applying the same slanted treatment to well-publicized criminal and political trials. The reference here is apparently to the Nečaev case, which Dostoevskij made use of as the basis for *Besy.* Also mentioned is Dostoevskij's treatment of Černyševskij in "Krokodil" ("The Crocodile").

Behind these rationalizations, another objection to Dostoevskij is clear: the distrust and rejection by the rationalist of whatever is not amenable to the discipline of reason. And reason, or reasonableness, is equated with health. (Here we have echoes of Černyševskij's stress upon the healthy demands of the personality and Pisarev's reliance upon the criterion of healthy common sense.) Mixajlovskij insists that Dostoevskij is maimed, and he points to Dostoevskij's epilepsy as a symptom of disease. Dostoevskij's subjectivity is also stressed, and the strain of the fantastic and arbitrary in his thinking is emphasized.

[40]   *Ibid.,* p. 426.
[41]   It is Dolinin's opinion that the figure of Rakitin is intended as a caricature of Kraevskij rather than of Blagosvetlov. See *F. M. Dostoevskij, materialy i issledovanija,* p. 59.

Having established the equivocal aspect of Dostoevskij's attitude toward suffering, Mixajlovskij proceeds to attack Dostoevskij's pretensions to expressing the Russian national spirit. He points out that Dostoevskij did not use the folk as a literary subject, except toward the end of his career and then in his role as journalist and philosopher and not as an artist. Mixajlovskij insists that *Zapiski iz mertvogo doma* (*Notes from the House of the Dead*) does not constitute a case in point since it deals only with a segment of the Russian folk, and Mixajlovskij suggests that those examples of the Russian folk to be found in penal servitude are scarcely to be considered typical. Mixajlovskij discerns in Dostoevskij's estimate of the Russian folk two elements, faith in the tsar (which, Mixajlovskij points out, is nothing new) and a love of suffering. This last, indeed, was new, but based neither upon observation or study, but subjectively. To drive home his point, Mixajlovskij contrasts the Vlas in Nekrasov's poem of that name with Dostoevskij's, as presented in the *Dnevnik pisatelja,* and again Mixajlovskij returns to the problem of suffering and the social as opposed to the personal attitude toward it. Speaking of Dostoevskij, Mixajlovskij writes: "And he never understood that deep characteristic not only of the Russian but of every national spirit by force of which the existence of sin creates an obligation not only to the passive act of personal suffering but to the active obligation to struggle with evil because it forces others to suffer." Mixajlovskij's final estimate is that "In general everything encouraged Dostoevskij to an apotheosis of suffering: reverence for the established order, a thirst for personal preaching, and a special cruelty of talent." [42]

Such are the principal points in Mixajlovskij's essay. There are also some interesting minor points: (1) so far as the typology of Dostoevskij's characters is concerned, Dostoevskij's handling of various types of rebels against the existing order has been mentioned. Mixajlovskij also notes the feminine type represented by Nastasja Filippovna in *Idiot*; (2) in the ranking of Dostoevskij's works, Mixajlovskij places *Zapiski iz mertvogo doma* first by a considerable distance as a special case, and *Prestuplenie i nakazanie* as the most satisfactory of the novels; (3) in addition to other characters already mentioned in this respect, Prince Myškin is added to the list of spokesman of Dostoevskij's ideas; (4) there is a disclaimer of a party attitude toward Dostoevskij and a denial that his ideas were stable and fixed, and a new

[42]   Mixajlovskij, *Sočinenija*, V, pp. 432, 427.

attitude toward Dostoevskij is suggested, one which was to be developed later by critics of a different temper; that is, that Dostoevskij was an eternal seeker after truth rather than someone who had found it. The principal importance of the essay is that it continues to insist upon the link joining Dostoevskij's novels and his journalism; it stresses the ambiguities and conflicts existent in Dostoevskij's thought. All of these ideas are developed further in Mixajlovskij's next essay, "Žestokij talant", which is actually an expansion and further development of ideas already stated.

As he had promised to do in his article "O Pisemskom i Dostoevskom", Mixajlovskij, the following year, returned to the discussion of Dostoevskij's work in "Žestokij talant". The two essays are closely and explicitly linked. In the earlier essay, Mixajlovskij concerned himself principally with Dostoevskij as an ideologue; in the latter one, with Dostoevskij as an artist. As Mixajlovskij had pointed out, these two aspects of Dostoevskij are inextricably intermingled, and the arguments encountered in the earlier essay reappear in the latter. The fundamental difference between the two essays lies in emphasis.

The main concern, then, of "Žestokij talant" is a consideration of Dostoevskij as an artist. In his earlier article, Mixajlovskij had pointed out the streak of cruelty existing in Dostoevskij's work, and this is the principal theme of "Žestokij talant". As usual, Mixajlovskij's essay is occasional, in the sense that the pretext for it was furnished by the appearance of volumes II and III of a collected edition of Dostoevskij's works, and Mixajlovskij's essay is based principally on the material published in these two volumes. It is Mixajlovskij's contention that in these early works are to be found the seeds of everything which was to flower later in Dostoevskij's more mature and powerful work and that from the beginning the phenomenon of cruelty had a powerful attraction for Dostoevskij.

In order to make quite clear to the reader precisely the point which he is attempting to establish, Mixajlovskij resorts to metaphor: "I think that no one in Russian literature has analyzed the sensations of a wolf devouring a sheep with such minuteness, such depth, such love, so to speak, as Dostoevskij". That such an opinion runs counter to that generally current concerning Dostoevskij, Mixajlovskij admits: "Sticking to our metaphor, others would say, if you like, that Dostoevskij, on the contrary, investigated with especial minuteness the feelings of the sheep devoured by the wolf." Mixajlovskij reconciles these opposites in the more comprehensive theory that, rather than in either the victim or the victimizer, Dostoevskij was interested fundamentally in the process of victimization. "Taking into consideration the whole literary career of Dostoevskij, we will have to come to the conclusion that he simply liked to torment the sheep with the wolf, but that during the first half of his activity, the sheep especially interested him, and during the second, – the wolf." [43] Thus, fundamentally, there was no change in Dostoevskij's interest, simply a shift in emphasis. To translate Mixajlovskij's contention into contemporary jargon, we might say that he wished to point out, in Dostoevskij's work, a pronounced streak of sado-masochism.[44] In order to establish his thesis, Mixajlovskij attempts to demonstrate two propositions: first, that Dostoevskij delighted in gratuitous cruelty, and second, that he detected elements of cruelty in relationships which are generally thought of as excluding it.

In order to demonstrate the first proposition, that Dostoevskij delighted in gratuitous cruelty, Mixajlovskij analyzes in considerable detail a whole series of early works: "Zapiski iz podpol'ja" ("Notes from Underground"), Selo Stepančikovo (A Friend of the Family), "Dvojnik" ("The Double"), "Čužaja žena i muž pod krovat'ju" ("Another Man's Wife"), and "Večnij muž" ("The Eternal Husband"). In the hero of "Zapiski iz podpol'ja" and Foma Fomič in Selo Stepančikovo, Mixajlovskij finds portraits of characters who torment others simply for their own pleasure. Mixajlovskij sketches the action of "Zapiski iz podpol'ja" and reaches the conclusion that the whole story is an exercise in the depiction of gratuitous cruelty. Mixajlovskij finds in the portrait of Foma Fomič in Selo Stepančikovo precisely the same element of pleasure in the infliction of gratuitous torment. "He is a pure artist, a poet of malice and tyranny, without the slightest utilitarian motive. And the more preposterous, the more unusual the project of cruelty which flashes through his head, the more welcome he finds it." [45] Furthermore, Mixajlovskij identifies the hero of "Zapiski iz podpol'ja" and Foma Fomič with Dostoevskij, at least so far as their interest in gratuitous cruelty is concerned. Just as the Underground Man and Foma Fomič delight in tormenting whoever is available, so Dostoevskij is given to tormenting his heroes beyond measure. As ex-

[43]   Ibid., pp. 6-7.
[44]   Corroboration for Mixajlovskij's point of view is to be found in Freud's "Dostoevsky and Parricide" (translated by D. F. Tait in The Realist, 1929), and Dostoevskij's position among those sharing the influence of the Marquis de Sade is discussed in Praz, The Romantic Agony, pp. 336-337. Cf. de Vogüé, Le roman russe, p. 251.
[45]   Mixajlovskij, Sočinenija, V, p. 25.

amples, Mixajlovskij takes the hero of "Dvojnik", Mr. Goljadkin, and Ivan Andreič, the hero of "Čužaja žena", and Mixajlovskij alludes to further examples in Dostoevskij's later work.

In order to substantiate his second proposition, that Dostoevskij detected an admixture of cruelty in emotions usually considered alien to it, Mixajlovskij points out the mixture of love and cruelty in the Underground Man's relationship with the prostitute. Also he points to that succession of feminine portraits running from Polina in *Igrok* (*The Gambler*) through Nastasja Filippovna in *Idiot* to Grušen'ka in *Brat'ja Karamazovy*, in whom the emotions of love and cruelty are inextricably mixed, and Mixajlovskij points to that mixture of friendship and cruelty in "Krokodil" and "Večnyj muž".

As minor substantiating points, Mixajlovskij points to a streak of gratuitous cruelty in Dostoevskij's publicistic writing, a point to which Mixajlovskij little more than alludes, since it was developed fully in his essay, "O Pisemskom i Dostoevskom". More suggestive, perhaps, is Mixajlovskij's assertion that Dostoevskij, not content with tormenting his characters, also torments his readers! This exercise of the author's sadism at the expense of the reader explains Dostoevskij's *longueurs,* his parenthetical scenes, his digressions (a stock complaint against Dostoevskij's style, but one it is now fashionable to explain on grounds other than technical incompetence), for Mixajlovskij contends that they serve no purpose but to subject his characters to cruelty or to exacerbate the nerves of the reader. When we remember that Belinskij was forced to admit that the last works of Dostoevskij with which he was acquainted were painful reading and that Dobroljubov professed his inability to do more than leaf through "Dvojnik", one wonders how much this effect upon the reader is due to Dostoevskij's sadistic propensities and how much to a possible exaggeration of favorite nineteenth century elaborations of narrative suspense devices, which are also a form of playing cat and mouse with the reader. That such abuses were noted by others than Mixajlovskij is clear, for example, from some of the observations of Trollope on the art of the novel as practiced in the nineteenth century.[46]

---

[46] "It may be allowed to the novelist to explain his views on a very important point in the art of telling tales. He ventures to reprobate that system which goes so far as to violate all proper confidence between the author and his readers, by maintaining nearly to the end of the third volume a mystery as to the fate of their favorite personage. Nay, more, and worse than this, is too frequently done. Have not often the profoundest efforts of genius been used to baffle the aspirations of the reader, to raise false hopes and false fears, and to give rise to ex-

Having demonstrated the display of an unusual interest in cruelty in Dostoevskij's work, what attitude does Mixajlovskij take toward it? Mixajlovskij does not deny the existence of cruelty, torment, and malice in real life, and since they exist and play an important role, they are a proper subject for the attention of the artist. Theoretically, Mixajlovskij is careful not to limit the scope permitted to the artist in the choice of his subject matter, but when it comes to the treatment of this subject matter, Mixajlovskij demands that the artist adopt an attitude toward what he depicts instead of simply calling the reader's attention to it. Since art is a reflection of life and since suffering exists, Mixajlovskij has no objection to its being the subject matter of a work of art, nor has he any objection to the emotions of sympathy and discontent aroused by such subjects, but he demands that this sympathy, this discontent be converted into motivation for action directed toward the elimination (insofar as possible) of suffering. It is precisely the gratuitous element in Dostoevskij's interest in suffering that Mixajlovskij objects to, and he objects to it on aesthetic grounds (it is not necessary to the action of the novel and it does not correspond to "living truth" – whatever that may be), on moral grounds (it has no moral significance), and on utilitarian grounds (it does not stir the reader to reflection). Apparently Mixajlovskij is able to accept the phenomenon of the existence of suffering only if it is given meaning by being used as a spur to social action. He is unequipped to deal with it in any other context. (One gets the picture of social progress as a sort of internal combustion engine, run on tears instead of gasoline!) Here, again, we come back to the difference between the attitudes of Dostoevskij and Mixajlovskij toward suffering as the crux of the quarrel between them.

The very existence of an attitude toward suffering like that of Dostoevskij is obviously deeply disturbing to Mixajlovskij, and in an attempt to come to terms with it somehow, to explain its existence as best he can, Mixajlovskij is tempted to make a biographical approach, but he shies off, pleading, in the first place, that the necessary biographical information is lacking (a lack to be supplied, at least partially, by the official biography of Dostoevskij, which Mixajlovskij discussed,

---

pectations which are never to be realized? Are not promises all but made of delightful horrors, in lieu of which the writer produces nothing but the most commonplace realities in his final chapter? And is there not a species of deceit in this to which the honesty of the present age should lend no countenance?" Trollope, *Barchester Towers*, I, p. 143; cf. Ortega y Gasset, *The Dehumanization of Art*, p. 72.

after it had appeared, in another and later article) and, in the second place, that he is discussing only Dostoevskij's work. What Mixajlovskij perceives there is a displacement of interest, a transfer from a desire to arouse sympathy for the unfortunate to a delight in the ability to arouse emotion in the reader, irrespective of any other considerations, a shift of emphasis from ends to means. In Mixajlovskij's opinion, it was the perception of this shift which motivated the change in Belinskij's evaluation of Dostoevskij's work.

Two factors made this shift possible: one was artistic, the other, personal and ideological. As an artist, Dostoevskij lacked a sense of measure and proportion; as an individual, he lacked a positive social ideal. Thus Mixajlovskij arrives at a discussion of Dostoevskij as an artist and as an ideologue.

Though Mixajlovskij's emphasis in this article is on Dostoevskij as an artist rather than as an ideologue, he insists that it is impossible to separate the two in Dostoevskij's case, and he recapitulates the arguments already familiar from his previous article: (1) that Dostoevskij had no coherent socio-political ideology and neither belonged to nor created a party, though he displayed certain Slavophile leanings, especially toward the end of his life; (2) that Dostoevskij had neither significance nor influence as an ideologue, though certain individuals claimed this significance for him; and (3) that Dostoevskij's journalism was compounded of sadism, reverence for the established order, an itch for preaching, and a tendency to pose all questions on purely personal grounds. If, ideologically, Dostoevskij was confused, aesthetically, his work is marred by that lack of a sense of proportion already mentioned, a lack which made his work extremely uneven. It is on the grounds of proportion, finish, that Mixajlovskij ranks *Zapiski iz mertvogo doma* as Dostoevskij's most satisfactory work, together with a few short stories: "Belye noči" ("White Nights"), "Malen'kij geroj" ("A Little Hero"), "Krotkaja" ("A Meek Soul").

In addition to pointing out a lack of a sense of proportion as Dostoevskij's principal aesthetic sin, Mixajlovskij makes other, less important observations about Dostoevskij's work. In establishing Dostoevskij's sadistic propensities, Mixajlovskij remarks the repetition of the feminine type Polina-Nastasja Filippovna-Grušen'ka. He also remarks the repetition of certain situations such as the relationship of Trusockij to Vel'čaninov (in "Večnyj muž") and that of Prince Myškin and Rogožin (in *Idiot*). And Mixajlovskij repeats the familiar accusation that Dostoevskij is fond of the unusual, the bizarre, the incredible.

Though Mixajlovskij agrees with Belinskij on this point, he differs with him in his estimate of Dostoevskij's success with humorous subjects.

Though Mixajlovskij shies off from a biographical approach to Dostoevskij's work, he insists that the Underground Man is a literary self-portrait, at least partially, and Mixajlovskij points out Dostoevskij's use of autobiographical elements in *Unižennye i oskorblennye*. The road to a biographical approach to Dostoevskij's work is obviously opened by such observations, and though Mixajlovskij refused to venture far down it, making only a preliminary reconnaissance, later critics were to exploit this approach. In this respect, Mixalovskij broke new ground (so far as the critics we have been studying are concerned). Also interesting, from the point of view of future developments, is Mixajlovskij's noting that Dostoevskij liked to pile up incidents, a tendency which Vjačeslav Ivanov was later to attribute to the influence of the drama upon Dostoevskij's novels.

Also interesting is Mixajlovskij's attempt to explain to his own satisfaction Dostoevskij's indubitable popularity. Mixajlovskij's explanation rests upon historical grounds. He comments that in times when society had before it problems of sufficient importance to engross its attention and some prospect of solving these problems, such a writer as Dostoevskij would pass relatively unnoted. But if such problems exist in a situation in which nothing can be done, then the resultant frustration may produce emotions gratified by the productions of a cruel talent. Here Dostoevskij's popularity is linked to the political doldrums through which Russia passed during the eighties.

Again in this essay, as in the previous one, Mixajlovskij discusses Dobroljubov's essay on Dostoevskij, this time at greater length and in greater detail, but the arguments are all already familiar: (1) Dobroljubov was in error in his estimate on Dostoevskij on two counts: first, he underrated Dostoevskij's talent and, second, he was in error as to Dostoevskij's *tendencija*; (2) Dobroljubov's critical errors are attributable to the fact that at the time he wrote, the corpus of Dostoevskij's work was far from complete. Actually, Mixajlovskij points out, Dobroljubov was not so very far wrong. His estimate of the stature of Dostoevskij's talent was accurate for the time when it was written. Furthermore, Dostoevskij never managed to rid himself of the artistic faults attributed to him by Dobroljubov: structural weakness and inability to dispense with lengthy digressions. So far as the humanitarian element is concerned, it was relatively prominent in most of Dostoevskij's early work. And if Dobroljubov was unable to detect the strain

of gratuitous cruelty which Mixajlovskij sees so clearly in such a work
as "Dvojnik", then there are two excuses: first, Mixajlovskij takes at
face value Dobroljubov's assertion that he had only leafed through
it, and second, the idea that a writer could have indulged in a taste
for gratuitous cruelty would have been simply unthinkable to Dobroljubov. For this blindness the spirit of the times was responsible. As
Mixajlovskij interprets the situation in which Dobroljubov worked and
wrote, Russian society, after a period of enforced inactivity, had an
opportunity to participate in socio-political activity, and immediate
problems were so pressing, the possible results of such activity so
promising, that it was simply taken for granted that art and science
should serve social interests. Dobroljubov so recombined the elements
of Dostoevskij's work that it became a protest against the social conditions obtaining at the time, and this was the real point and importance
of Dobroljubov's essay.

In 1883 the appearance of the official biography of Dostoevskij,
accompanied by letters and extracts from his notebooks, furnished
Mixajlovskij with the occasion and the ammunition for a further attack
upon Dostoevskij as an ideologue.[47] In addition, Mixajlovskij attacked
Straxov and Miller, the authors of the biography as well as the editors
of the accompanying material, both as inept biographers and as ideological adherents of Dostoevskij's ideas. Mixajlovskij's article appeared
in the *Otečestvennye zapiski* in January, 1884, as part of the series,
"Pis'ma postoronnego v redakciju 'Otečestvenny zapisok' " ("Letters
of an Outsider to the Editors of *Fatherland Notes*"), and it is clearly
a pendant to his earlier article, "Žestokij talant", to which explicit
reference is made.

The biography, obviously intended to enhance Dostoevskij's reputation, produced, in Mixajlovskij's opinion, rather the opposite effect.
The impression that the reader of this book gets of Dostoevskij is
scarcely one compatible with the image of a powerful spiritual leader.
Three types of evidence are contained in the book under discussion:
the biography, Dostoevskij's letters, and extracts from his notebooks.
Mixajlovskij reviews each of these in turn in order to examine the
image reflected in it.

First Mixajlovskij discusses the extracts from Dostoevskij's notebooks and reaches the conclusion that these do not reflect the image of
a *vlastitel' dum* (master of minds): "A man, ripe of years, not having

---

[47]   Miller and Straxov, *Biografija, pis'ma, i zametki iz zapisnoj knižki Dostoevskogo.*

worked out for himself any fixed and serious political convictions and, in addition, discussing political themes – here you have the author of this notebook." [48] Here one finds clearly reflected the assumption so characteristic of the Russian political left-wing that man's first duty is to arrive at clear political convictions. (It is amusing to reflect that this same accusation of a lack of fixed and clear political convictions could be leveled at Belinskij with considerable justice and that there is some difference of opinion as to just what Pisarev's political opinions were.)

Mixajlovskij finds an equally unflattering image reflected in the correspondence published together with the biography. Part of the letters date from the period before Dostoevskij's exile in Siberia. What does Mixajlovskij find reflected in them? A rather grubby preoccupation with money and effusions of over-weening vanity. Mixajlovskij does not deny that Dostoevskij was pressed for money at this period in his life, but he argues that this state of affairs was attributable to Dostoevskij's own improvidence rather than to lack of adequate financial resources. No letters are reproduced from the period of Dostoevskij's Siberian exile, but there are letters dating from after that period in Dostoevskij's life. Again Mixajlovskij stresses Dostoevskij's preoccupation with money. Mixajlovskij is careful to point out that Dostoevskij's chronic impecuniousness was in part occasioned by creditable actions on his part, such as the assumption of the debts of his dead brother Mixail, but he emphasizes the fact that they were in part also due to Dostoevskij's inveterate gambling. Mixajlovskij comes to the following conclusion: "An unfortunate man, and at the same time, a weak man, a man who is pitiable – this is the conclusion most creditable to Dostoevskij that can be arrived at on the basis of his letters." [49]

There remains the biography itself. Here the situation is complicated by the intervention of Dostoevskij's biographers. Mixajlovskij accuses them of the attempt to exploit Dostoevskij's prestige to their own profit. Mixajlovskij raises no serious objection, in principle, to this procedure; rather he takes Miller and Straxov to task for ineptness in execution. They wanted to establish themselves as the orthodox repositories of Dostoevskij's ideological succession, and to this end, they confuse the issue, so far as a clear understanding of Dostoevskij's ideas is concerned. Such a result might well be expected, since their own ideas are ambiguous and ill-defined, and it is of no service to Dostoevskij's reputation as an ideological leader.

---

[48]   Mixajlovskij, *Sočinenija*, V, p. 881.
[49]   *Ibid.*, p. 887.

Discounting, then, the intervention of the biographers, Mixajlovskij turns to the evidence of the life itself. But, first, he is careful to point out that Dostoevskij's testimony, whether in regard to himself or to others, is not reliable. As evidence, Mixajlovskij points out that what Dostoevskij wrote in 1877 about the conditions under which *Bednye ljudi* was composed is contradicted by his letters of the period and that Dostoevskij's own explanation of the reasons for his having received so relatively light a punishment for his share in the Petraševskij affair is unconvincing and highly improbable. Also Mixajlovskij points out the inconsistencies in Dostoevskij's accounts of his relations with Belinskij as given in 1862 and 1871. That Dostoevskij's attitude toward Belinskij may well have altered, Mixajlovskij considers very possible on the basis of Dostoevskij's change in attitude toward Gercen. Shifts of opinion were not uncommon in Dostoevskij's case, but in their desire to present Dostoevskij as consistent, the biographers minimize or ignore these ideological shifts of Dostoevskij's. Thus Mixajlovskij raises the issue as to whether Dostoevskij's ideological development represents a zigzag or a straight line, a problem which later critics were to ruminate.

With the review of Dostoevskij's official biography, Mixajovskij had had his say, essentially, on the subject of Dostoevskij. Not that he never returned to Dostoevskij but that his opinion, once worked out and clearly and completely stated, did not alter fundamentally, and later references to Dostoevskij were always *à propos* something else, for example, Merežkovskij's book on Dostoevskij.[50]

In order to sample Mixajlovskij's later pronouncements on the subject of Dostoevskij, it will, perhaps, be sufficient here to glance at a couple of articles published in 1894, ten years after the appearance of the last essay studied. The first of these is a general review of the current state of Russian letters intended for a European rather than a Russian audience. In this article Mixajlovskij discusses Dostoevskij principally as an ideologue rather than as a creative artist and denies the influence of Dostoevskij's ideas and the contention that Dostoevskij represents the "soul" of the Russian people. While he admits the power of Dostoevskij's talent, Mixajlovskij refers to it as "son talent cruel".[51]

The second essay is entitled " 'Vydajuščaja ženščina' g. Ardova i Raskol'nikov Dostoevskogo" ("Mr. Ardov's 'An Outstanding Woman'

[50]   Mixajlovskij, *Poslednye sočinenija*, II, pp. 284-308.
[51]   Mixajlovskij, "Le mouvement littéraire", p. 184.

and Dostoevskij's Raskol'nikov") and it appeared in July, 1894.[52] In this essay Dostoevskij's *Prestuplenie i nakazanie* is used for purposes of comparison with E. Ardov's novel which had appeared in the number of the *Russkaja Mysl'* for May, 1894. Mixajlovskij is still concerned with Dostoevskij as an ideologue and stresses his hostility to progressive ideas. It is clear that Mixajlovskij is continuing the struggle, begun by Pisarev, to disassociate Raskol'nikov and his ideas from the radical movement. He does not deny that Raskol'nikov might have existed or might now exist. The point is that he is not typical, representative. This is precisely the point made in Mixajlovskij's attack on *Besy*, that the characters of the conspirators are not typical, and again we hear an echo of the distrust of Dostoevskij as the creator of the atypical. Mixajlovskij keeps abreast of current intellectual fashions by pointing out that *Prestuplenie i nakazanie* contains an exposition of dual morality (that is, one appropriate to superior people and another for the remainder of humanity) and that the crux of the novel is Raskol'nikov's testing whether or not he belongs among the superior. (This position is in clear opposition to the contention of Pisarev that Raskol'nikov's theories are irrelevant to his acts.) Mixajlovskij indicates the existence of similar ideas expressed in other European literatures and especially in the work of Nietzsche, who was becoming influential in Russia at this time. And though he disapproves of Dostoevskij's ideology, Mixajlovskij remains constant in his insistence upon the power and importance of Dostoevskij's work.

The disappearance of Mixajlovskij from the Russian scene marked the end of a line of succession. Ivanov-Razumnik writes: "N. K. Mixajlovskij was the last of the Mohicans in the famous file of representatives of Russian journalism and criticism in the second half of the past century." [53] The place that he left vacant remained unoccupied. Russian literature did not know another individual who spoke with a similar broad authority until the later years of Gorkij's life, and then, as a semi-official government spokesman, Gorkij occupied a rather different position from that of Mixajlovskij, whose voice had been that of the not too overtly disloyal opposition.

[52] Mixajlovskij, *Literaturnye vospominanija i sovremennaja smuta*, II, pp. 366-378.
[53] Ivanov-Razumnik, *Literatura i obščestvennost'*, p. 13. Cf. Klejnbort, "N. K. Mixajlovskij", p. 2 and Nevedomskij, "N. K. Mixajlovskij", p. 32. Trockij continues the succession through Plexanov. See *Literature and Revolution*, p. 209.

CONCLUSION

Lacking a viable native tradition of formal literary criticism, the Belinskij School (as exemplified by the work of Belinskij, Černyševskij, Dobroljubov, Pisarev, and Mixajlovskij), by dint of judicious borrowing of ideas from Western European sources, an ingenious adaptation of them to the specific socio-political conditions obtaining in Russia in the nineteenth century, and intense preoccupation with the development of Russian literature succeeded in producing an original contribution to the national culture. The school was characterized by an overweaning interest in social problems which, so far as literature was concerned, tended toward the substitution of social for aesthetic value as a criterion. A number of factors contributed to this development: (1) an organic view of the world; (2) a faith in progress and an idealistic estimate of the potentialities of human nature together with the conviction that the world order was both rational and moral; (3) a conviction that the fundamental problem confronting the Russian nation was social and a desire to bring about necessary social change by whatever means possible in a political situation which, on the whole, inhibited socio-political activities.

We have seen that, keen as Belinskij's aesthetic sensibilities were, he confessed, toward the end of his career, that in a work of art social values had come to be more important to him than aesthetic values. Černyševskij and Dobroljubov attempted to effect a substitution of values, to insist that the proper content of a work of art was the "interesting" rather than the "beautiful". Pisarev carried this process further by defining the "interesting" as the "useful". Since Pisarev considered art of dubious usefulness, he was willing to dispense with it altogether (at least, theoretically). The extremism of the position adopted by Pisarev (and especially by his followers) tended to discredit the whole system, and Mixajlovskij retreated to a safer position which recognized both aesthetic and social criteria but continued to treat social values as paramount.

The Belinskij School vacillated between two contradictory ideas of the function of the writer: between the concept of the artist as the social as well as the cultural leader of his people and the idea of the artist as someone who accepts the ideological leadership of others. Having inherited from the German romantics an idea of the writer as the leader, the critics of the Belinskij School gradually became convinced, as their own social ideology ripened, that the writer was not necessarily qualified for this role and that when, in their opinion, he did not adequately carry out this role, it was up to the critics to supplant him in it.

The result was a struggle for supremacy between critics and creative writers, a struggle which took various forms. At one extreme, members of each group attempted on occasion (and usually without conspicuous success) to invade the proper domain of their opponents. On their own ground, the critics took several tacks in dealing with writers. Their principal practical problem was a dearth of literary works of first importance which exemplified their ideas. Whenever they found works which did so, the critics tended to minimize the aesthetic deficiencies of such works and to exaggerate their artistic importance. In dealing with works whose ideology differed from their own, the critics attempted, often, to demonstrate that the content of the work in question actually contradicted the significance attributed to it by its author and accorded with the ideology of the critics. They thus used works of art as a sort of raw material for the propagation of their own ideas, in effect re-writing creative works so as to make them conform to the ideology of the critics. On occasion, creative writers were treated simply as ideological opponents. Dostoevskij's work was subjected to each of these procedures at different times. Whatever the attitude of the critics toward individual writers or to individual works, these critics (with the possible exception of Pisarev) always considered literature as important, even if only as the sole available lever by means of which desired social change might be effected.

When Belinskij became acquainted with Dostoevskij's first novel, he thought he had discovered a writer who exemplified his ideas. He hailed the young Dostoevskij as a writer who expressed social protest and stimulated faith in the human dignity of the socially humble. At this point Belinskij was willing to defend Dostoevskij both as an artist and as an ideologue, but as succeeding works of Dostoevskij demonstrated a different ideological trend, Belinskij became increasingly disillusioned with Dostoevskij as an artist. In this case we see a linking of social and aesthetic values in which social values are clearly paramount.

Černyševskij, when he substituted the "interesting" for the "beautiful" as the content of art, tried to find a theoretical basis for the substitution of social values in place of aesthetic ones as a criterion for judging works of art. But his system was unable to reconcile man's "needs" and his "desires" and resulted in a situation in which the artist was forced to choose between satisfying man's "desires" and his "needs". For Černyševskij, as well as for Dobroljubov and Pisarev, man's "needs" took clear precedence in importance over his "desires". Dobroljubov, though suspicious of Dostoevskij's ideology, tried to treat Dostoevskij's work as Belinskij had done, as social protest, though he admitted Dostoevskij's aesthetic short-comings, which he professed to consider as irrelevant to the social value of Dostoevskij's work.

By the time Pisarev came to deal with Dostoevskij's work, it was clear that Dostoevskij must be considered as an ideological opponent of the social philosophy of the Belinskij School. Pisarev, therefore, attempted to turn Dostoevskij's *Prestuplenie i nakazanie* inside out, to re-interpret the content of the work so that it served as substantiation of the ideas of Pisarev rather than those of the author. Like Pisarev, Mixajlovskij saw Dostoevskij as an ideological opponent, and he sought to discredit Dostoevskij as a social ideologue by pointing out a morally unattractive aspect of Dostoevskij's work, its sado-masochistic tendencies, which Mixajlovskij's view of human nature permitted him to admit only as an aberration.

In his own literary criticism, Dostoevskij put his finger squarely on the pretension of the Belinskij School to sole ideological social leadership. Dostoevskij did not deny the proposition that art should serve society; he simply challenged the right of the critics of the Belinskij School to act as sole judges as to what was socially useful. Further, he insisted that aesthetic weakness in a work of art inhibited its social usefulness. At the same time as he disputed the right of the Belinskij School to be sole arbiter of what was socially useful, he blandly assumed that right himself and did not hesitate to castigate the social ideology of fellow creative writers, his contemporaries Turgenev and Tolstoj, for example. Indeed, in the main, Dostoevskij adopted the basic assumptions and the critical procedures of the Belinskij School, with the important exception of their right to exert ideological leadership. Throughout his career, except at its very beginning, Dostoevskij's work was marked by conflict with the social ideology of the Belinskij

School. Belinskij, himself, however, left an impression upon Dostoevskij which can be traced throughout his work.

Though the ideological leadership of the Belinskij School was continually challenged, especially by the emergence of the "decadent" movement toward the end of the nineteenth century, many of the basic tenets of the school continue to echo in Soviet criticism down to the present, and its ideas about and attitudes toward Dostoevskij are still strongly reflected in Soviet literary criticism of his work.

BIBLIOGRAPHY

The bibliography for a work which covers as much ground as the present one must of unfortunate necessity be partial and selective. Bibliographical information is given for works cited in the footnotes. Additional items are suggested points of departure for further pursuit of topics discussed and do not appear in Muratova, *Istorija russkoj literatury xix veka: bibliografičeskij ukazatel'*. Relevant material has doubtless escaped the author's attention or has not been available to him.

The bibliography is divided into sections as follows:

    I.   Works dealing with Russian history, the history of Russian literature, journalism, and literary criticism, Russian aesthetics, philosophy, and intellectual history.

    II.   Works dealing with Dostoevskij.

    III. Works dealing with Belinskij, the forties, and the revolutionary democrats as a group.

    IV. Works dealing with Černyševskij and the sixties.

    V.   Works dealing with Dobroljubov.

    VI. Works dealing with Pisarev.

    VII. Works dealing with Mixajlovskij and the period after the sixties.

    VIII. Miscellaneous works.

In the interest of brevity, the following abbreviations have been used:

ANSSSR   Akademija nauk SSSR.
Gosizdat   Gosudarstvennoe izdatel'stvo.
GIXL   Gosudarstvennoe izdatel'stvo "Xudožestvennaja literatura", Gosudarstvennoe izdatel'stvo xudožestvennoj literatury, Izdatel'stvo "Xudožestvennaja literatura".
Učpedgiz   Gosudarstvennoe učebno-pedagogičeskoe izdatel'stvo Ministerstva prosveščenija RSFSR.

I

ANSSSR, *Istorija russkoj kritiki*, 2 vols. (Moskva, ANSSSR, 1958).
——, *Istorija russkoj literatury*, 10 vols. (Moskva, ANSSSR, 1941-1956).
——, Institut filosofii, *Istorija filosofii*, II (Moskva, ANSSSR, 1957).
Akademija xudožestv SSSR, *Očerki marksistsko-leninskoj èstetiki* (Moskva, Akademija xudožestv SSSR, 1960).

——, *Voprosy teorii sovetskogo izobraziteľnogo iskusstva* (Moskva, Akademija xudožestv SSSR, 1950).

Aničkov, E., "Očerk razvitija èstetičeskix učenij", *Voprosy teorii i psixologii tvorčestva*, VI, 1-242 (Xar'kov, Mirnyj trud, 1915).

Berestnev, V. F. (ed.), *Iz istorii èstetičeskoj mysli novogo vremeni* (Moskva, ANSSSR, 1959).

Borozdin, A. K., *Literaturnye xarakteristiki devjatnadcatogo veka*, II, Part I (Sankt-Peterburg, M. V. Pirožkov, 1905).

Galaktionov, A. and P. Nikandrov, *Istorija russkoj filosofii* (Moskva, Izdatel'stvo social'no-èkonomičeskoj literatury, 1961).

Gorodeckij, B. P., "O sozdanii istorii russkoj literaturnoj kritiki", *Izvestija ANSSSR, Otdelenie literatury i jazyka*, July-August, 1958, pp. 316-330.

Istorija Rossii v xix v., 9 vols. (Sankt-Peterburg, A. i I. Granat).

Ivanov-Razumnik, R. V., *Istorija russkoj obščestvennoj mysli*, 2 vols. (Sankt-Peterburg, M. M. Stasjulevič, 1907).

Kagan, M., "O putjax issledovanija specifiki iskusstva", *Voprosy èstetiki*, III (1960), pp. 46-84.

Kogan, P., *Očerki po istorii novejšej russkoj literatury*, I, III (Moskva, Gosizdat, 1929).

Koyré, Alexandre, *Études sur l'histoire de la pensée philosophique en Russie* (Paris, Librairie philosophique, J. Vrin, 1950).

Leningradskij gosudarstvennyj universitet, *Očerki po istorii russkoj žurnalistiki i kritiki*, II (Leningrad, Leningradskij gosudarstvennyj universitet, 1965).

Lukács, Georg, *Beiträge zur Geschichte der Aesthetik* (Berlin, Aufbau, 1954).

Lunačarskij, A. V. and P. I. Lebedev-Poljanskij (eds.), *Očerki po istorii russkoj kritiki*, 2 vols. (Moskva, Gosizdat, GIXL, 1929-1931).

Mandel'štam, R. S. (ed.), *Xudožestvennaja literatura v ocenke russkoj marsistskoj kritiki* (Moskva, Gosizdat, 1923).

Masaryk, T. G., *The Spirit of Russia*, 2 vols., translated by Eden and Cedar Paul (London, George Allen and Unwin, 1955).

Miljukov, P. N., *Iz istorii russkoj intelligencii* (Sankt-Peterburg, A. E. Kolpinskij, 1902).

——, *Očerki po istorii russkoj kuľtury*, II, Part I (Pariž, Sovremennye zapiski, 1931).

——, *Outlines of Russian Culture*, translated by Valentine Ughet and Eleanor Davis (Philadelphia, University of Pennsylvania Press, 1948).

Mirsky, D. S., *A History of Russian Literature* (New York, A. A. Knopf, 1927).

——, *Contemporary Russian Literature* (New York, A. A. Knopf, 1926).

Mordovčenko, N. I., *Russkaja kritika pervoj četverti xix veka* (Moskva, ANSSSR, 1959).

Moskovskij gosudarstvennyj universitet, Fakuľtet žurnalistiki, *Iz istorii russkoj žurnalistiki* (Moskva, Moskovskij universitet, 1959).

——, Filosofskij fakuľtet, *Iz istorii russkoj filosofii* (Leningrad, Gosudarstvennoe izdateľstvo političeskoj literatury, 1951).

Muratova, K. D. (ed.), *Istorija russkoj literatury xix v.: bibliografičeskij ukazateľ* (Moskva, Mir, 1908-1910).

Ovsjaniko-Kulikovskij, D. N. (ed.), *Istorija russkoj literatury xix veka*, 5 vols. Moskva, Mir, 1908-1910).

Plexanov, G. V., *Literatura i èstetika*, 2 vols. (Moskva, GIXL, 1958).

Protopopov, M. A., "Iz istorii našej literaturnoj kritiki", *Russkaja mysľ*, August, 1892, 129-148; September, 104-125.

Radlov, E., *Očerki istorii russkoj filosofii* (Petrograd, Nauka i škola, 1920).

Simmons, Ernest J. (ed.), *Continuity and Change in Russian and Soviet Thought* (Cambridge, Harvard University Press, 1955).

Slonim, Marc, *The Epic of Russian Literature* (New York, Oxford University Press, 1950).

——, *Modern Russian Literature* (New York, Oxford University Press, 1953).

Vengerov, S. A., *Očerki po istorii russkoj literatury* (Sankt-Peterburg, Obščest-vennaja pol'za, 1907).

Volynskij, A. L. (A. L. Flekser), *Russkie kritiki* (Sankt-Peterburg, M. Merkušev, 1896).

Zapadov, A. V. (ed.), *Istorija russkoj žurnalistiki xviii-xix vekov* (Moskva, Gosu-darstvennoe izdatel'stvo "Vysšaja škola", 1963).

Zen'kovskij, V. V., *Aus der Geschichte der aesthetischen Ideen in Russland im 19. und 20. Jahrhundert* ('s-Gravenhage, Mouton & Co., 1958).

——, *Istorija russkoj filosofii*, 2 vols. (Pariž, YMCA Press, 1948-1950).

——, *A History of Russian Philosophy*, 2 vols. translated by George L. Kline (London, Routledge and Kegan Paul, 1953).

II

Since a convenient check-list of material in English on Dostoevskij is available (Beebe and Newton, "Dostoevsky in English"), the listing of such items is confined to works quoted or not listed there.

Dostoevskij, F. M., *Polnoe sobranie sočinenij* (Sankt-Peterburg, Brat'ja Pantelee-vye, 1891-1892).

——, *The Diary of a Writer*, 2 vols., translated by Boris Brasol (London, Cassell, 1949).

——, *Notes from Underground and the Grand Inquisitor*, translated by Ralph E. Matlaw (New York, E. P. Dutton, 1960).

——, *Pis'ma*, 4 vols. (Moskva, GIXL, 1928-1959).

ANSSSR, *Literaturnoe nasledstvo, LXXVII, F. M. Dostoevskij v rabote nad romanom "Podrostok"* (Moskva, Nauka, 1965).

Arsen'ev, K., "Mnogostradal'nyj pisatel' ", *Vestnik Evropy*, January, 1884, pp. 322-342.

Beebe, Maurice and Christopher Newton, "Dostoevsky in English", *Modern Fiction Studies*, IV, No. 3 (Autumn, 1958), pp. 271-291.

Belkin, A. A. (ed.), *F. M. Dostoevskij v russkoj kritike* (Moskva, GIXL, 1956).

Bem, A. L. (ed.), *Dostojewski* (Praha, Melantrich, 1931).

——, (ed.), *O Dostoevskom*, 3 vols. (Praga, Legiografie, Petropolis, 1929-1936).

Borščevskij, S., *Ščedrin i Dostoevskij* (Moskva, GIXL, 1956).

Čukovskij, K., "Dostoevskij i plejada Belinskogo", *Nekrasov* (Leningrad, Kubič, 1926), pp. 326-349. Also N. A. Nekrasov, *Tonkij čelovek i drugie neizdan-nye proizvedenija* (Moskva, Federacija, 1928), pp. 187-268.

Dolinin, A. S. (ed.), *F. M. Dostoevskij, materialy i issledovanija* (Leningrad, 1935).

—— (ed.), *F. M. Dostoevskij v vospominanijax sovremennikov*, 2 vols. (Moskva, GIXL, 1964).

——, *Poslednie romany Dostoevskogo* (Moskva, Sovetskij pisatel', 1963).

Dostoevsky, Aimée, *Fyodor Dostoevsky* (London, William Heinemann, 1921).

Fanger, Donald, *Dostoevsky and Romantic Realism* (Cambridge, Harvard University Press, 1965).

Freud, Sigmund, "Dostoevsky and Parricide", F. M. Dostoevsky, *Stavrogin's Confession*, translated by Virginia Woolf and S. S. Koteliansky (New York, Lear Publishers, 1947), pp. 87-114.

Fridlender, G. M., *Realizm Dostoevskogo* (Moskva, Nauka, 1964).

Golosovker, Ja. È., *Dostoevskij i Kant* (Moskva, ANSSSR, 1963).

Gosudarstvennaja akademija xudožestvennyx nauk, *Trudy, Literaturnaja seksija, vyp. III* (1928), *Dostoevskij*.

Grossman, L., *Dostoevskij* (Moskva, Molodaja gvardija, 1962).

Gus, M., *Idei i obrazy Dostoevskogo* (Moskva, GIXL, 1962).

Hesse, Hermann, *Blick ins Chaos* (Berne, Seldwyla, 1922).

Jackson, Robert L., *Dostoevsky's Quest for Form* (New Haven, Yale University Press, 1966).

Kirpotin, V., *Dostoevskij i Belinskij* (Moskva, Sovetskij pisatel', 1960).

——, *Dostoevskij v šestidesjatye gody* (Moskva, GIXL, 1966).

Komarovič, V. L., "Junost' Dostoevskogo", *Byloe*, No. 23 (1924), pp. 3-43.

Koz'min, B. P., "Brat'ja Dostoevskie i proklamacija 'Molodaja Rossija' ", *Pečat' i revoljucija*, Nos. 2-3 (1929), pp. 69-77.

Magarshack, David, *Dostoevsky* (London, Secker and Warburg, 1962).

Miller, O. and N. N. Straxov (eds.), *Biografija, pis'ma i zametki iz zapisnoj knižki Dostoevskogo* (Sankt-Peterburg, 1883).

Payne, Robert, *Dostoevsky* (New York, A. A. Knopf, 1961).

Rammelmeyer, A., "Dostojevskijs Begegnung mit Belinskij", *Zeitschrift für slavische Philologie* (1951), pp. 1-21; (1952), pp. 273-292.

Seduro, V., *Dostoevskovedenie v SSSR* (München, Institut po izučeniju istorii i kul'tury SSSR, 1955).

Simmons, Ernest J., *Dostoevski* (London, Oxford University Press, 1940).

Solov'ev, Vsevolod, "Vospominanija o Dostoevskom", *Istoričeskij vestnik*, March, 1881, pp. 602-616; April, pp. 839-853.

Troyat, Henri, *Firebrand*, translated by Norbert Guterman (London, William Heinemann, 1946).

Van der Eng, J., *Dostoevskij romancier* ('s-Gravenhage, Mouton & Co., 1957).

Vetrinskij, Č. (V. E. Češixin) (ed.), *F. M. Dostoevskij v vospominanijax sovremennikov, pis'max i zametkax* (Moskva, I. D. Sytin, 1912).

Wasiolek, Edward, *Dostoevsky* (Cambridge, M.I.T. Press, 1964).

Yarmolinsky, Avraham, *Dostoevsky* (London, Arco, 1957).

Zamotin, I. I., *F. M. Dostoevskij v russkoj kritike*, I (Varšava, Okružnyj štab, 1913).

III

Belinskij, V. G., *Sobranie sočinenij*, 3 vols. (Moskva, GIXL, 1948).

——, *Polnoe sobranie sočinenij*, 13 vols. (Sankt-Peterburg–Leningrad, various publishers, 1900-1948).

——, *Polnoe sobranie sočinenij*, 13 vols. (Moskva, ANSSSR, 1953-1959).

——, *Èstetika i literaturnaja kditika, 2 vols.* (Moskva, GIXL, 1959).

ANSSSR, *Belinskij i sovremennost'* (Moskva, Nauka, 1964).

——, *Literaturnoe nasledstvo*, Vols. LV-LVII (Moskva, ANSSSR, 1948-1951).

Annenkov, P. V., *Literaturnye vospominanija* (Leningrad, Academia, 1928).

Baltalon, C., *Èstetika V. G. Belinskogo* (Moskva, A. I. Mamontov, 1898).

——, *Principy kritiki V. G. Belinskogo* (Moskva, A. L. Samovaja, 1898).

Berezina, V., "K učastiju V. G. Belinskogo v izdanijax N. I. Nadeždina", *Russkaja literatura*, No. 3 (1962), pp. 51-94.

——, "Ob izučenii nasledija Belinskogo", *Novyj mir*, No. 6 (1961), pp. 257-262.

——, *Russkaja žurnalistika vtoroj četverti xix veka* (Leningrad, Izdatel'stvo Leningradskogo universiteta, 1965).

Berlin, Isaiah, "A Marvellous Decade", *Encounter*, June, 1955, pp. 27-39; November, pp. 21-29; December, pp. 22-43.

Boborykin, P., "Krasota, žizn' i tvorčestvo", *Voprosy filosofii i psixologii*, January, 1893, pp. 71-108; March, pp. 30-62.

Bowman, Herbert E., *Vissarion Belinski* (Cambridge, Harvard University Press, 1954).

Brown, Edward J., "The Circle of Stankevich", *The American Slavic and East European Review*, October, 1957, pp. 349-368.

——, "Stankevich and Belinskij", *American Contribution to the Fourth International Congress of Slavicists* ('s-Gravenhage, Mouton and Co., 1958), pp. 19-39.

——, *Stankevich and his Moscow Circle* (Stanford, Stanford University Press, 1966).

Bursov, B., *Voprosy realizma v èstetike revoljucionnyx demokratov* (Moskva, GIXL, 1953).

Černyševskij, N. G., *Očerki gogolevskogo perioda russkoj literatury* (Sankt-Peterburg, V. A. Tixonov, 1893).

Čiževskij, D. I., *Gegel' v Rossii* (Pariž, Dom knigi i Sovremennye zapiski, 1939).

D'jačenko, M., "Èvoljucija literaturnyx i obščestvennyx vzgljadov Belinskogo", *Russkaja starina*, May, 1911, pp. 291-328.

Evlaxov, A. M., "Principy èstetiki Belinskogo", *Varšavskie universitetskie izvestija*, October, November, December, 1912, pp. 1-16, 17-32, 33-38.

Fejder, V. (ed.), *O Belinskom: k 75-letnej godovščine so dnja smerti* (Moskva, Gosizdat, 1923).

Filippov, M., "Sud'by russkoj filosofii, VI", *Russkoe bogatstvo*, September, 1894, pp. 149-176, November, pp. 41-56.

Glagolev, N. A., "Za leninskuju kritiku vzgljadov Plexanova na Belinskogo", *Marksistsko-leninskoe iskusstvoznanie*, No. 2, 1932, pp. 3-33.

Glinskij, B., *Vissarion Grigor'evič Belinskij i čestvovanie ego pamjati* (Sankt-Peterburg, A. S. Suvorin, 1898).

Golovenčenko, F. M., *Belinskij* (Moskva, GIXL, 1948).

Grigorov, G., "Gegel'janstvo V. G. Belinskogo", *Novyj mir*, November, 1931, pp. 128-140.

Grigorovič, D. V., *Literaturnye vospominanija* (Leningrad, Academia, 1928) (also Moskva, GIXL, 1961).

Guljaev, N., "Literaturno-èstetičeskie vzgljady N. A. Polevogo", *Voprosy literatury*, No. 12, 1964, pp. 69-87.

——, *V. G. Belinskij i zarubežnaja èstetika ego vremeni* (Kazan, Izdatel'stvo Kazanskogo universiteta, 1961).

Harper, Kenneth E., "Criticism of the Natural School in the 1840's", *The American Slavic and East European Review*, October, 1956, pp. 400-414.

Ivanov-Razumnik, R. V., *Velikie iskanie* (Sankt-Peterburg, Prometej, 1912).

Jakowenko, B., *Ein Beitrag zur Geschichte der Hegelianismus in Russland* (Prague, 1938).

Karaban, S. I., *V. G. Belinskij* (Minsk, Belorusskaja akademija nauk, 1936).

Kogan, P., *Mirosozercanie Belinskogo* (Moskva, V. Č. Znamenskij, 1911).

Kornilov, A., "K biografii Belinskogo", *Russkaja mysl'* (June, 1911), part II, pp. 18-45.

——, *Molodye gody Mixaila Bakunina* (Moskva, M. i S. Sabašnikovy, 1915).

Kovalevskij, M., "Šellingianstvo i gegel'janstvo v Rossii", *Vestnik evropy*, November, 1915, pp. 133-170.

Kozlovskij, A. A. and K. I. Tjun'kin (eds.), *V. G. Belinskij v vospominanijax sovremennikov* (Moskva, GIXL, 1962).

Kozmin, N. K., "Nadeždin i ego otnošenija k Belinskomu", *Izvestija, Otdelenie russkogo jazyka i slovesnosti, Imperatorskoj akademii nauk*, No. 4, 1905, pp. 303-311.

——, *Nikolaj Ivanovič Nadeždin* (Sankt-Peterburg, M. A. Aleksandrov, 1912).

Kresky, Elizabeth, "Soviet Scholarship on Belinskij", *The American Slavic and East European Review*, October, 1948, pp. 269-275.

Kubikov, I., *V. G. Belinskij* (Moskva, Gosizdat, 1924).

Kulešov, V. I., *Natural'naja skola v russkoj literature xix veka* (Moskva, Prosveščenie, 1965).

——, "Novye knigi o Belinskom", ANSSSR, *Izvestie Otdelenija literatury i jazyka*, No. 3, 1961, pp. 231-237.

Lavreckij, A., *Belinskij, Černyševskij, Dobroljubov v bor'be za realizm* (Moskva, GIXL, 1941).

——, "Belinskij v bor'be za realističeskoe iskusstvo", *Literaturnyj kritik*, No. 6, 1936, pp. 137-163.

Lebedev-Poljanskij, P. I., *V. G. Belinskij* (Moskva, ANSSSR, 1945).

Legavka, M. P. (ed.), *Russkaja literatura xix v., vypusk II: Literaturnoe dviženie 1826-1848 gg.* (Xar'kov, Xar'kovskij gosudarstvennyj universitet, 1961).

Lepta Belinskogo (Moskva, D. I. Inozemcev, 1892).

Ljaskoronskij, V. G., "Filisofskie i èstetičeskie vozzrenija V. G. Belinskogo", *Filologičeskie zapiski*, Nos. 5-6, 1912, pp. 770-783.

Luppol, I., "Filosofskij put' V. G. Belinskogo", *Pod znamenem marksizma*, October, 1938, pp. 112-135.

Malia, Martin E., "Schiller and the Early Russian Left", *Harvard Slavic Studies, IV, Russian Thought and Politics* ('s-Gravenhage, Mouton & Co., 1957), pp. 169-200.

Makedonov, A., "Realizm i romantizm v èstetike Belinskogo", *Literaturnyj kritik*, No. 10, 1935, pp. 3-33.

Malnick, Bertha, "V. G. Belinsky", *The Slavonic and East European Review*, May, 1949, pp. 363-380.

Mann, Ju., "N. I. Nadeždin-predšestvennik Belinskogo", *Voprosy literatury*, No. 6, 1962, pp. 143-166.

——, "Poèzija kritičeskoj mysli", *Novyj mir*, No. 5, 1961, pp. 230-245.

——, "Valerijan Majkov", *Voprosy literatury*, No. 11, 1963, pp. 103-123.

Matlaw, Ralph E. (ed.), *Belinsky, Chernyshevsky, and Dobroljubov: Selected Criticism* (New York, E. P. Dutton, 1962).

Merežkovskij, D. S., *Zavet Belinskogo* (Petrograd, Prometei, 1915).

Mezencev, P., *Belinskij i russkaja literatura* (Moskva, Prosveščenie, 1965).

Nečaeva, V. S., *V. G. Belinskij*, 4 vols. (Moskva, ANSSSR, 1949-1961).

Panaev, I. I., *Literaturnye vospominanija i vospominanija o Belinskom* (Sankt-Peterburg, V. Kovalevskij, 1876).

Plexanov, G. V., *V. G. Belinskij* (Geneva, Sojuz russkix social'demokratov, 1899).

——, *V. G. Belinskij* (Moskva, Gosizdat, 1923).

Poljakov, M., *Vissarion Belinskij* (Moskva, GIXL, 1960).

——, *Vissarion Grigor'evič Belinskij* (Moskva, Učpedgiz, 1960).

Pospelov, G. N., *Èpoxa rascveta kritičeskogo realizma* (Moskva, Moskovskij universitet, 1958).

Pravduxin, V., "Vissarion Belinskij – osnovopoložnik social'noj èstetiki", *Sibirskie ogni*, May-June, 1923, pp. 179-202.

Prijma, F., "Ob èzopovskom jazyke V. G. Belinskogo", *Russkaja literatura*, No. 1, 1962, pp. 107-125.

Sakulin, P., "Psixologija Belinskogo", *Golos minuvšego*, April, 1914, pp. 85-121.
Schultze, Bernhard, *Wissarion Grigorjewitsch Belinskij* (München, Anton Pustet, 1958).
Setschkareff, W., *Schellings Einfluss in der russischen Literatur der 20er und 30er Jahre des xix Jahrhunderts* (Berlin, C. Schultze, 1939).
Silberstein, Leopold, "Belinskij und Černyševskij", *Jahrbücher für Kultur und Geschichte der Slaven*, Neue Erfolge, VII, 2 (1931), pp. 163-189.
Smirnova, Z., *Voprosy xudožestvennogo tvorčestva v èstetike russkix revoljucionnyx demokratov* (Moskva, Izdatel'stvo social'no-èkonomičeskoj literatury, 1958).
Solov'ev, E., *V. G. Belinskij v ego pis'max i sočinenijax* (Sankt-Peterburg, Nadežda, 1898).
Solov'ev, N., "Kritika kritiki", *Otečestvennye zapiski*, September, 1865, part II, pp. 284-313.
Stepanov, V. I., *Filosofskie i sociologičeskie vozzrenija V. G. Belinskogo* (Minsk, Belgosuniversitet, 1959).
Struve, Gleb, "A Belinsky Centenary Bibliography", *The Slavonic and East European Review*, XXVII, No. 69 (May, 1949), pp. 546-555.
Ščerbina, V., "Problemy realizma v èstetike V. G. Belinskogo", *Teatr*, December, 1938, pp. 13-36.
——, "Velikij russkij myslitel' V. G. Belinskij", *Voprosy filosofii*, No. 2, 1948, pp. 171-194.
Trubačev, S., "Predšestvennik i učitel' Belinskogo", *Istoričeskij vestnik*, August, 1889, pp. 307-330; September, pp. 499-527.
Turgenev, Ivan, *Literary Reminiscences and Autobiographical Fragments*, translated by David Magarshack (London, Faber and Faber, 1959).
Vetrinskij, Č. (V. E. Češixin), *V sorokovyx godax* (Moskva, A. D. Karčagin, 1899).
Vorovskij, V. V., *Russkaja intelligencija i russkaja literatura* (Xar'kov, Proletarij, 1923).
von Laziczius, L., "Fr. Hegels Einfluss auf V. Belinskij", *Zeitschrift für slavische Philologie*, V, 3-4 (1928), pp. 339-355.

IV

Černyševskij, N. G., *Polnoe sobranie sočinenij*, 10 vols. (Sankt-Peterburg, Č. Krajz, 1906).
——, *Izbrannye sočinenija: èstetika, kritika* (Moskva, GIXL, 1934).
——, *Èstetika* (Moskva, Iskusstvo, 1939) (also Moskva, GIXL, 1958).
——, *Èstetika i literaturnaja kritika* (Moskva, GIXL, 1951).
——, *Èstetičeskie otnošenija iskusstva k dejstviteľnosti* (Moskva, Gosudarstvennoe izdatel'stvo političeskoj literatury, 1948).
ANSSSR, *Literaturnoe nasledstvo*, XXV-XXVI (Moskva, Žurnal'no-gazetnoe ob"edinenie, 1936); LXVII (Moskva, ANSSSR, 1959).
Asmus, V. F., "Èstetika Černyševskogo", *Znamja*, February, 1935, pp. 226-252.
Astaxov, V. G., *G. V. Plexanov i N. G. Černyševskij* (Stalinabad, 1961).
Barghoorn, Frederick C., "The Philosophic Outlook of Chernyshevski", *The American Slavic and East European Review*, December, 1947, pp. 42-56.
Baskakov, V. G., *Mirovozzrenie Černyševskogo* (Moskva, ANSSSR, 1956).
Belik, A. P., "Černyševskij kak istorik èstetičeskix učenij", *Vestnik istorii mirovoj kuľtury*, July-August, 1959, pp. 149-162.

——, *Èstetika Černyševskogo* (Moskva, Vysšaja škola, 1961).

Bel'čikov, N., "Černyševskij i Dostoevskij", *Pečat'* i *revoljucija*, July-August, 1928, pp. 35-53.

Bowman, Herbert E., "Art and Reality in Russian 'Realist' Criticism", *The Journal of Aesthetics and Art Criticism*, March, 1954, pp. 386-392.

Bursov, B. I., *Masterstvo Černyševskogo-kritika* (Leningrad, Sovetskij pisatel', 1956).

Corbet, Charles, "Černyševskij esthéticien et critique", *Revue des études slaves*, Nos. 1-4, 1948, pp. 107-128.

Denisjuk, N. (ed.), *Kritičeskaja literatura o proizvedenijax Černyševskogo, Čast'*, I (Moskva, A. S. Panfidin, 1908).

Èl'sberg, Ja. E., *Osnovnye ètapy razvitija russkogo realizma* (Moskva, GIXL, 1961).

Ikov, V. K., *Èstetika N. G. Černyševskogo* (Moskva, Izdatel'stvo Associacii xudožnikov revoljucii, 1929).

Jaroslavskij, E., "O žizni i dejatel'nosti N. G. Černyševskogo", *Istorik-marksist*, No. 5, 1939, pp. 15-37.

Kagan, M. S., *Èstetičeskoe učenie Černyševskogo* (Leningrad, Iskusstvo, 1958).

——, "Problema prekrasnogo v èstetičeskom učenii N. G. Černyševskogo", *Zvezda*, August, 1953, pp. 152-169.

Kamenev, L. B., *Černyševskij* (Moskva, Žurnal'no-gazetnoe ob"edinenie, 1933).

Koz'min, B. P., *N. G. Černyševskij, 1829-1889, kratkij ukazatel' literatury* (Moskva, Narkompross, 1939).

Lavreckij, A., "N. G. Černyševskij – teoretik i istorik literatury", *Èstetičeskie vzgljady russkix pisatelej* (Moskva, GIXL, 1963), pp. 201-261.

Lebedev-Poljanskij, P. I., *N. G. Černyševskij* (Moskva, GIXL, 1939).

Lejkina-Svirskaja, V., "N. G. Černyševskij i 'Zapiski iz mertvogo doma'", *Russkaja literatura*, No. 1, 1962, pp. 212-215.

Lemke, M., *Političeskie processy v Rossii 1860-x gg.* (Moskva, Gosizdat, 1923).

Ležnev, I., "Èstetika Černyševskogo", *Krasnaja nov'*, October-November, 1939, pp. 204-228.

Ljackij, E. A., "N. G. Černyševskij i učitelja ego mysli", *Sovremennyj mir*, October, 1910, pp. 136-163; November, pp. 135-154.

Messer, R., "Klassovaja bor'ba v kritike 60-x godov", *Krasnaja nov'*, February, 1936, pp. 237-250.

Mirov, V., "Černyševskij i Plexanov v ix èstetičeskix vozzrenijax", *Pečat'* i *revoljucija*, July-August, 1928, pp. 19-34.

Mixajlov, A., "K voprosu ob èstetičeskoj teorii Černyševskogo", *Pod znamenem marksizma*, November, 1928, pp. 103-112.

Naumova, M., "Černyševskij i Fejerbax", *Bol'ševik*, No. 22, 1944, pp. 45-53.

Oksman, Ju. G. (ed.), *N. G. Černyševskij v vospominanijax sovremennikov*, 2 vols. (Saratov, Saratovskoe knižnoe izdatel'stvo, 1958-1959).

Piksanov, N. K. and O. V. Cexnovicer (eds.), *Šestidesjatye gody* (Moskva, ANSSSR, 1940).

Plexanov, G. V., *N. G. Černyševskij* (Sankt-Peterburg, Šipovnik, 1910).

Pokusaev, E. I., *Nikolai Gavrilovič Černyševskij* (Moskva, Učpedgiz, 1960).

Protopopov, M. A., "Ètika i èstetika", *Russkaja mysl'*, April, 1893, pp. 126-146.

——, "Umnaja kniga", *Russkaja mysl'*, January, 1893, pp. 100-121.

Rjurikov, B., *N. G. Černyševskij* (Moskva, GIXL, 1961).

Rozental', M., "Kritika Gegelja v èstetike Černyševskogo", *Novyj mir*, October, 1944, pp. 145-154.

Solov'ev, Vladimir, "Pervyj šag k položitel'noj èstetike", *Vestnik Evropy*, January, 1894, pp. 294-302.

Steklov, Ju. M., *N. G. Černyševskij*, 2 vols. (Moskva, Gosizdat, 1928).
Ščerbina, V., "Učenie Černyševskogo o krasote", *Zvezda*, August, 1938, pp. 165-181.
Taubin, R. A., "K voprosu o roli N. G. Černyševskogo", *Istoričeskie zapiski*, No. 39, 1952, pp. 59-97.
Zapadov, A. V. (ed.), *Iz istorii russkoj žurnalistiki vtoroj poloviny xix v.* (Moskva, Izdatel'stvo Moskovskogo universiteta, 1964).
Zivel'činskaja, L., "Èstetičeskie vozzrenija Černyševskogo", *Pod znamenem marksizma*, November, 1928, pp. 113-122.

V

Dobroljubov, N. A., *Polnoe sobranie sočinenij*, 9 vols. (Sankt-Peterburg, Dejatel', 1912-1913).
——, *Sobranie sočinenija*, 9 vols. (Moskva, GIXL, 1961-1964).
——, *Sočinenija*, 4 vols. (Sankt-Peterburg, P. P. Sojkin, 1901).
——, *Izbrannoe* (Moskva, Gosudarstvennoe izdatel'stvo detskoj literatury Ministerstva prosveščenija RSFSR, 1961).
——, *Literaturnaja kritika* (Moskva, GIXL, 1961).
ANSSSR, *Izvestija, Otdelenie obščestvennyx nauk: N. A. Dobroljubov*, Nos. 1-2, 1936, pp. 33-379.
Bibikov, P. A., *O literaturnoj dejatel'nosti N. A. Dobroljubova* (Sankt-Peterburg, Iosofat Ognizko, 1862).
Corbet, Charles, "Dobroljubow als Literaturkritiker", *Zeitschrift für slavische Philologie*, XXIV, 1 (1955), pp. 156-173.
——, "La critique de Dobroljubov", *Revue des études slaves*, XXXIX (1952), 34-53.
Efremenko, E. L., "Raskrytie avtorstva", ANSSSR, Institut mirovoj literatury, *Voprosy tekstologii*, vyp. II (Moskva, ANSSSR, 1960), pp. 52-99.
Egorev, B. F., "Dobroljubov – polemist", *Učenye zapiski Tartuskogo gosudarstvennogo universiteta*, vyp. 67 (1958), pp. 163-193.
——, "O forme literaturno-kritičeskix statej N. A. Dobroljubova", *Učenye zapiski Tartuskogo gosudarstvennogo universiteta*, vyp. 43 (1956), pp. 185-204.
Evgen'ev-Maksimov, V. (ed.), *N. A. Dobroljubov: sto let so dnja roždenija (1836-1936): pamjatka* (Leningrad, GIXL, 1936).
Glagolev, N., "Istoriko-literaturnye vzgljady N. A. Dobroljubova", *Novyj mir*, No. 2, 1936, pp. 263-277.
——, "Kritik – borec", *Oktjabr'*, January, 1933, pp. 185-204.
Gol'cev, V. A., "O literaturnoj dejatel'nosti N. A. Dobroljubova", *Russkaja mysl'*, December, 1885, pp. 97-109.
Gor'kovskij gosudarstvennyj universitet, *Učenye zapiski, N. A. Dobroljubov: stat'i i materialy*, vyp. 71 (1965).
Kirpotin, V. Ja., "Dobroljubov – kritik", *Literaturnaja učeba*, No. 3, 1936, pp. 11-24.
Kogan, L., "K voprosu o formirovanii mirovozzrenija Dobroljubova", *Literaturnyj kritik*, September-October, 1938, pp. 273-292.
Kotljarevskij, N. A., "Iz istorii obščestvennogo nastroenija šestidesjatyx godov: Nikolaj Aleksandrovič Dobroljubov", *Vestnik Evropy*, December, 1911, pp. 249-285.
Kružkov, V. S., "Èstetika i literaturnaja kritika N. A. Dobroljubova", *Znamja*, September, 1949, pp. 161-180.

Lavreckij, A., "Problema realizma v kritike Dobroljubova", *Literaturnyj kritik*, No. 2, 1936, pp. 52-73.

Lebedev-Poljanskij, P. I., *N. A. Dobroljubov* (Moskva, Gosizdat, 1926) (also Academia, 1933; GIXL, 1935).

——, "Političeskij smysl' literaturno-kritičeskoj dejatel'nosti N. A. Dobroljubova", *Literatura i marksizm*, No. 5, 1931, pp. 3-31; No. 6, pp. 3-46.

Leningradskij gosudarstvennyj universitet, *N. A. Dobroljubov– kritik i istorik russkoj literatury* (Leningrad, Izdatel'stvo Leningradskogo universiteta, 1963).

Makedonov, A., "Literaturnye vzgljady Dobroljubova", *Znamja*, No. 2, 1936, pp. 263-285.

Messer, R., "Èstetičeskie principy Dobroljubova", *Zvezda*, March, 1947, pp. 159-169.

Naumova, M. A., *Sociologičeskie, filosofskie i èstetičeskie vzgljady N. A. Dobroljubova* (Moskva, ANSSSR, 1960).

Protopopov, M., "Dobroljubov", *Russkaja mysl'*, December, 1896, pp. 224-241.

Pypin, A. N., "Moi zametki", *Vestnik Evropy*, March, 1905, pp. 5-58.

Rejser, S., *Letopis' žizni i dejatel'nosti N. A. Dobroljubova* (Moskva, Gosudarstvennyj izdatel'stvo kul'turno-prosvetitel'noj literatury, 1953).

—— (ed.), *N. A. Dobroljubov v vospominanijax sovremennikov* (Leningrad, GIXL, 1961).

Sokolov, N. I., *Nikolaj Aleksandrovič Dobroljubov* (Moskva, Prosveščenie, 1965).

Solov'ev, G., *Èstetičeskie vzgljady N. A. Dobroljubov* (Moskva, GIXL, 1963).

Vitenson, M., "Èstetika Dobroljubova", *Zvezda*, No. 2, 1936, pp. 196-211.

Zel'dovič, M. G. and M. V. Černjakov, *N. A. Dobroljubov: Seminarij* (Xar'kov, Xar'kovskij gosudarstvennyj universitet, 1961).

Ždanov, V. V., "Istoriko-literaturnye vzgljady Dobroljubova", *Literaturnyj kritik*, February, 1936, pp. 74-106.

——, *N. A. Dobroljubov* (Moskva, GIXL, 1961).

VI

Pisarev, D. I., *Sočinenija*, 6 vols. (Sankt-Peterburg, Obščestvennaja pol'za, 1894).

——, *Sočinenija*, 6 vols. and supplement (Sankt-Peterburg, Obščestvennaja pol'za and others, 1904-1907).

——, *Sočinenija*, 6 vols. (Sankt-Peterburg, Šmidt and others, 1909-1913).

——, *Sočinenija*, 4 vols. (Moskva, GIXL, 1955-1956).

——, *Izbrannye filosofskie i obščestvenno-političeskie stat'i* (Gosudarstvennoe izdatel'stvo političeskoj literatury, 1949).

——, *Izbrannye socinenija*, 2 vols. (Moskva, GIXL, 1934-1935).

Ballod, P. D., "Zametka o dele D. I. Pisareva", *Katorga i ssylka*, No. 3, 1924, pp. 47-55.

Bel'čikov, N. F., "Bazarov v ponimanii Pisareva", *Literaturnaja učeba*, November, 1940, 39-60.

Coquart, Armand, *Dmitri Pisarev (1840-1868) et l'idéologie du nihilisme russe* (Paris, Institut d'études slaves de l'université de Paris, 1946).

——, "La sage enfance du nihiliste Pisarev", *Revue des études slaves*, XXII, Nos. 1-4 (1949), pp. 128-161.

Četunova, N., "Čto razrušil 'nigilist' Pisarev?", *Literaturnyj kritik*, August, 1938, pp. 3-50.

Kazanovič, E., "D. I. Pisarev posle kreposti", *Zven'ja*, IV (Moskva, Academia, 1936), pp. 625-649.

——, "Nekrasov i Pisarev", *Pečat'* i *revoljucija*, No. 1, 1925, pp. 79-95.
——, "Turgenev: perepiska s D. I. Pisarevym", *Raduga: Al'manax Puškinskogo doma* (Petrograd, Kooperativnoe izdatel'stvo literatorov i učenyx, 1922), pp. 207-225.
Kırpotın, V. Ja., *Radikal'nyj ruznočineu D. I. Pisarev* (Leningrad, Priboj, 1929).
Kovalev, I., "D. I. Pisarev i carskaja cenzura", *Krasnyj arxiv*, 1940, pp. 198-201.
Koz'min, B. P., "Pamjati D. I. Pisareva", *Novyj mir*, July, 1938, pp. 239-246.
——, "Pis'ma D. I. Pisareva iz kreposti", *Krasnyj arxiv*, 1924, pp. 248-257.
——, "Raskol v nigilistax", *Literatura i marksizm*, No. 2, 1928, pp. 51-107. Also *Iz istorii revoljucionnoj mysli v Rossii* (Moskva, ANSSSR, 1961), pp. 20-67.
Kružkov, V. S., "Filosofskie vzgljady D. I. Pisareva", *Pod znamenem marksizma*, April, 1938, pp. 101-123.
Kuznecov, F. F., *Žurnal "Russkoe slovo"* (Moskva, GIXL, 1965).
——, " 'Žurnal'nyj èkspluatator' ili revoljucionnyj demokrat?", *Russkaja literatura*, No. 3, 1960, pp. 60-83.
Maslin, A. N., *Materializm i revoljucionno-demokratičeskaja ideologija v Rossii v 60-x godax xix veka* (Moskva, VPS i AON pri CK KPSS, 1960).
Meščerjakov, N. L., "Èvoljucija mirosozercanija D. I. Pisareva", *Izvestija ANSSSR, Otdelenie literatury i jazyka*, No. 1, 1941, pp. 8-21.
Pereverzev, V., "Teoretičeskie predposylki pisarevskoj kritiki", *Vestnik Kommunističeskoj akademii*, XXX, No. 1 (Moskva, Kommunističeskaja akademija, 1929), pp. 35-46.
Plotkin, L., *D. I. Pisarev* (Leningrad, GIXL, 1940).
——, *D. I. Pisarev: žizn' i dejatel'nost'* (Moskva, GIXL, 1962).
——, *Pisarev i literaturno-obščestvennoe dviženie šestidesjatyx godov* (Leningrad, ANSSSR, 1945).
Pustovojt, P. G., *Roman I. S. Turgeneva "Otcy i deti" i idejnaja bor'ba 60-x godov xix veka* (Moskva, Moskovskij universitet, 1960).
Stanis, L. Ja., *Osnovnye čerty mirovozzrenie D. I. Pisareva* (Moskva, Vysšaja škola, 1963).
Vorob'ev, V., *D. I. Pisarev* (Xar'kov, Xar'kovskij gosudarstvennyj universitet, 1953).
Zonin, A., "Obščestvennye tendencii kritiki Pisareva", *Obrazy i dejstvitel'nost'* (Moskva, Moskovskij rabočij, 1930), pp. 136-163.

VII

Mixajlovskij, N. K., *Sočinenija*, 6 vols. (Sankt-Peterburg, B. M. Vol'f, 1896-1897).
——, *Poslednie sočinenija*, 2 vols. (Sankt-Peterburg, N. N. Klobukov, 1905).
——, *Literaturnye vospominanija i sovremennaja smuta*, 2 vols. (Sankt-Peterburg, B. M. Vol'f, 1900).
——, *Literaturno-kritičeskie stat'i* (Moskva, GIXL, 1957).
——, "Le mouvement littéraire en Russie", *Revue des revues*, 15 January, 1894, pp. 89-95; 1 February, pp. 181-188.
Aleksandrovič, Ju., *Istorija novejšej russkoj literatury (1880-1910)*, Part I (Moskva, Sfinks, 1911).
Aleksandrovskij, G. V., *Čtenija po novejšej russkoj literature*, Part I (Kiev, N. Ja. Oglobin, n.d.).
Billington, James H., "The Intelligentsia and the Religion of Humanity", *The American Historical Review*, July, 1960, pp. 807-821.

——, *Mikhailovsky and Russian Populism* (London, Oxford University Press, 1958).

Bogdanovič, A. O., *Gody pereloma (1895-1906)* (Sankt-Peterburg, Mir božij, 1908).

Černov, V. (Ju. Gardenin), *Pamjati N. K. Mixajlovskogo* (Geneva, Partija socialistov-revoljucionerov, 1904) (also Sankt-Peterburg, Zemlja v volja, 1906 and Moskva, 1917).

Esin, B. I., *Russkaja žurnalistika 70-80-x godov xix veka* (Moskva, Izdatel'stvo Moskovskogo universiteta, 1963).

Faresov, A. I., "N. K. Mixajlovskij", *Istoričeskij vestnik*, March, 1904, pp. 1028-1044.

Ivanov-Razumnik, R. V., *Russkaja literatura ot semidesjatyx godov do našix dnej* (Berlin, Skify, 1923).

Klejnbort, A., "N. K. Mixajlovskij kak publicist", *Mir božij*, June, 1904, Part II, pp. 1-22.

Korolenko, V. G., "Nikolaj Konstantinovič Mixajlovskij", *Polnoe sobranie sočinenij*, II, pp. 283-293 (Sankt-Peterburg, A. F. Marks, 1914).

Mendel, Arthur P., "N. K. Mikhailovsky and his Criticism of Russian Marxism", *The American Slavic and East European Review*, October, 1955, pp. 331-345.

Merežkovskij, D. S., *O pričinax upadka i o novyx tečenijax sovremennoj russkoj literatury* (Sankt-Peterburg, B. M. Vol'f, 1893).

Na slavnom postu (1860-1900) (Sankt-Peterburg, N. N. Klobukov, 1900).

Nevedomskij, M., "N. K. Mixajlovskij", *Mir božij* (April, 1904), Part II, pp. 1-32.

Pedler, Anne, "Going to the People: The Russian Narodniks in 1874-1875", *The Slavonic Review*, June, 1927, pp. 130-142.

Plexanov, G. V., *K voprosu o razvitii monističeskogo vzgljada na istoriju* (Sankt-Peterburg, Obščestvennaja pol'za, 1906).

Raškovskij, N. S., *N. K. Mixajlovskij pered sudom kritiki* (Odessa, Odesskie novosti, 1889).

Rusanov, N. S., " 'Politika' N. K. Mixajlovskogo", *Byloe*, No. 7, 1907, pp. 124-138.

Strannik, Ivan, *La pensée russe contemporaine* (Paris, Librairie Arman Colin, 1903).

Ščetinin, B. A., "N. K. Mikajlovskij i moskovskoe studentčestvo", *Istoričeskij vestnik*, No. 3, 1914, pp. 948-953.

Veresaev, V. V., "N. K. Mixajlovskij", *Vospominanija* (Moskva, GIXL, 1936).

VIII

ANSSSR, *Literaturnoe nasledstvo*, XLIII-XLIV (Moskva, ANSSSR, 1941).

—— Institut russkoj literatury, *Problemy realizma v russkoj literatury xix veka* (Moskva, ANSSSR, 1961).

Antonovič, M. A., *Izbrannye stat'i* (Leningrad, GIXL, 1938).

——, *Literaturno-kritičeskie stat'i* (Moskva, GIXL, 1961).

Cross, J. W., *Life of George Eliot* (New York, Y. Crowell, 1904).

Čalyj, D. V., *Realizm russkoj literatury* (Kiev, Naukova dumka, 1964).

de Voguë, E. M., *Le roman russe* (Paris, E. Plon, Nourrit, 1886).

Družinin, A. V., *Sobranie sočinenij*, VII (Sankt-Peterburg, Imperatorskaja akademija nauk, 1865).

Gol'cev, V. A., *Literaturnye očerki* (Moskva, I. N. Kušnerov, 1895).

Gončarov, I. A., *Sobranie sočinenij*, 8 vols. (Moskva, GIXL, 1955).

Goriély, Benjamin, *Science des lettres soviétiques* (Paris, Éditions des portes de France, 1947).

Grigor'ev, Apollon, *Sočinenija*, I (Sankt-Peterburg, Obščestvennaja pol'za, 1876).

Hare, Richard, *Pioneers of Russian Social Thought* (London, Oxford University Press, 1951).

——, *Portraits of Russian Personalities between Reform and Revolution* (London, Oxford University Press, 1959).

Huxley, Aldous, *The Genius and the Goddess* (New York, Harper and Bros., 1955).

Ivanov-Razumnik, R. V., *Literatura i obščestvo* (Sankt-Peterburg, M. Stasjulevič, 1910).

Kaun, Alexander and Ernest J. Simmons (eds.), *Slavic Studies* (Ithaca, Cornell University Press, 1943).

Kavelin, K. D., *Sobranie sočinenij*, 3 vols. (Sankt-Peterburg, N. Glagolev, n.d.).

Koni, A. F., *Za poslednye gody* (Sankt-Peterburg, A. S. Suvorin, 1898).

Kropotkin, P., *Russian Literature: Ideals and Realities* (London, Duckworth, 1916).

Lampert, Evgenij, *Studies in Rebellion* (London, Routledge and Kegan Paul, 1957).

Lebedeva, M. (ed.), *Kratkij slovar' po éstetike* (Moskva, Izdatel'stvo političeskoj literatury, 1963).

Lukács, George, *Studies in European Realism*, translated by Edith Bone (London, Hillway, 1950).

Lunačarskij, A. V., *Russkaja literatura* (Moskva, GIXL, 1947).

——, *Stat'i o literature* (Moskva, GIXL, 1957).

Murry, John Middleton, *Discoveries* (London, W. Collins Sons, 1924).

Ortega y Gasset, José, *The Dehumanization of Art* (New York, Doubleday and Co., 1956).

Piksanov, N. K., *Dva veka russkoj literatury* (Moskva, Gosizdat, 1923).

Praz, Mario, *The Hero in Eclipse in Victorian Fiction* (London, Oxford University Press, 1956).

——, *The Romantic Agony* (London, Oxford University Press, 1951).

Protiv bezidejnosti v literature (Leningrad, Sovetskij pisatel', 1947).

Puškin, A. S., *Polnoe sobranie sočinenij*, 10 vols. (Moskva, ANSSSR, 1949).

Pypin, A. N., *Istoričeskie očerki* (Sankt-Peterburg, M. M. Stasjulevič, 1890).

——, *N. A. Nekrasov* (Sankt-Peterburg, M. M. Stasjulevič, 1905).

Rjurikov, B. S., *O bogatstve iskusstva* (Moskva, Sovetskij pisatel', 1956).

Rozanov, V. V., *Literaturnye očerki* (Sankt-Peterburg, M. Merkušev, 1899).

Skabičevskij, A., *Sočinenija*, 2 vols. (Sankt-Peterburg, Novost', 1890).

Solov'ev, N. I., *Iskusstvo i žizn'*, Part I (Moskva, Gračev, 1869).

Struve, P., *Patriotica* (Sankt-Peterburg, Obščestvennaja pol'za, 1911).

Šelgunov, N. A., *Sočinenija*, 3 vols. (Sankt-Peterburg, O. N. Popova, 1904).

Timofeev, L. I. and N. Vengrov, *Kratkij slovar' literaturovedčeskix terminov* (Moskva, Učpedgiz, 1952).

Trollope, Anthony, *Barchester Towers* (Stratford-upon-Avon, Shakespeare Head Press, 1929).

Trotsky, Leon, *Literature and Revolution* (New York, Russell and Russell, 1957).

Uspenskij, Gleb, *Polnoe sobranie sočinenij*, VI (Sankt-Peterburg, A. F. Marks, 1908).

Vexi (Moskva, V. M. Sablin, 1909).

Volynskij, A. L. (A. L. Flekser), *Kniga velikogo gneva* (Sankt-Peterburg, Trud, 1904).

Vorovskij, V. V., *Literaturnye očerki* (Moskva, Novaja Moskva, 1923).
Vvedenskij, A. A., *Literaturnye xarakteristiki* (Sankt-Peterburg, M. P. Mel'nikov, 1903).
Wellek, René, *A History of Modern Criticism*, III, IV (New Haven, Yale University Press, 1965).
Willey, Basil, *Nineteenth Century Studies* (London, Chatto and Windus, 1949).
Wilson, Edmund, "Comrade Prince", *Encounter*, July, 1955, pp. 10-20.
Yarmolinsky, Avrahm, *Road to Revolution* (New York, Macmillan, 1959).
Zajcev, V. A., *Izbrannye sočinenija*, I (Moskva, Izdatel'stvo Vsesojuznogo obščestva politkatoržan i ssyl'no-poselencev, 1934).
Zen'kovskij, V. V., *Russkie mysliteli i Evropa* (Pariž, YMCA Press, 1926).
Ždanov, I. N., Sočinenija, II (Sankt-Peterburg, Imperatorskaja akademija nauk, 1907).

SLAVISTIC PRINTINGS AND REPRINTINGS

Edited by C. H. van Schooneveld

43. RENÉ WELLEK: Essays on Czech Literature. Introduced by Peter De-metz. 1963. 214 pp., portrait. Cloth. Glds. 28.—

44. HONGOR OULANOFF: The Serapion Brothers: Theory and Practice. 1966. 186 pp. Glds. 28.—

48. Russkaja Proza, pod redakčiej B. Ejchenbauma i Ju. Tynjanova. Sbornik statej. Photomechanic reprint. 1963. 265 pp. Cloth. Glds. 36.—

51. ROMAN JAKOBSON and DEAN S. WORTH (eds.): Sofonija's Tale of the Russian-Tatar Battle on the Kulikovo Field. 1963. 71 pp., 49 plates. Cloth. Glds. 26.—

52. WACŁAW LEDNICKI: Tolstoj between War and Peace. 1965. 169 pp., 4 plates. Cloth. Glds. 28.—

53. TATJANA ČIŽEVSKA: Glossary of the Igor' Tale. 1966. 405 pp. Glds. 73.—

55. FRANCES DE GRAAFF: Sergej Esenin: A Biographical Sketch. 1966. 178 pp. Glds. 39.—

56. N. S. TRUBETZKOY: Dostoevskij als Künstler. 1965. 178 pp. Cloth. Glds. 33.—

57. F. C. DRIESSEN: Gogol as a Short-Story Writer. A Study of his Tech-nique of Composition. Translated from the Dutch by Ian F. Finlay. 1965. 243 pp. Cloth. Glds. 40.—

58. V. ŽIRMUNSKIJ: Introduction to Metrics: The Theory of Verse. Translated from the Russian by C. F. Brown. Edited with an introduc-tion by Edward Stankiewicz and W. N. Vickery. 1966. 245 pp. Glds. 36.—

59. DALE L. PLANK: Pasternak's Lyric: A Study of Sound and Imagery. 1966. II + 121 pp. Glds. 21.50

60. HENRY M. NEBEL, JR.: N. M. Karamzin: A Russian Sentimentalist. 1967. 190 pp. Glds. 32.—

62. CARL R. PROFFER: The Comparison in Gogol's Dead Souls. 1967. 230 pp. Glds. 28.—

65. DAVID J. WELSH: Russian Comedy, 1765-1823. 1966. 133 pp. Glds. 21.50

66. Poètika: Sbornik statej. 1966. 163 pp. Photomechanic reprint of the first edition, Leningrad, 1926. Glds. 25.—

67. P. A. LAVROV: Materialy po istorii vozniknovenija drevnejšej slavan-skoj pis'mennosti. 1966. L + 200 pp. Photomechanic reprint of the edition Leningrad, 1930. Glds. 34.—

72. ROBERT L. BELKNAP: The Structure of The Brothers Karamazov. 1967. 128 pp. Glds. 22.—

MOUTON & CO. · PUBLISHERS · THE HAGUE